R I V E R
REFLECTIONS

AN ANTHOLOGY
edited by Verne Huser

The East Woods Press Inc.
Charlotte, North Carolina
Boston • New York

River reflections.
Includes index.
1. Rivers—United States—Addresses, essays, lectures. 2. United States—
Description and travel— Addresses, essays, lectures. 3. Rivers—United States—
Literary collections. 4. American prose literature. 5. Rivers—Alaska—
Addresses, essays, lectures. 6. Alaska—Description and travel—Addresses,
essays, lectures. 7. Rivers—Alaska—Literary collection.
I. Huser, Verne.
E161.5.R58   1984   973'.0916'93   84-48040
ISBN 0-88742-014-1

Cover design by Sophia Geronimus
Illustrations by Ann Zwinger
Typography by Raven Type
Printed in the United States of America

East Woods Press Books
Fast & McMillan Publisher, Inc.
429 East Boulevard
Charlotte, North Carolina 28203

Table of Contents:

Dedicated to the memory of David Sumner,
writer, photographer, river runner and friend,
who died too young.

Introduction

This book is about rivers. It is a collection of nearly fifty writings about rivers: the different ways of seeing and feeling and experiencing rivers. It is a very personal book, an outgrowth of five decades of my own experience with rivers and river writings. I have chosen the passages, but the essence of the book is nearly two centuries of other people's writings about rivers.

My fascination with rivers began as a boy growing up in south-central Texas. My rivers were Fosters Creek, the Navidad River and Rocky Creek. They sometimes flooded, providing clean sand (our fathers and older brothers would occasionally haul some home in washtubs for our sandboxes), offering cool swimming holes, sandy shallows for wading, and deep, dark pools for fishing. These streams watered vast bottomlands, where pecan groves rained down delicious nuts in the fall and where I first hunted squirrel. Here I came to know the wildlife and plants of the rivers and learned to appreciate the cool shade and avoid the poisonous plants and snakes that might do me harm.

As I grew up and traveled more widely, I swam in the clear, cool San Marcos and Guadelupe, fished the muddy Brazos and Colorado (where I lost a friend to a drowning—he had been drinking one Saturday night and accepted a challenge to swim the river near La Grange). I went to Boy Scout camp in the Big Thicket, where we had to chase the alligators out of the swimming hole by thrashing through the water before our daily swim.

Still later, I marveled at the breadth of the Mississippi, its load of silt, its freight barges, at the dams and locks that allowed the great river to be utilized to meet the needs of the nation. As I moved west, I came to know the grandiose hydroelectric projects and irrigation systems that harnessed the latent energy of the rivers, dewatering or drowning vast valleys and canyons. I have always regretted that I came west too late to have known Glen Canyon before it was submerged beneath Lake Powell.

During all these years of growing up I was reading: stories of the voyageurs, of early explorers and mountain men, of trappers and settlers, of river men and pioneers. I read *The Last of the Mohicans* and *Huckleberry Finn*, Thoreau's *The Maine Woods* and *A Week on the Concord and Merrimack Rivers*, the journals of Lewis and Clark, of Powell and of Doane; I read Eric Sevareid's *Canoeing with the Cree* and Hemingway's "Big Two-Hearted River," Sigurd Olson and Wallace Stegner, later Edward Abbey and John McPhee. To each new book I brought a different me, and each new book changed me.

I was born—somewhat like John Denver—in the summer of my twenty-seventh year when I discovered Jackson Hole and the Snake River, spent several months there absorbing history, climbing the Teton peaks, floating the Snake, getting to know the fauna and flora. It was there that I began my career as a professional river guide and began to read river literature with greater interest and direction.

In Jackson Hole I discovered the magic of water. Loren Eisley, in his now-famous and frequently-quoted passage from *The Immense Journey*, says, "If there is magic on this planet, it is contained in water." The late Roderick L. Haig-Brown, English fisherman and writer who lived most of his adult life in western Canada, writes in *A River Never Sleeps*, "I have never yet seen a river that I could not love. Moving water, even in a pipeline or a flume, has a fascinating vitality." I can sit for hours and watch a river flow by, listen to its song, trace its current with bits of bark.

There is much about rivers in North American literature—from the journals of the voyageurs and early explorers, the diaries of pioneer settlers and military leaders to the works of great writers, such as Irving, Melville, Thoreau, Twain, Hemingway, Faulkner, Steinbeck.

When the first explorers reached these shores, they traveled inland by water routes. Farley Mowat tells us that the Vikings penetrated to the very heart of Eskimo northern Canada, and we have ample evidence of their presence in the area of the Great Lakes. Many of these early visitors and colonizers used native craft—canoe, kayak, umiak, bullboat, dugouts—adapting these traditional boats for their own. They brought with them, or developed as the need grew, other crafts: the piroque, the freight canoe, the johnboat, the flatboat, keelboat, steamboat, barge and scow.

Copying the Indians, the earliest European settlers built their homes along the rivers. They established their mills and early industry where the rivers dropped enough to generate power. As roads and, later, railroads developed, they too followed the river valleys, and new water routes were created by digging canals to reach places rivers did not go. Traders and trappers followed rivers to the interior, to the Great Lakes and beyond: north and south and always west in search of the passage to the Orient.

I have said that this is a very personal book. I know many of the writers presented here on a personal basis, have run rivers with many of them and become acquainted with others through correspondence over the years. This book belongs to all the writers, as well as to me, for it is their work that fills it. I am grateful for their counsel and encouragement.

Part I

The Pioneers—Before the Twentieth Century

The Lonely Land
Sigurd F. Olson

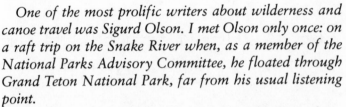

One of the most prolific writers about wilderness and canoe travel was Sigurd Olson. I met Olson only once: on a raft trip on the Snake River when, as a member of the National Parks Advisory Committee, he floated through Grand Teton National Park, far from his usual listening point.

Several of his numerous books might have been represented in this collection, but I have selected the introductory chapter to The Lonely Land, *the story of a canoe trip in the heart of Canada. The book revives the days of the voyageurs, quotes Alexander Mackenzie, David Thompson, George Simpson and others who wrote much of the early history of Canada.*

This opening chapter offers a resume of those days. While it is hardly representative of the range of Olson's thought or the depth of his imagination, this selection distills the essence of the man whose writings have inspired generations of North Americans on both sides of the border.

There are few places left on the North American continent where men can still see the country as it was before Europeans came and know some of the challenges and freedoms of those who saw it first, but in the Canadian Northwest it can still be done. A thousand miles northwest of Lake Superior are great free rivers, lakes whose horizons disappear, countless unnamed waterways, and ridges and forested valleys still largely unknown. Most of it is part of the Canadian Shield, an enormous outpouring of granitic lava that extends from the bleak coasts of Labrador in the east, almost to the Mackenzie River valley in the west and then on into the Arctic North.

It is a vast and lonely land, for as yet only its southern fringes have been occupied. The rest is neither settled nor pierced by roads. Though planes have mapped most of it and jets fly high above with vapor trails floating even over the tundras south of the Arctic coast, though a few mining camps serviced by air can be found far in the interior, few men know it well. Hudson's Bay Posts and installations of the

Royal Canadian Mounted Police are scattered throughout it and at such locations are often found the missions of the Oblate Fathers of Montreal and the Anglican Church of Canada. There are Indian settlements, the Crees and Chippewyans, the Yellow Knives, the Dog Ribs, and Hares, along the great rivers that have always been their major routes of travel and migration, but the land itself has changed little since the days of the fur trade and exploration.

This was the region the French voyageurs explored and traveled after they knew the country between the St. Lawrence and the Great Lakes. Beyond Lake Superior until 1650, the Northwest was the vast unknown, perhaps the fabled passage to the Pacific, the greatest frontier of the new world. For two hundred years these intrepid canoemen probed its farthermost reaches trading wherever they went, establishing posts at strategic points, weaving a vast network of influence over the entire region. During those days fortunes in fur were carried across the portages and paddled down the waterways to satisfy the markets of the east. In the two or three thousand miles between Montreal and the far Northwest, these French Canadians lived and traveled with a spirit, sense of adventure and pride in their calling that balanced its enormous distances and hardships. These wiry little men—seldom more than five feet four or five—dressed in breech cloth, moccasins and leather leggings reaching to thighs, a belted shirt with its inevitable colored pouch for tobacco and a pipe, topped off with a red cap and feather. They were a breed apart. From dawn until dark they paddled their great canoes and packed enormous loads, facing storms, wild uncharted rivers, hostile Indians and ruthless rivals with a joy and abandon that has possibly never been equaled in man's conquest and exploitation of any new country.

Each spring at the breakup of ice on the St. Lawrence, great brigades of canoes left Montreal for the west, hundreds of gay and colorful craft fashioned from birchbark, cedar, and spruce. There were the huge thirty-five foot Montreals with a crew of fourteen, the Bastard Canoes with a crew of ten, the twenty-five foot North Canoes and the Half Canoes, for such inland waters as those beyond Grand Portage. Decorated in gaudy designs, each brigade with its own insignia, vermilion-tipped paddles moving in rhythm to the chansons of Old France, here was a pageant such as the New World had never known and will never see again.

In command of each brigade was the Bourgeois whose word was law. It was he who decided when to start and stop and where to go. In his charge was the precious cargo of trade goods and the responsibility of converting it into fur. These men were usually of Scotch or

English origin—Mackenzies, McGillivrays, McTavishes, Simpsons, and McLeods. To them this country and its vast resources were there to be exploited. While they left voluminous diaries and meticulous journals, there is little in them of appreciation of the life they led. To them the country meant fur and fur meant profit. Indians were the means of acquiring it and the voyageurs merely a source of power for the sole purpose of transporting trade goods into the interior and furs back either to Montreal on the St. Lawrence or to York Factory on Hudson Bay. With the exception of a few men such as Peter Pond, Samuel Hearne, or David Thompson, they were seldom impressed with the stark beauty of romance of the land they traversed. To them the fur trade was a business proposition and if at the end of a season the books balanced with a profit, that was all that mattered. Still, without the shrewdness, indomitable will, and vision of these men— the partners and clerks of the various companies, the free traders, and the Bourgeois of the brigades—this commerce would not have developed on the continental scale that it did.

Thousands of men were in the trade from the early sixteen hundreds until approximately a hundred years ago. The routes they traveled were as familiar to them as our transcontinental highways are to us. Nothing was thought of leaving Montreal or the Bay for such distant points as Grand Portage on Lake Superior, Cumberland House in the Saskatchewan country, or Fort Chippewyan at the end of Lake Athabasca. A few thousand miles of travel by canoe was as accepted a procedure in those days as taking an automobile trip today.

For a century and a half the French were in control, but after 1760 and the conquest of Canada by the British, the ancient emblem of France, the Fleur-de-lis, was seen no more in the far country. Grace Lee Nute says:

"Kings came and went, governments rose and fell, wars were fought and boundary lines placed at will, but the border country cared little. Its life went on as before, full of activity, danger, adventure, the struggle of existence, the round of ordinary life in a region that was virtually a law unto itself."

The last century of the trade was a time of fierce competition and the men of the various companies, particularly the North West and Hudson's Bay companies, as well as the free traders, fought bitterly for fur. While it is true the voyageurs sang as they paddled their canoes and made merry with the Indians at the encampments, they also fought pitched battles with their enemies, ambushed rivals and stole their supplies and fur. It was a common practice to intercept bands of Indians taking fur to rival posts, fur that had already been paid for by others. Nothing was thought of piracy or of debauching the Indians with rum to make them amenable. There was bloodshed on lakes and portages, and camp sites. Murder went unpunished for there was no law that extended into the hinterlands. The gathering of fur was a deadly serious business to everyone except the voyageurs themselves.

George Simpson of the Hudson's Bay Company must have been very conscious of this as he worked his way up the Churchill in 1820.

"Embarked at half past three AM; passed Fourteen N.W. Canoes. I could not help remarking with much concern the striking contrast between our Brigade and that of our Opponents; all their Canoes are new and well built of good materials, ably manned, a water proof arm chest and casette for fineries in each, and the baggage covered with new oil cloths, in short well equipped in every respect: on the other hand, our Canoes are old, crazy, and patched up, built originally of bad materials without symmetry and neither adapted for stowage nor expedition; manned chiefly by old infirm creatures or Porkeaters unfit for the arduous duty they have to perform. . . . At four O'Clock observed a half loaded Canoe pushing across the River towards us, it turned out to be Simon McGillivray who merely came alongside to make his observations; This Gentleman I understand has been most active in every nefarious transaction that has taken place in Athabasca, he is notorious for his low cunning, has made Mr. Clarke a prisoner twice and threatens to have him soon again . . . next to Black he is more to be dreaded than any member of the N.W. Coy.; he was the principal leader of the lawless assemblage of Halfbreeds and Indian assassins at the Grand Rapid this season; a day of retribution I trust is at hand for this worthy."

With the absorption of the North West Company and other rivals by the Hudson's Bay Company in 1821, competition came to an end. Gradually the trade declined, due partly to the settlement of the west, changing fashions in fur, and because many parts of the country had been exhausted by heavy trapping and hunting. While the Hudson's Bay Company still has far-flung outposts, the old days are gone forever.

All that is left of those colorful days of the past are crumbling forts, old foundations, and the names the voyageurs gave to lakes and rivers and portages. But there is something that will never be lost; the voyageur as a symbol of a way of life—the gay spirit with which he traveled, his singing as he paddled his canoe, and a love of the wilderness that practically depopulated the struggling pioneer settlements along the St. Lawrence during the heyday of the trade.

Grace Lee Nute in her book *The Voyageur* sums up the feeling of them all in one trenchant paragraph from an old journal:

"Said one of these men, long past seventy years of age: 'I could carry, paddle, walk and sing with any man I ever saw. I have been twenty four years a canoe man, and forty-one years in the service; no portage was ever too long for me. Fifty songs could I sing. I have saved the lives of ten voyageurs. Have had twelve wives and six running dogs. I spent all my money in pleasure. Were I young again, I should spend my life the same way over. There is no life so happy as a voyageur's life.' "

Ghosts of those days stalk the portages and phantom brigades move down the waterways, and it said that singing still can be heard on quiet nights. I wonder when the final impact of the era is weighed on the scales of time if the voyageur himself will not be remembered longer than anything else. He left a heritage of the spirit that will fire the imaginations of men for centuries to come.

For a long time I dreamed of the Northwest, of exploring it by canoe as I had explored the lake country of the Quetico-Superior. The beautiful waterways I had come to know so well along the Minnesota-Ontario border seemed the answer to my own need of wilderness and my interest in the voyageurs until the summer I made an expedition with a group of Canadian friends along the old La Vérendrye route from Grand Portage on Lake Superior to Fort Francis almost three hundred miles away. Along that route something happened to us that made us determined to follow the ancient trail we had begun far into the Northwest.

The urge began the moment we pitched our tents near the rebuilt North West Company stockade on the north shore of Lake Superior. Gagnon's Island lay like a watchdog off the entrance to Grand Portage Bay. Hat Point with the gnarled old Witches Tree at its tip was waiting as always for the brigades to come by. In the blue distance was the shadowy outline of Isle Royale. It was the same as the day in 1731 when La Vérendrye and his voyageurs made the terrible nine-mile carry around the rapids of the Pigeon River toward the unknown country beyond for the first time. That night those men were with us and when the haze of our campfire drifted along the beach, it seemed to join with the smoke or long forgotten fires and lay like a wraith over the canoes, tepees, and tents along the shore.

When we broke camp the following morning and toiled up the Grand Portage to the top of the first plateau, they moved beside us. When we stopped to rest and looked back at the blue sparkling expanse of Lake Superior, we saw it through their eyes. That day we struggled through bogs and muskegs with them, fought our way over hills and rocks and ledges, suffered from black flies and mosquitoes, made the same poses or rests after each half mile, and dreamed of the moment we would glimpse blue water, drop our loads, and take to the canoes once more.

Though there were no shouts of welcome at the landing, voyageurs were still with us. All along the trail Vérendrye blazed was a consciousness of them and of the land to which the Quetico-Superior was but the gateway. More and more our thoughts became involved with them, until by the time the trip was over at the far end of Rainy Lake, we knew that within a year or two we must follow them into the Northwest.

The plan for our first expedition into the Lonely Land was born at a gathering of the veterans of the La Vérendrye route at Ottawa during the following winter. We met around a table spread with maps, pictures, and diaries and as we talked of Athabasca, Great Slave, and the Churchill River country, this hitherto nebulous land became real to us and its names began to have meaning. None of us had forgotten the previous summer and how the men of the old brigades had been with us. As we read from their diaries, the wild country they had explored became alive.

Somewhere in northwestern Saskatchewan, near the height of land between the waters flowing north into the Arctic and those flowing east into Hudson Bay, would be our starting point. We would travel downstream as though we had wintered there, beginning at the historic old post at Ile à la Crosse close to the headwaters of the Churchill River, follow it for five hundred miles across the top of the province and then southeast to Flin Flon or possibly Cumberland House. It was one of the most famous routes of all and so well traveled that during the days of the trade it was considered a major highway from the Mackenzie.

We chose it because it was the way the Athabasca brigades had come on their way to the Quetico-Superior to meet those from Montreal at Grand Portage. Nowhere in the Northwest could we find a route that had seen more of the life of that era. Every portage, every camp site, every mile of that great waterway was steeped in the annals of trade and exploration. Here if anywhere we might capture the feel of the old days.

It is a difficult thing to recapture the sense of any time that is gone, hard to realize the meaning of Daniel Boone's Wilderness Trail, the route of Lewis and Clark, or of Coronado, unless you can travel as those men did, see the terrain as they saw it, and live in the same primitive way. Only in a region of great unbroken distances where men can travel for weeks or months away from roads and towns can this be done. The Churchill River country was still relatively unchanged.

We had no idea of emulating the voyageurs or performing their feats. We had traveled enough together in the Quetico-Superior and other areas to know our limitations. We considered ourselves experienced on rivers and lakes and portages and knew what we could do as modern voyageurs. Our standard load for instance would seldom be more than a hundred pounds, while they never carried less than one hundred and eighty, and often more. Ours was the best of modern equipment, sixteen-foot Prospector canoes made by Peterborough instead of birchbarks, tents with mosquito netting, insect bombs and repellents, down sleeping bags instead of a shoddy blanket for each, air mattresses, waterproof rain gear and ponchos, the best of dehydrated foods, but more important than all else were our excellent maps.

We seldom got under way in the morning before six or seven and always made camp well before dark. They often started before dawn, paddled several hours before breakfast and continued until nine or ten o'clock at night. We would average twenty or thirty miles a day, while they often doubled and sometimes even tripled that distance, because they had more paddlers and were on the water from fourteen to sixteen or even eighteen hours a day. We would attempt no such heroic feats for we wanted to enjoy the wilderness and try to catch something of the drama of the era of which those men were a part.

We would paddle the same lakes, however, run the same rapids and pack over the same portages. We would know the wind and the storms and see the same sky lines, and because it was our first expedition into the far Northwest we might feel some of the awe and wonderment and even the fear and delight at the enormous expanses and the grandeur of a new land.

The quotations preceding each chapter and interspersed throughout are taken mostly from the diaries of a number of men who traveled the route between 1770 and 1870. Their records give us a sense of personal relationship that somehow bridges the gap between those days and the present. Although place names have changed many times since then—sometimes to English, French, or Cree—and most of the journals, particularly those of Alexander Mackenzie and George Simpson, were made coming upstream rather than downstream, they cover the general area of our experience and in all of them is the color and flavor of the country itself.

If a man can pack a heavy load across a portage, if he can do whatever he has to do without complaint and with good humor, it makes little difference what his background has been. And if he can somehow keep alive a spark of adventure and romance as the old-time voyageurs seem to have done, then any expedition becomes more than a journey through wild country. It becomes a shining challenge and an adventure of the spirit.

Without exception on all of the trips we have made, laughter has been the rule and in each case we have accomplished what we set out to do. Since the Churchill there have been others: the God's Lake-Hayes River route toward Hudson Bay, the Reindeer-Athabasca, Methye Portage and the Clearwater, the Camsell River from Great Slave to Great Bear, and the Mackenzie. On those I have been privileged to make, my companions have been men who not only did what was expected of them but who also contributed some unique and special quality that made each venture a memorable one. With me on the Churchill were men who had traveled widely and played a vital role in the affairs of their time. They found in our shared wilderness experience something deeply satisfying that more than compensated for the hardship and work involved.

On the Churchill expedition described in this book were: Dr. Anthony J. Lovink, then Netherland's Ambassador to Canada; Major General Elliot Rodger of the Canadian Army; Eric Morse, executive director of the Associated Clubs of Canada; Dr. Omond Solandt, chairman of the Defence Research Board of Canada; and Denis Coolican, president of the Canadian Bank Note Company, Ltd.

Tony, dean of the diplomatic corps at Ottawa, had served all over the world and was steeped in the give-and-take of international affairs. He was tall, lean, and rangy. Even in his bush outfit he was a diplomat, but on the trip his greatest attributes were a philosophical turn of mind, a slight Dutch accent, and the skill with which he set up the tent he shared with me. His all-important task, however, was supplying us with what we needed in the way of fish.

Elliot had a great knowledge of the rivers and lakes of his far-flung command. Beloved of his men, compact, lithe, and adventurous, he liked white water, and to hear him laugh after running a rapids was a joy. He was possessed of boundless energy and zest. Whenever we stopped, he headed into the bush and returned with treasures—caribou horns, Indian relics, strange formations of rock or wood. But it was as second cook and helper around the fire that he really came into his own, for he had a good soldier's intuitive efficiency and sense of priorities.

Eric, student of voyageur history, was in charge of all the careful research and planning that went into the expedition. With a temperament and enthusiasm that matched Elliot's, the two made a good team, serving as scouts ranging far and wide off the trail, coming back like bird dogs to report their findings. It was Eric who roused the voyageurs each morning with the historic call *"Lèvi lèvi lèvi, nos gens"* and then, no matter how cold it was, plunged into the water with much splashing. Possibly more significant, however, was his reading to us from the diaries of the explorers who had traveled our route.

Omond, with a scientist's accurate turn of mind and almost infallible judgment, was in charge of charts, logistics, and calculations. Solidly built and imperturbable, with a deep sense of humor, he had a stabilizing influence. Because of his unquestioned integrity, one of the major responsibilities was delegated to him. This was to uphold a tradition of the trade, doling out to weary voyageurs after a hard day, a meticulously calibrated dram of rum from the little "Dutchman."

Denis, formerly of the Canadian Navy, was as fluent in French as in English, his a patois and a rare sense of habitant perception no disaster could dampen. With a powerful set of shoulders that could all but lift a canoe out of the water, he was a good bowman, and to see him boring into a gale made adverse winds unimportant. When a landing was made for the night, it was his immediate task to find rocks to support the grate and kindling for the fire, and if there was any daylight left after supper, to keep the expedition's diary.

I was designated as the Bourgeois which was what the voyageurs always called their leaders in the old fur-trading days. Having once been a professional guide with wilderness experience and a background in geology and ecology, the indulgent members of our expedition insisted I be responsible for major decisions. When all was said and done, however, my real contribution was as the party's cook.

I shall not attempt to give any reactions other than my own. To try and tell how my companions felt seems to me presumptuous, but this I do know, that what I felt and saw was colored and enriched by them so that my interpretation of the country and our experiences in traveling through it is, in a sense, a composite of our combined feelings. Alone, I would have seen the country, but it would have been without the completion and joy that now is mine.

There were no heroics in our travels and we took few chances, believing that desperate adventures were the result of lack of knowledge and foolhardiness. There were few flies or mosquitoes because we deliberately chose the latter part of the summer when they were gone. Many of the portages were long and difficult, and the larger lakes were dangerous at times. We were often cold, wet, and weary, but this was the price we expected to pay and the paying itself was good. To those who have never been in the bush or traversed the wilderness hinterlands by canoe, our expedition might seem like a formidable undertaking, while to old-timers just as to the voyageurs of the past, it would be merely a routine trek.

I do not entertain the illusion that a few short expeditions into the northwest makes me an authority on the country, or that this book is an accurate, carefully documented travel guide. All I want to do is give the reader some feel of this land as we saw it and to share with him some of its rewards and the sense of fulfillment that comes to men traveling the bush together. If he can catch in addition, something of the great silences still to be found in the Lonely Land, the heightened awareness that comes with a certain amount of danger, and the sense of wilderness as a counterbalance to the tensions and pressures of our age, then I shall be happy indeed.

Omond Solandt, when asked upon his return from the Churchill why he went along, answered:

"I went along to iron out the wrinkles in my soul," which is perhaps as good an explanation as any I know for a venture such as ours.

River Crossings

Rivers offer routes of passage, but they also serve as barriers that must be boated or bridged, forded or swum. Numerous early writers left records of their experiences at river crossings. The following excerpts illustrate the problems they encountered.

Astoria *is an account of the 1811–12 expedition John Jacob Astor sent to the mouth of the Columbia River to establish a trading post. Irving, better known for his "Legend of Sleepy Hollow" and "Rip van Winkle," was the first American writer accepted by the literary world of Europe. In this passage, a party of Astorians makes a river crossing that becomes a 91-mile float trip down the Snake River.*

John Kirk Townsend was a young naturalist traveling with the renowned English botanist, Thomas Nuttall, to the mouth of the Columbia in 1834. His Narrative of a Journey across the Rocky Mountains to the Columbia, *published in 1839, tells of his experiences traveling overland with a party of mountain men that included the New Englanders Nathaniel Wyeth and Osborne Russell.*

Two passages from Osborne Russell's Journal of a Trapper [1834–1843] *follow. Unlike Townsend, who was only passing through, Russell stayed on to become one of the latter-day mountain men. His journal entries offer a slightly different perspective.*

Excerpts from the Diary of Amelia Stewart Knight record a covered wagon journey from Iowa to Oregon by a family of nine. Their progress from April through mid-September in 1853, is marked by river crossings.

The final account in this section tells of the Nez Perce crossing of the Snake River in Hells Canyon during their 1877 exodus. General O.O. Howard had just ordered the Nez Perce to leave their homeland in the Wallowa Valley and move onto the reservation. Howard gave them only a month to make the move. The account begins with Chief Joseph's reply to Howard.

Astoria

Washington Irving

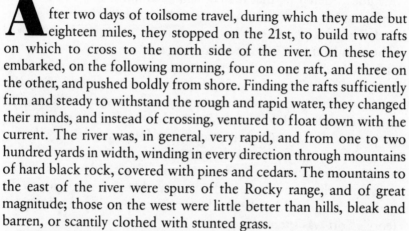

After two days of toilsome travel, during which they made but eighteen miles, they stopped on the 21st, to build two rafts on which to cross to the north side of the river. On these they embarked, on the following morning, four on one raft, and three on the other, and pushed boldly from shore. Finding the rafts sufficiently firm and steady to withstand the rough and rapid water, they changed their minds, and instead of crossing, ventured to float down with the current. The river was, in general, very rapid, and from one to two hundred yards in width, winding in every direction through mountains of hard black rock, covered with pines and cedars. The mountains to the east of the river were spurs of the Rocky range, and of great magnitude; those on the west were little better than hills, bleak and barren, or scantily clothed with stunted grass.

Mad River, though deserving its name from the impetuosity of its current, was free from rapids and cascades, and flowed on in a single channel between gravel banks, often fringed with cotton-wood and dwarf willows in abundance. These gave sustenance to immense quantities of beaver, so that the voyagers found no difficulty in procuring food. Ben Jones, also, killed a fallow deer and a wolverine, and as they were enabled to carry the carcasses on their rafts, their larder was well supplied. Indeed, they might have occasionally shot beavers that were swimming in the river as they floated by, but they humanely spared their lives, being in no want of meat at the time. In this way, they kept down the river for three days, drifting with the current and encamping on land at night, when they drew up their rafts on shore. Towards the evening of the third day, they came to a little island on which they descried a gang of elk. Ben Jones landed, and was fortunate enough to wound one, which immediately took to the water, but, being unable to stem the current, drifted above a mile, when it was overtaken and drawn to shore. As a storm was gathering, they now encamped on the margin of the river, where they remained all the next day, sheltering themselves as well as they could from the rain and snow—a sharp foretaste of the impending winter. During their encampment, they employed themselves in jerking a part of the elk for future supply. In cutting up the carcass, they found that the animal had been wounded by hunters, about a week previously, an arrow head and a musket ball remaining in the wounds. In the wilderness, every trivial circumstance is a matter of anxious speculation. The Snake Indians have no guns; the elk, therefore, could not have been wounded by one of them. They were on the borders of the country infested by the Blackfeet, who carry firearms. It was concluded, therefore, that the elk had been hunted by some of that wandering and hostile tribe, who, of course, must be in the neighborhood. The idea put an end to the transient solace they had enjoyed in the comparative repose and abundance of the river.

For three days longer they continued to navigate with their rafts. The recent storm had rendered the weather extremely cold. They had now floated down the river about ninety-one miles, when finding the mountains on the right diminished to moderate sized hills, they landed, and prepared to resume their journey on foot. Accordingly, having spent a day in preparations, making moccasins, and parceling out their jerked meat in packs of twenty pounds to each man, they turned their backs upon the river on the 29th of September and struck off to the northeast, keeping along the southern skirt of the mountain on which Henry's Fort was situated.

Narrative of a Journey

John Kirk Townsend

May 3, 1834. We were on the move early the next morning, and at noon arrived at the Kanzas River, a branch of the Missouri. This is a broad and not very deep stream, with the water dark and turbid, like that of the former. As we approached it, we saw a number of Indian lodges, made of saplings driven into the ground, bent over and tied at top, and covered with bark and buffalo skins. These lodges, or wigwams, are numerous on both sides of the river. As we passed them, the inhabitants, men, women, and children, flocked out to see us, and almost prevented our progress by their eager greetings. Our party stopped on the bank of the river, and the horses were unloaded and driven into the water. They swam beautifully, and with great regularity, and arrived safely on the opposite shore, where they were confined in a large lot, enclosed with a fence. After some difficulty, and considerable detention, we succeeded in procuring a large flat bottomed boat, embarked ourselves and goods in it, and landed on the opposite side near our horse pen, where we encamped. The lodges are numerous here, and there are also some good frame houses inhabited by a few white men and women, who subsist chiefly by raising cattle, which they drive to the settlements below. They, as well as the Indians, raise an abundance of good corn; potatoes and other vegetables are also plentiful, and they can therefore live sufficiently well.

The canoes used by the Indians are mostly made of buffalo skins, stretched, while recent, over a light frame work of wood, the seams sewed with sinews, and so closely, as to be wholly impervious to water. These light vessels are remarkably buoyant, and capable of sustaining very heavy burthens.

Journal of a Trapper

Osborne Russell

Here we were obliged to cross Lewis fork which is about 300 yds. wide and might be forded at a low stage of water, but at present was almost overflowing its banks and running at the rate of about 6 mls per hour. We commenced making a boat by sewing two raw Bulls hides together which we stretched over a frame formed of green willow branches and then dried it gradually over a slow fire during the night 22d Our boat being completed we commenced crossing our equippage and while 5 of us were employed at this a young man by the name of Abram Patterson attempted to cross on horse back in spite of all the advice and entreaty of those present his wild and rash temper got the better of his reason and after a desperate struggle to reach the opposite bank he abandoned his horse made a few springs and sunk to rise no more—he was a native of Penna. about 23 years of age. We succeeded in crossing our baggage and encamped on the East side for the night.

Here we again attempted to cross Lewis' fork with a Bull skin boat July 4th Our boat being completed we loaded it with baggage and crossed to the other side but on returning we ran it into some brush when it instantly filled and sunk but without further accident than the loss of the boat we had already forded half the distance accross the river upon horse back and were now upon a other shore We now commenced making a raft of logs that had drifted on the Island on this when completed we put the remainder of our equipments about 2 oclk P.M and 10 of us started with it for the other side but we no sooner reached the rapid current than our raft (which was constructed of large timber) became unmanageable and all efforts to reach either side were vaine and fearing lest We should run on to the dreadful rapids to which we were fast approaching we abandoned the raft and committed ourselves to the mercy of the current. We being all tolerable good swimmers excepting myself, I would fain have called for help but at this critical period every one had to Shift for himself fortunately I scrambled to the shore among the last swimmers. We were now on the side from whence we started without a single article of bedding except an old cloth tent whilst the rain poured incessantly. Fortunately we had built a large fire previous to our departure on the raft which was still burning

The night at length came on and we lay down to await the events of the morrow day light appeared and we started down along the shore in hopes of finding something that might get loose from the raft and drift upon the beach—We had not gone a mile when we discovered the raft lodged on a gravel bar which projected from the Island where it had been driven by the current—we hastened thro. the water waist deep to the spot where to our great surprise and satisfaction we found everything safe upon the raft in the same manner we had left it. we also discovered that the river could with some difficulty be forded on horseback at this place. Accordingly we had our horses driven accross to us packed them up mounted and crossed without further accident and the day being fair we spent the remainder of it in and the following day in drying out equippage 7th Left the river followed up a stream called the "Grosvent fork" in an East direction about 2 Mils this stream was very high and rapid in fording it we lost 2 Rifles

Diary of Mrs. Amelia Stewart Knight

Amelia Stewart Knight

Friday, May 6th, 1853 . . . Here we passed a train of wagons on their way back, the head man had been drowned a few days before, in a river called Elkhorn, while getting some cattle across and his wife was lying in the wagon quite sick, and children were mourning for the father gone. With sadness and pity I passed those who perhaps a few days before had been well and happy as ourselves. Came 20 miles today.

Saturday, May 7th ... Cold morning, thermometer down to 48 in the wagon. No wood, only enough to boil some coffee. Good grass for the stock. We have crossed a small creek, with a narrow Indian bridge across it. Paid the Indians 75 cents toll. My hands are numb with cold. . .

Sunday, May 8th ... Still in camp. Waiting to cross [Elkhorn]. There are three hundred or more wagons in sight and as far as the eye can reach, the bottom is covered, on each side of the river, with cattle and horses. There is no ferry here and the men will have to make one out of the tightest wagon-bed (every company should have a water-proof wagon-bed for this purpose.) Everything must now be hauled out of the wagons head over heels (and he who knows where to find anything will be a smart fellow.) Then the wagons must be all taken to pieces, and then by means of a strong rope stretched across the river with a tight wagon-bed attached to the middle of it, the rope must be long enough to pull from one side to the other, with men on each side of the river to pull it. In this way we have to cross everything a little at a time. Women and children last, and then swim the cattle and horses. There were three horses and some cattle drowned while crossing this place yesterday. It is quite lively and merry here this morning and the weather fine. We are camped on a large bottom, with the broad, deep river on one side of us and a high bluff on the other.

Monday, May 9th ... Morning cold, within 4 degrees of freezing; we are all on the right side of the river this morning. . .

Thursday, May 12th Thursday Noon ... Beautiful weather, but very dusty. We are camped on the bank of Loup Fork, awaiting our turn to cross. There are two ferry boats running, and a number of wagons ahead of us, all waiting to cross. Have to pay three dollars a wagon for three wagons and swim the stock. Traveled 12 miles today. We hear there are 700 teams on the road ahead of us. Wash and cook this afternoon.

Wednesday, June 15th ... passed Independence Rock this afternoon, and crossed Sweetwater River on a bridge. Paid 3 dollars a wagon and swam the stock across. The river is very high and swift. . .

Wednesday, June 29th ... Cold and cloudy. The wagons are all crowded up to the ferry waiting with impatience to cross. There are 30 or more to cross before us. Have to cross one at a time. Have to pay 8 dollars for a wagon; 1 dollar for a horse or a cow. We swim all our stock. . .

Sunday, July 17th . . . We are traveling through the Digger Indians' country, but have not seen any yet. (We crossed Swamp Creek this morning, and Goose Creek this afternoon. Goose Creek is almost straight down, and then straight up again. Several things pitched out of the wagons into the Creek. Travel over some very rocky ground. Here Chat fell out of the wagon, but did not get hurt much.)

Friday, August 5th . . . (Snake River) . . . Our turn to cross will come sometime tomorrow. There is one small ferry boat running here, owned by the Hudson's Bay Company. Have to pay three dollars a wagon. Our worst trouble at these large rivers is swimming the stock over. Often after swimming half way over the poor things will turn and come out again. At this place, however, there are Indians who swim the river from morning till night. There is many a drove of cattle that could not be got over without their help. By paying them a small sum, they will take a horse by the bridle or halter and swim over with him. The rest of the horses all follow and by driving and hurrahing to the cattle they will almost always follow the horses, sometimes they fail and turn back. This Fort Boise is nothing more than three new buildings, its inhabitants, the Hudsons Bay Company officials, a few Frenchmen, some half-naked Indians, half breeds, etc.

Friday, September 2nd . . . Came 5 miles this morning, and are now crossing Fall (or Deschutes it is called here) River on a ferry boat. Pay 3 dollars a wagon and swim the stock. This river is very swift and full of rapids. . .

A few days later my eighth child was born. After this we picked up and ferried across the Columbia River, utilizing skiff, canoes and flatboat to get across, taking three days to complete. Here husband traded two yoke of oxen for a half section of land with one-half acre planted to potatoes and a small log cabin and lean-to with no windows. This is the journey's end.

(finis)

Snake River Of Hells Canyon

Johnny Carrey, Cort Conley, Ace Barton

After listening to the complaints of settlers and missionaries, General O.O. Howard ordered Joseph's band onto the Lapwai reservation. The Indians were given one month to make the move. Joseph replied:

War can and ought to be avoided. I want no war. My people have always been friends of the white men. Why are you in such a hurry? I can not get ready to move in thirty days. Our stock is scattered and the Snake River is very high. Let us wait till fall, then the river will be low. We want time to hunt up our stock and gather supplies for the winter.

General Howard was unmoved by the plea. "If you let the time run over one day, the soldiers will be there to drive you on the reservation and cattle outside the reservation at that time will fall into the hands of the white men."

The Indians went into the canyons and draws to gather their horses and cattle with heavy-hearted haste.

When the Indians arrived on the bank with their stock they found the river in full spring flood. They made rafts from tightly rolled skins lashed together and loaded with packs. Riders used horses to tow the rafts across the powerful current. The skilled horsemen and range-wise horses accomplished the crossing without loss of life. While most of the Nez Perce are believed to have crossed at Dug Bar, a few may have crossed upriver at Pittsburg Landing. They trailed their stock up Divide Creek, crossed the ridge, went down across the turbulent Salmon.

The Big Sky
A.B. Guthrie, Jr.

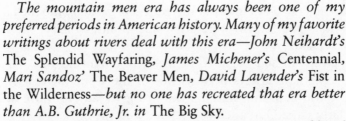

> *The mountain men era has always been one of my preferred periods in American history. Many of my favorite writings about rivers deal with this era—John Neihardt's* The Splendid Wayfaring, *James Michener's* Centennial, *Mari Sandoz'* The Beaver Men, *David Lavender's* Fist in the Wilderness—*but no one has recreated that era better than A.B. Guthrie, Jr. in* The Big Sky.
>
> *When that book was made into a movie, it was filmed on the upper Snake River in Jackson Hole, Wyoming, where a few years later I began my career as a professional river guide. Our launch site for river trips was the cut bank used by the movie company to launch the* Mandan, *the keelboat that took Boone Caudil into the beaver country near the headwaters of the Missouri River.*
>
> *Guthrie's books,* The Big Sky, The Way West, *which won a Pulitzer Prize,* These Thousand Hills, *and* Arfive, *paint a vivid picture of the northern Rockies and their rivers.*

The Missouri was boiling. It overran its bed, clucking among the willow and the cottonwood. It gouged at the bluffs, undercutting the shore. Great sections of bank had slid into it or toppled over, making slow splashes which the current caught up and carried on and lost in its own hurry. Trees came down when the banks gave, falling slow at first and then faster, to the sound of torn air, and lying out in the water, anchored to the broken shore, making dams against which the drift piled. The water moved up against the dams, climbing as it felt for weaknesses, and turned and raced around, breaking white as it found its course again. Out in the channel the current rose, like the back of a snake.

The Missouri was a devil of a river; it was a rolling wall that reared against the *Mandan* and broke around her and reared against her again; it was no river at all but a great loose water that leaped from the mountains and tore through the plains, wild to get to the sea.

As far as a man could see, rain was falling—falling small-dropped and steady, so that the air itself was watery and came into the lungs wet and weak. Looking up river, feeling the breeze square on his face, Jourdonnais lost the river in the mist. The far shore was a shadow. He could see the towline, running from the mast through the bridle, bellying of its own weight, and going on to nothing, toward the crew that was a slow-moving blur upshore.

It was no time for boating, no time for sail or oars or poles or line. A man could lose his boat before he knew it. A shelving bank would wreck her, or a planter, or a sawyer. Most of all, Jourdonnais feared sawyers. A half a dozen times this day he had seen the moving water break and the great limbs spring out like thrashing legs, standing for a moment against the current, naked and huge, and then yielding again and sinking from sight. One leg under the *Mandan* would be enough. Jourdonnais watched the dark water as if he might see beneath it. Romaine stood ahead of him in the bow, a watchful giant of a man who handled his long pole as if it were no heavier than a cane.

It was no time to be moving, but the *Mandan* had to move—ten miles a day, five miles, one, whatever they could strain out. And so they had rowed and poled and towed and put up sail and had to haul it down and put it up again, hoping for long reaches and favorable winds. They had worked from dawn to dark, snatching breakfast and dinner aboard and making camp only when the light was done. Where the shore water was deep they had moved into the bank and the men had stood on the *passe avant* and on the decks, grasping for the brush, pulling the *Mandan* ahead hand over hand.

There was complaint among the crew. They looked at Jourdonnais—not directly, but out of the corners of their eyes—and he had heard them grumbling over their food at night and in their blankets of a morning, waking to the dawn sore and resentful. Every morning now and every night he passed the whisky jug. He led them in songs and made jokes and swore at them and praised them, as if they were children. He and Summers talked at night when they were camped, telling about the Pawnees, who were bad when they found a white man alone. It was just last year, Summers said, that two deserters had gone under on the Platte.

The rain fell in a tiny lisp against the cargo box and ran down the sides. The deck was filmed with water. Pretty soon they would have to bail. Jourdannais felt uneasy about Teal Eye, though she had a robe to sit on and an extra blanket, and he himself had rearranged the buffalo hide that made her little lodge. It would not do for her to get sick. He must save her from sickness and the men. *Mon Dieu*, the men! He would tell them again and have Summers stare at each with that so-hard eye of his. The cats in the cage on the box looked small with their hair wet. They moved around, mewing, not liking the rain. There were only four of them left now. Two had been taken by Francis Chouteau, the trader on the Kansas, for the price of a good plew each, for the price of an Ashley beaver. Painter was in the stern with Teal Eye, protected by the robe.

Jourdonnais squeezed the water from his mustache with the knuckle of his forefinger. April nearly at the half, and the Platte still ahead! He shook his head, thinking about it. How far was it to the Blackfoot Nation, past the Roche Jaune, past the Milk and the Musselshell, maybe clear to the Great Fall? Twenty-three hundred miles? Twenty-five? It was a long summer's work, that was sure. The *Mandan* wouldn't make it unless they used every minute, or maybe would make it late, maybe in time to be frozen in, in country so cold the air cracked like ice and the sun froze and even the *Pieds Noirs* kept to their lodges, dreaming ahead to summer and war parties while they sharpened their scalping knives.

Les Pieds Noirs! A little cold lump came into a man's bowels when he thought about them. Even Lisa had had to give up, and the bones of Immel and Jones and how many others rotted in the Trois Forches or along the Roche Jaune? Jourdonnais shook himself, pushing uneasiness from his mind. It could all be accounted for. The Blackfeet knew Lisa as the friend of their enemies, the Crows. Immel and Jones had set their traps in country forbidden. And neither Lisa nor the others had had Teal Eye, the little squaw who was daughter of a chief. The white trader was bringing her home because the white trader was kind and wanted to be a brother to the Blackfeet. He had journeyed many sleeps and encountered many dangers just to get her back, and he brought with him a red uniform with gold facings and silver buttons that would mark the chief as the great man he was in the nation. Also, he had for his brothers beads and vermilion and guns and powder and some of the drink called firewater. He had brought them past the Sioux, past the Rees, past the Assiniboines, so that his friends, the Blackfeet, might have what other nations had.

All would be well, Jourdonnais told himself again, if only the *Mandan* got there, and got there in time. He would manage. Starting from nothing, as a common voyageur, he had worked himself up, by labor, by saving, by being bolder than other men. And now, along with Summers, he was a bourgeois, for all that he served as his own patron, trader with all his savings and borrowed money, too, invested in an old boat and in traders' goods. He had a chance, a gambler's chance, to make very many dollars, and he would manage. He would push ahead as he had always pushed ahead, and by and by perhaps he and his Jeanette could build themselves a big house far away from Carondelet, and who could call him a *Vide Poche* then?

Out of the bushes along the shore the hunter appeared. He waded out and came aboard as Jourdonnais brought the boat in. His wet buckskins hugged his body. He said, "Jesus!"

"Bad," Jourdonnais agreed.

Summers said "Jesus!" again. "This bank ain't made for the cordelle."

"Or the bed for poling, or the current for rowing, or the wind for the sail. We move, a little, anyway."

"The damn trees, right down to the water."

Jourdonnais looked at the sky. "The river she's straight now, above the Nishnabotna, and the wind wrong, like always."

"*Embarras* ahead," Summers announced.

"Another?"

"Worst yet."

Jourdonnais swore. He looked toward the far shore, across the brown flood and its traffic of drift. "We waste the time going back and forth like a damn ferry. All the time, point to point, we cross and cross again."

Summers' eyes were inquiring.

"Maybe we try, anyhow."

The hunter moved his head dubiously. "The mast might go, or the line, I'm thinking."

"It is not safe, even to cross," Jourdonnais answered, pointing across the water.

"Risky, all right."

"I look, anyhow."

For a hundred feet from shore the fallen tree dammed the current. Drift was piled deep against it, soggy cottonwoods and cedar and dwarf pine from far up river and willow still swollen with buds, making a litter that pulsed with the current and drove tight against the bar of the tree, so that a man might walk on it. Around the end the water swept, smooth-muscled at first and then broken, flying in foam and spray, filling the ears with a steady gushing. The air stank a little with decay, from the bloated bodies of buffaloes that had drowned up river and now were caught in the jam and made little hills of brown in the drift and sometimes pushed around it and ran bobbing in the waves.

Jourdonnais signaled for a halt below the *embarras*. He studied, it, his lids half-drawn over his eyes. "We have to drop back, to cross," he said to Summers, and waited for the reply.

The hunter only nodded.

"Even so, we run the risk." He motioned again toward the channel. "We could be wreck' there, also."

Summers grinned, but his eyes were sober. "I'm thinking we would tie up if we had a fool hen's sense."

Jourdonnais said, "*Non*! Mother of God! Do we spend the summer on the bank?"

"Let's try 'er, then," the hunter said. "You need three men anyhow in the boat, but we need as many hands as we can git on the line."

"Go on. Romaine and I, we will handle her."

Romaine poled the boat toward the bank, and Summers splashed ashore. "We'll take a hitch around a tree and then r'ar at her," he called to Jourdonnais. Romaine was working the *Mandan* out again. Jourdonnais came down from the cargo box and gave him a hand, ignoring Romaine's heavy frown. He saw Summers stride along the bank, walking as a man of purpose walks, his figure blurring with rain as he drew away.

Summers waved his hat. "Ready," Jourdonnais said to Romaine, and climbed back to the helm.

The *Mandan* inched ahead while the water boiled against her nose. The cordelle straightened from its sag, running almost in a line. The rain was thinner now, and Jourdonnais could see the crew, bent and scrambling on the rough and cluttered shore.

The boat came close to the dam, came even with it, out from it by a dozen feet but still in the tow of the current that raced around it. The *Mandan* began to swing like a kite, running out and suddenly turning back toward shore, getting her nose to one side as if to swing around and then overanswering to the towing line and the bridle and the steering oar in Jourdonnais' hand. Romaine jumped from side to side, swinging his pole around with him.

Jourdonnais heard himself saying "*Fort! Fort!*" His body strained to urge her ahead, but she lay at the crest of the sweep, running before it but not pushing into it, like a scared horse before a fence. "*Fort! Fort!*" The men could pull her well enough but for the lack of footing. He saw water squeezing out from the cordelle and standing in beads like sweat. The mast arched with the strain on it. The rain was thick again, making a blur of the crew. He should have told them to take a shorter hold on the line, for the power it would give them.

"*Fort!*" he grunted again, between his teeth, and fell ahead, seeing the brown current streaking under him while his hands clawed for a lashing. Romaine made a splash in the water, and came up and began pawing for shore, bending his streaming face around to see the *Mandan*.

She had reared and spun around as the bridle broke and now she lay tilted while the water beat against her side, held by the line and the mast bending to it. Sprawled on the cargo box, clutching a rope, Jourdonnais said, "O mon Dieu! Mon Dieu!" The boat ran in and out, like the weight at the end of a pendulum. He saw the mast arching over him, the mast that he had insisted be made of hickory, and felt the slant of the cargo box under his belly. "Line! Give line! Easy!" he shouted, knowing he couldn't be heard above the water. He saw Romaine pull himself from the river and stand dripping for a minute, staring at the *Mandan*, and then begin lunging up shore through the mud.

He worked himself off the cargo box and crawled to the spare pole and got it over the side while he braced himself on the slope by one foot and a knee. He forced the pole through the water and felt for the bottom, hoping to bring the *Mandan* part way round. The *Mandan* and all that he might be and all his years of work and purpose tilted on the brink of nothing, held by a hickory stick and a string, tilted for a minute, for an hour, for a lifetime that seemed as long as forever and no longer than yesterday. He heard himself shouting, crying for the crew to ease up.

His voice seemed prisoned, kept within the *Mandan* herself by the rush of water on her side, or lost beyond her in the little, busy rain, but at last he felt the line give, felt the boat rock and come to balance against the cordelle again, and saw the *embarras* easing upstream.

He poled her in after a while, and Romaine came up, puffing, and made her fast to a tree. After him came Summers and the crew.

Jourdonnais turned and looked the boat over. "The cats," he said "I did not see them go." And suddenly he thought, "Teal Eye!" and jumped to the *passe avant* and ran along it to the stern. He saw Painter, standing stiff-legged on a blanket. He yelled, "Gone! Look, everybody! Along the bank. She is gone. Teal Eye!"

He jumped from the boat and plunged ashore, motioning. "All! All! Look!" He started running. "You, Summers, you have eyes like the Indian."

They scattered into the brush and came out of it farther down and looked out at the water and along the banks. "Go on! Go on! Farther down! She could be farther."

It was the young Kentuckian, Caudill, who found her. They heard him shout and ran to meet him and found him carrying her through the brush. "She was holdin' to a loose log," he said. "Near done in, too. I had to swim for her." He looked down at his dripping jeans.

Jourdonnais took charge of her. "We get some dry clothes, little one," he said, "and then the fire and food." She looked at him, saying nothing, her eyes melting in the thin face that seemed all the thinner now. Her clothes hung to her small limbs. "She look like the wet cat but chic, still," Jourdonnais thought. Aloud he said, "Tell her to get dry and change clothes, Summers. She understand you better. She get the fever, maybe."

The girl seemed to understand. She barely nodded. Jourdonnais lifted her into the stern.

He walked away then and stopped when he came even with the nose of the *Mandan* and looked across the rolling water and up it, feeling tired but glad with a fierce gladness. "Four cats," he said. "You great big damn tough river, you only get four cats." He turned back. "Come on. We all have a drink."

The Lost Journal of John Colton Sumner

Jack Sumner was chief boatman on Major John Wesley Powell's first exploration of the canyons of the Green and Colorado rivers in 1869. At Powell's request Sumner kept a journal that is often more colorful, if less scientific, than Powell's. It contains many of Powell's observations and measurements and was used in part as a source for Powell's own journal because certain segments of his journal were lost.

Three of Powell's men left the expedition, carrying with them, at Powell's request, certain expedition documents which were lost when the men were killed by Indians. Sumner's notes, which were fortunately sent out and published disappeared into the labyrinth of Powell's office. We are indebted to Otis "Dock" Marston, Colorado River historian, for digging these excerpts out of the archives of the Democrat.

Because Powell's Journal has appeared in many forms and excerpts, I have not included it in this collection. The Sumner material is fresh and alive. For more of the Sumner flavor, read Robert Brewster Stanton's Colorado River Controversy, *recently republished by Westwater Books (1982). Stanton interviewed Sumner shortly before the latter's death in 1907, in an attempt to clear up the mystery of the separation and deaths of the men who left the 1869 expedition.*

Adaily journal of the Colorado Exploring Expedition (Jack Sumner's Diary of the First Powell Expedition from Green River, Wyoming, to the Uinta Basin)

May 24, 1869.—After many weeks of weary waiting, today sees us all ready for the adventures of an unknown country. Heretofore all attempts in exploring the Colorado of the West, throughout its entire course, have been miserable failures. Whether our attempt will turn out the same time alone can show. If we fail it will not be for the want of a complete outfit of material and men used to hardships.

After much blowing off of gas and the fumes of bad whiskey, we were all ready by two o'clock and pulled out into the swift stream. The Emma Dean, a light four-oared shell, lightly loaded, carrying as crew Professor J.W. Powell, W.H. Dunn, and a trapper,[1] designed as a scouting party, taking the lead. The "Maid of the Canon" followed close in her wake, manned by Walter H. Powell and George Y. Bradley, carrying two thousand pounds of freight. Next on the way was "Kitty Clyde's Sister," manned by as jolly a brace of boys as ever swung a whip over a lazy ox, W.H. Rhodes, of Missouri, and Andrew Hall, of Fort Laramie, carrying the same amount of freight. The last to leave the miserable adobe village was the "No Name" (piratic craft) manned by O.G. Howland, Seneca Howland, and Frank Goodman. We make a pretty show as we float down the swift, glossy river. As Kitty's crew have been using the whip more of late years than the oars, she ran on the sand-bar in the middle of the river, got off of that, and ran ashore on the east side, near the mouth of Bitter creek, but finally got off and came down to the rest of the fleet in gallant style, her crew swearing she would not "gee" or "haw" a "cuss." We moved down about seven miles and camped for the night on the eastern shore where there is a large quantity of cord wood. As it was a cold, raw night, we stole a lot of it to cook with. Proff., Walter, and Bradley spent a couple of hours geologising on the east side. Howland and Dunn went hunting down the river; returned at dark with a small sized rabbit. Rather slim rations for ten hungry men. The balance of the party stopped in camp, and exchanged tough stories at a fearful rate. We turned in early, as most of the men had been up for several proceding nights, taking leave of their many friends, "a la Muscovite." The natural consequence were fog[g]y ideas and snarly hair.

May 26th.—All afloat early; went about three miles, when we came to our first rapid. It cannot be navigated by any boat with safety, in the main channel, but the river being pretty high, it made a narrow channel, under the overhanging willows on the west shore, so that we were not delayed more than twenty minutes, all the boats but Kitty's Sister getting through easily. She getting on a rock, compelled Rhodes to get overboard and pry her off. About 4 o'clock, came to a meadow of about a thousand acres, lying between Green River and Henry's Fork. Camped for the night on the east shore, about a mile above the mouth of Henry's Fork.* Passed the mouth of Black's Fork of the Green River today; it is but little wider at the mouth than at Fort Bridger, but deep. Henry's Fork is a stream about thirty feet wide, and is fed by the snows of the Uinta Mountains, about seventy-five miles northwest of this camp; it has some good pasturage on it, but no farming land, as it is at too great an altitude. At the mouth is a good place for one or two ranches. There are about three hundred acres of good land, but is inundated nearly every spring by freshets. There is a large stack of hay standing in the meadow, that has been left over from last year's crop.

May 29th.—Proff. [Powell] climbed the hill on the east side of the canyon and measured it with a barometer; h[e]ight above the river 1140 feet, not perpendicular. There is a cliff on the west side that is fifty feet higher, and perpendicular. The rock is hard, fiery-red sandstone. It has been named Flaming Gorge.

May 30.—Professor, Bradley, Senica, and Hall went up the river five miles, measuring a geological section. All in camp by three o'clock, when we loaded up and pulled on again into a channel as crooked as a street in Boston. Passed out of Flaming Gorge into Horseshoe Canon, out of Horseshoe Canon into Kingfisher Canon. While rounding a bend, we came on a herd of mountain sheep, that scampered up a steep, rocky side of the canon at an astonishing rate. The crews of the freight boats opened a volley on them that made the wilderness ring, reminding us all of other scenes and times, when we were the scampering party. Passed the mouth of a small stream coming in from the west, which we named King Fisher Creek, as there was a bird of that species perched on the branch of a dead willow, watching the finny tribe with the determination of purpose that we often see exhibited by politicians while watching for the spoils of office.[4] Killed two geese, and saw a great number of beavers today, but failed to get any of them. No sooner would we get within gun-shot, than down they would go with a plumping noise like dropping a heavy stone into the water. Made seven miles today, and camped for the night on the west bank opposite a huge grayish white sandstone that loomed up a thousand feet from the water's edge, very much the shape of an old-fashioned straw beehive, and we named it "Beehive Point." Saw the tracks of elk, deer and sheep on the sand. Near our camp, Goodman saw one elk, but missed it.

June 2d.—All out early to breakfast; dispatched it, and let Kitty's Sister over the falls as we did the small boat. Then came the real hard work, carrying the freight a hundred yards or more over a mass of loose rocks, tumbled together like the ruins of some old fortress. Not a very good road to pack seven thousand pounds of freight. Got the loads of the two boats over, loaded them, and moved down three hundred yards to still water; tied up and returned to the other boats, to serve them the same; got everything around in still water by 11 o'clock; had dinner and smoked all round; distance from Bee-hive Point unknown; course east of south continuous canyon of red sand-stone; estimated height of one thousand feet; three highest perpendicular walls estimated at two thousand two hundred feet; named Red Canyon; on a rock the east side there is the name and date—"Ashley, 1825"—scratched on evidently by some trapper's knife: all aboard, and off we go down the river; beautiful river, that increases its speed as we leave the fall, till it gets a perfect rapid all the way, but clear of sunken rocks; so we run through the waves at express speed; made seventeen miles through Red Stone canyon in less than an hour running time, the boats bounding through the waves like a school of porpoise. The Emma being very light is tossed about in a way that threatens to shake her to pieces, and is nearly as hard to ride as a Mexican pony. We plunge along singing, yelling, like drunken sailors, all feeling that such rides do not come every day. It was like sparking a black-eyed girl—just dangerous enough to be exciting. About three o'clock we came suddenly out to a beautiful valley about two by five miles in extent. Camped about the middle of it, on the west side, under two large pine trees: spread our bedding out to dry, while we rested in the shade. Two of the party came in at sunset, empty handed except the Professor, he being fortunate enough to get a brace of grouse. Spread our blankets on the clean, green grass, with no roof but the old pines above us, through which we could see the sentinel stars shining from the deep blue pure sky, like happy spirits looking out through the blue eyes of a pure hearted woman.

June 5th.—This morning we were all awakened by the wild birds singing in the old tree above our heads. The sweet songs of birds, the fragrant odor of wild roses, the low, sweet rippling of the ever murmuring river at sunrise in the wilderness, made everything as lovely as a poet's dream. I was just wandering into paradise; could see the dim shadow of the dark-eyed houris, when I was startled by the cry, "Roll out; bulls in the corral; chain up the gaps"—our usual call to breakfast. The hour is vanished, and I rolled out to fried fish and hot coffee.

June 8th.—Pulled out early and entered into as hard a day's work as I ever wish to see. Went about a half a mile when we came to a terrible rapid, and had to let our boats down with ropes. Passed about a dozen bad rapids in the forenoon. Camped for dinner on the east side at the foot of a perpendicular rose-colored wall, about fifteen hundred feet;

pulled out again at one o'clock; had proceeded about half a mile when the scouting boat came to a place where we could see nothing but spray and foam. She was pulled ashore on the east side and the freight boats instantly signaled to land with us. The Maid and Kitty's Sister did so but the No Name being too far out in the current and having shipped a quantity of water in the rapid above, could not be landed, though her crew did their best in trying to pull ashore at the head of the rapid, she struck a rock and swung into the waves sideways and instantly swamped. Her crew held to her while she drifted down with the speed of the wind; went perhaps 200 yards, when she struck another rock that stove her bow in; swung around again and drifted toward a small island in the middle of the river; here was a chance for her crew, though a very slim one. Goodman made a spring and disappeared; Howland followed next, and made the best leap I ever saw made by a two-legged animal, and landed in water where he could touch the rocks on the bottom; a few vigorous strokes carried him safe to the island. Seneca was the last rat to leave the sinking ship, and made the leap for life barely in time; had he stayed aboard another second we would have lost as good and true a man as can be found in any place. Our attention was now turned to Goodman, whose head we could see bobbing up and down in a way that might have provoked a hearty laugh had he been in a safe place. Howland got a pole that happened to be handy, reached one end to him and hauled him on the isle. Had they drifted thirty feet further down nothing could have saved them, as the river was turned into a perfect hell of waters that nothing could enter and live. The boat drifted into it and was instantly smashed to pieces. In half a second there was nothing but a dense foam, with a cloud of spray above it, to mark the spot.

June 20th.—All hands in today, taking a general rest. Wrote our names on Echo rocks opposite the camp. The entire distance from the southern end of the valley called Brown's Hole to the mouth of the Bear river is a canyon, except at two creeks on the west side, where there is a gorge cut through by the water of each. It has been named Ladore canyon by the Professor, but the idea of diving into musty trash to find names for new discoveries on a new continent is un-American, to say the least. Distance through it, 25 miles; general course, 25 degrees west of south; average h[e]ight on both sides about 1700 feet; highest cliff measured (Black Tail Cliff) 2307 feet. There are many still higher but having enough other work on our hands to keep us busy, we did not attempt to measure them.[11]

June 27th.—Off again at seven, down a river that cannot be surpassed for wild beauty of scenery, sweeping in great curves through magnificent groves of cottonwood. It has an average width of two hundred yards and depth enough to float a New Orleans packet. Our easy stroke of eight miles an hour conveys us just fast enough to enjoy the scenery, as the view changes with kaleidescopic rapidity. Made sixty-three miles today, and camped on the west side, at the mouth of a small, dirty creek. Killed eight wild geese on the way.

[1] The title of trapper was of high standing from 1824 to 1840 when the mountain men were stripping the fur-bearing animals from the Upper Colorado River Basin, and Sumner was accepting this status in the third person.*

*Site of first rendezvous of mountain men (trappers)—1825.

[4] The stream later acquired the name Sheep Creek. Beehive Point is opposite.*

[11] The Canyon of Lodore was measured as eighteen and one-half miles by the 1922 survey.*

*Notes by Otis Dock Marston.

Snake River Exploration of 1876–1877

Lt. G. C. Doane

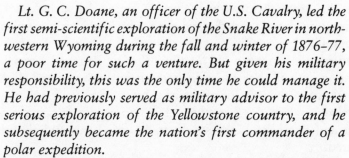

Lt. G. C. Doane, an officer of the U.S. Cavalry, led the first semi-scientific exploration of the Snake River in north-western Wyoming during the fall and winter of 1876–77, a poor time for such a venture. But given his military responsibility, this was the only time he could manage it. He had previously served as military advisor to the first serious exploration of the Yellowstone country, and he subsequently became the nation's first commander of a polar expedition.

Only a few months before his Snake River Expedition, Doane had been at Little Bighorn the day after the battle to evacuate the wounded. Soon after his return, he chased the Nez Perce tribes trying to reach Canada. His Snake River Expedition was a more personally rewarding goal than Indian fighting, but it was doomed from the start. He and his men covered little more than a tenth of the 1053-mile length of the Snake. Their experience, however, is worth reading about.

Tuesday, *November 7, twenty-eighth day.* Started the loaded boat in the stream but had to unload her and pack the animals with the property. The stream led into a small canon immediately and descended over granite ledges half a mile with a fall of two hundred feet or more in that distance. The water merely trickled over this wide granite slope, and the boat we dragged over it by hand. Hard and slow work. Came out in a little valley marshy in the summer time, and camped. Distance 3 m. Weather fine.

Wednesday, November 8, twenty-ninth day. Clear cold day. 23°. Worked very hard all day dragging the boat over rocks in a channel where she would not float at any point. Used a mule part of the time and wore out the bottom of the boat as well as ourselves making three miles. Abandoned one horse and one mule. Left the boat at sundown and went on to camp. Distance 6 m.

Thursday, November 9, thirtieth day. Went back after the boat and dragged it to camp during the day. The Sergeant took all the heavier stuff three miles below to the head of a canon and returned.

The basin through which we have been travelling since leaving the lake is mostly timbered, but contains large spaces of crossed foothills. The valleys are marshy and grownup with willows. There has been a great deal of work done along all the water courses by Beaver. The country is very rough being a mass of converging ridges descending from the great divide which curves around between the Upper Yellowstone above the Lake and the Snake River basin in which we are travelling.

Saturday, November 18, thirty-ninth day. Reached camp in the forenoon with all the calking melted out of the seams and all the ice thawed out of the interior of the boat by the floods of boiling water passed through in the river channel just above. Took her out of the water and put her on the stocks to be dried out and thoroughly repaired.

Her bottom was a sight to behold. The green pine planks were literally shivered by pounding on the rocks. The tough stripping of the seams, two inches or more in thickness was torn away. Two of the heaviest planks were worn through in the waist of the vessel, and three holes were found in her sides. The stern was so bruised and stove that we had to hew out a new one. We took out the seats, floor and bulkheads, and this gave us lumber enough to put on a new bottom. Mended the holes with tin and leather. Recalked her, using candles and pitch mixed for the filling. Split young pines and put a heavy strip on each seam and made her stronger than ever. This occupied the 19th which was a stormy day, and the 20th, which was clear long enough to enable us to finish the boat.

When it is remembered that the wood had to be dry before the pitch would adhere, and that we were obliged to keep a bed of coals under the boat constantly to effect this, on ground saturated with snow water and with the snow falling most of the time, it can be realized that the labor was of the most fatiguing description. Half of the party worked while the others cared for the animals and slept.

Warren here came out as an invaluable member of the party. He kept the camp full of trout and we fared sumptuously.

The problem was to get where the boat could carry the property and make distance before the animals gave out. Also to get to settlements before rations were exhausted. I know we had the formidable "Mad River Canon" of the old trappers between us and human habitations.[15] With plenty of large game in range, this would have caused no uneasiness, but we were descending daily and leaving the game behind.

At sundown a black ousel or water canary lit on a rock near camp and sang for an hour, the most wonderful flood of melody I ever heard any bird pour forth. Its notes were similar to those of a canary, but many times louder. These birds are solitary in habit, do not sing in the summer time, frequent water falls, and are scarce. This one was evidently not migrating, but entirely at home. It was the size of an ordinary blackbird.[16]

Tuesday, December 12, sixty-third day. The River was becoming better, the ice foot more uniform and the channel free from frozen pools when all of a sudden the boat touched the margin, turned under it, and the next instant was dancing end over end in the swift bold current. All of the horse meat, all the property, arms, instruments and note books were in the roaring stream. A few hundred yards below there was a narrow place where the ice foot almost touched the middle of the river. We ran thither and caught whatever floated. The clothing bags, valise, bedding, bundles, and the lodge were saved. All else, excepting one hind quarter of the old horse meat went to the bottom and was seen no more. All the rubber boots were gone excepting mine. The warm clothing all floated and was saved. We dragged in the boat by the tow line and pulled her out of the water and far up on a ledge of rock. 6 miles.

Started the Sergeant and Warren at once on their way down the river. The rest of us dried out the property and rested until morning.

Wednesday, December 13, sixty-fourth day. Last night was bitterly cold, and we slept by a roaring fire on a ledge of rock. We were camped at a place where several dead pines had fallen in a mass of broken up fire wood and dried out what was left of our sadly diminished outfit with less trouble than usual. We had our sheath knives left, and matches. Cooked our horse meat on sticks, Indian fashion. Started early and worked over frozen pools and open rapids, all day without accident. Toward evening had a fine open river. Pulled the boat out as usual at night. Seven miles. A cold night as usual. Canon very deep and the descent rapid.

Thursday, December 14, sixty-fifth day. Moved on as before. Frozen pools and rapids. Hundreds of otter played around us on the ice. The boat is becoming ice bound and we have no axes or hatchets with which to chip out the rapidly accumulating ice. She floats all right but is cranky.

After working hard all day we came to an open space with two rapids. Passed them both successfully but the boat was filled as it came to the bank. We bailed her out and went on. Travelled as long as we could see, all of us walking on the ice foot excepting Applegate, who remained in the boat to balance her and keep her off the rocks and away from the ice foot. Camped in a pocket in the canon and pulled the boat into what we thought a place secure from ice gorges. We had eaten our last horse meat for breakfast, and had no food left. 6 miles. Dried out bedding as usual and all slept soundly.

Friday, December 15, sixty-sixth day. Morning intensely cold. Stowed away the bedding in rolls with the valise, high up among the rocks and started, unarmed, without food, and in an unknown wilderness to find settlements seven miles up on a stream which we had no positive assurance of being able to recognize when we came to its mouth.

[15]"Mad River" was the name given to the canyon below the mouth of the Hoback River by the French Canadian voyageurs with Wilson Price Hunt's party of Astorians in 1811. These experienced canoemen took one look at the canyon and shook their heads—they considered it unnavigable. (Washington Irving, *Astoria*)

[16]This chunky, slate-colored bird loves the rushing mountain streams. From a precarious perch on a slippery, mid-stream rock, he bobs energetically until he spots a choice bit in the water and makes his dive. The bird sings year round.

Along Alaska's Great River
Frederick Schwatka

Frederick Schwatka (1849–1892), a West Point graduate and career Army officer, became one of America's first Arctic explorers. In 1883 he led a secret military expedition down the Yukon River, traveling more than 1300 miles by log raft. He wrote about his experiences in terms river runners understand today, a century after his pioneering venture.

Lake Marsh gave us four days of variable sailing on its waters, when, on the 29th of June, we emerged from it and once more felt the exhilaration of a rapid course on a swift river, an exhilaration that was not allowed to die rapidly away, by reason of the great amount of exercise we had to go through in managing the raft in its many eccentric phases of navigation. On the lakes, whether in storm or still weather, one man stationed at the stern oar of the raft had been sufficient, as long as he kept awake, nor was any great harm done if he fell asleep in a quiet breeze, but once on the river an additional oarsman at the bow sweep was imperatively needed, for at short turns or sudden bends, or when nearing half-sunken bowlders or tangled masses of driftwood or bars of sand, mud or gravel, or while steering clear of eddies and slack water, it was often necessary to do some very lively work at both ends of the raft in swinging the ponderous contrivance around to avoid these obstacles, and in the worst cases two or three other men assisted the oarsmen in their difficult task. Just how much strength a couple of strong men could put on a steering sweep was a delicate matter to gauge, and too often in the most trying places our experiments in testing the questions were failures, and with a sharp snap the oar would part, a man or two would sit down violently without stopping to pick out the most luxurious places, and the craft like a wild animal unshackled would go plowing through the fallen timber that lined the banks, or bring up on the bar or bowlder we had been working hard to avoid. We slowly became practical oar makers, however, and toward the latter part of the journey had some crude but effective implements that defied annihilation.

As we leisurely and lazily crept along the lakes somebody would be driving away *ennui* by dressing down pins with a hatchet, boring holes with an auger and driving pins with an ax, until by the time the lakes were all passed I believe that no two logs crossed each other in the raft that were not securely pinned at the point of juncture with at least one pin, and if the logs were large ones with two or three. In this manner our vessel was as solid as it was possible to make such a craft, and would bring up against a bowlder with a shock and swing dizzily around in a six or seven mile current with no more concern that if it were a slab in a mill race.

I believe I have made the remark in a previous chapter that managing a raft—at least our method of managing a raft—on a lake was a tolerably simple affair, especially with a favorable wind, and to tell the truth, one can not manage it at all except with a favorable wind. It was certainly the height of simplicity when compared with its navigation upon a river, although at first sight one might perhaps think the reverse; at least I had thought so, and from the conversation of the whites and Indians of southeastern Alaska, I knew that their opinions coincided with mine; but I was at length compelled to hold differently from them in this matter, as in many others. Especially was this navigation difficult on a swift river like the Yukon, and I know of none that can maintain a flow of more even rapidity from source to mouth than this great stream. It is not very hard to keep a raft or any floating object in the center of the current of a stream, even if left alone at times, but the number of things which present themselves from time to time to drag it out of this channel seems marvelous.

Old watermen and rafting lumbermen know that while a river is rising it is hard to keep the channel, even the driftwood created by the rise clinging to the shores of the stream. Accordingly they are anxious for the moment when this driftwood begins to float along the main current and out in the middle of the stream, for then they know the water is subsiding, and from that point it requires very little effort to keep in the swiftest current. Should this drift matter be equally distributed over the running water it is inferred that the river is at "a stand-still," as they say. An adept can closely judge of the variations and stage of water by this means.

In a river with soft or earthy banks (and in going the whole length of the Yukon, over two thousand miles, we saw several varieties of shores), the swift current, in which one desires to keep when the current is the motive power, nears the shores only at points or curves, where it digs out the ground into steep perpendicular banks, which if at all high make it impossible to find a camping place for the night, and out of this swift current the raft had to be rowed to secure a camp at evening, while breaking camp next morning we had to work it back into the current again. Nothing could be more aggravating than after leaving this swift current to find a camp, as evening fell, to see no possible chance for such a place on the side we had chosen and to go crawling along in slack water while trees and brushes swept rapidly past borne on the swift waters we had quitted.

If the banks of a river are wooded—and no stream can show much denser growth on its shores than the Yukon—the trees that are constantly tumbling in from these places that are being undermined, and yet hanging on by their roots, form a series of *chevaux de frise* or *abatis*, to which is given the backwoods cognomen of "sweepers," and a man on the upper side of a raft plunging through them in a swift current almost wishes himself a beaver or a muskrat so that he can dive out and escape.

Often when camped in some desolate spot or floating lazily along, having seen no inhabitants for days, we would be startled by the sound of a distant gun-shot on the banks, which would excite our curiosity to see the savage sportsman; but we soon came to trace these reports to the right cause, that of falling banks, although not until after we had several times been deceived. Once or twice we actually saw these tremendous cavings in of the banks quite near us, and more frequently than we wanted we floated almost underneath some that were not far from the crisis of their fate, a fate which we thought might be precipitated by some accidental collision of our making. By far the most critical moment was when both the current and a strong wind set in against one of these banks. On such occasions we were often compelled to tie up to the bank and wait for better times, or if the danger was confined to a short stretch we would fight it out until either the whole party was exhausted or our object was attained.

Whenever an island was made out ahead and it appeared to be near the course of our drifting, the conflicting guesses we indulged in as to which shore of the island we should skirt would indicate the difficulty of making a correct estimate. It takes a peculiarly well practiced eye to follow with certainty the line of the current of the stream from the bow of the raft beyond any obstruction in sight a fair distance ahead, and on more than one occasion our hardest work with the oars and poles was rewarded by finding ourselves on the very bar or flat we had been striving to avoid. The position of the sun, both vertical and horizontal, its brightness and the character of the clouds, the clearness and swiftness of the water, the nature and strength of the wind, however lightly it might be blowing, and a dozen other circumstances had to be taken into account in order to solve this apparently simple problem. If we would determine at what point in the upper end of the island the current was parted upon either side (and at any great distance this was often quite as difficult a problem as the other), one could often make a correct guess by projecting a tree directly beyond and over this point against the distant hills. If the tree crept along these hills to the right, the raft might pass to the left of the island, and vice versa; this would certainly happen if the current was not deflected by some bar or shoal between the raft and the island. And such shoals and bars of gravel, sand and mud are very frequent obstructions in front of an island—at least it was so on the Yukon—indeed the coincidence was too frequent to be without significance. These bars and shoals were not merely prolongations from the upper point of the island, but submerged islands, so to speak, just in front of them, and between the two a steamboat could probably pass. Using tall trees as guides to indicate on which side of the island the raft might pass was, as I have said, not so easy as appears at first sight, for unless the tree could be made out directly over the dividing point of the current, all surmises were of little value. The tall spruce trees on the right and left flanks of the island in sight were always the most conspicuous, being fewer in number, and more prominent in their isolation, than the dense growth of the center of the island, as it was seen "end on" from above. People were very prone to use these convenient reference marks in making their calculations, and one can readily perceive when the trees were near and the island fairly wide, both of the outer trees would appear to diverge in approaching, and according as one selected the right or the left of the two trees, one would infer that our course was to the left or right of the island. As one stood on the bow—as we always called the down-stream end of the raft, although it was shaped no differently from the stern—and looked forward on the water flowing along, the imagination easily conceives that one can follow up from that position to almost any thing ahead and see the direction of the current leading straight for it. Eddies and slack currents, into which a raft is very liable to swing as it rounds a point with an abrupt turn in the axis of the current, are all great nuisances, for though one may not get into the very heart of any of them, yet the sum total of delay in a day's drift is often considerable, and by a little careful management in steering the raft these troubles may nearly always be avoided. Of course, one is often called upon to choose between these and other impediments, more or less aggravating, so that one's attention is constantly active as the raft drifts along.

In a canal-like stream of uniform width, which gives little chance for eddies or slack water—and the upper Yukon has many long stretches that answer to this description—everything goes along smoothly enough until along toward evening, when the party wishes to go into camp while the river is tearing along at four or five miles an hour. I defy anyone who has never been similarly situated, to have any adequate conception of the way in which a ponderous vessel like our raft, constructed of large logs and loaded with four or five tons of cargo and crew, will bring up against any obstacle while going at this rate. If there are no eddies into which it can be rowed or steered and its progress thereby stopped or at least slackened, it is very hard work indeed to go into camp, for should the raft strike end on, a side log or two may be torn out and the vessel transformed by the shock into a lozenge-shaped affair. Usually, under these circumstances, we would bring the raft close in shore, and with the bow oar hold its head well out into the stream, while with the steering oar the stern end would be thrown against the bank and there held, scraping along as firmly as two or three men could do it, and this frictional brake would be kept up steadily until we slowed down a little, when one or two, or even half-a-dozen persons would jump ashore at a favorable spot, and with a rope complete the slackening until it would warrant our twisting the rope around a tree on the bank and a cross log on the raft, when from both places the long rope would be slowly allowed to pay out under strong and increasing friction, or "snubbing" as logmen call it, and this would bring the craft to a standstill in water so swift as to boil up over the stern logs, whereupon it would receive a series of snug lashings. If the position was not favorable for camping we would slowly "drop" the craft down stream by means of the rope to some better site, never allowing her to proceed at a rate of speed that we could not readily control. If, however, we were unsuccessful in making our chosen camping ground and had drifted below it, there was not sufficient power in our party, nor even in the strongest rope we had, ever to get the craft up stream in the average current, whether by tracking or any other means, to the intended spot.

Good camping places were not to be had in every stretch of the river, and worse than all, they had to be selected a long way ahead in order to be able to make them, with our slow means of navigation, from the middle of the broad river where we usually were.

Oftentimes a most acceptable place would be seen just abreast of it, having until then been concealed by some heavily wooded spur or point, and then of course it would be too late to reach it with our slow craft, while to saunter along near shore, so as to take immediate advantage of such a possible spot, was to sacrifice a good deal of our rapid progress. To run from swift into slacker water could readily be accomplished by simply pointing the craft in the direction one wanted to go, but the reverse process was not so easy, at least by the same method. I suppose the proper way to manage so clumsy a concern as a raft, would be by means of side oars and rowing it end on (and this we did on the lakes in making a camp or in gaining the shore when a head wind set in), but as our two oars at bow and stern were the most convenient for the greater part of the work, we used them entirely, always rowing our bundle of logs broadside on to the point desired, provided that no bars or other obstacles interfered. We generally kept the bow end inclined to the shore that we were trying to reach, a plan that was of service, as I have shown, in passing from swift to slack water, and in a three mile current by using our oars rowing broadside on we could keep at an angle of about thirty degrees from the axis of the stream as we made shoreward in this position. The knowledge of this fact enabled us to make a rough calculation as to the point at which we should touch the bank. The greater or less swiftness of the current would of course vary this angle and our calculations accordingly.

Our bundles of effects on the two corduroy decks made quite high piles fore and aft, and when a good strong wind was blowing—and Alaska in the summer is the land of wind—we had by way of sail power a spread of broadside area that was incapable of being lowered. More frequently than was pleasant the breeze carried us along under "sweepers" or dragged us over bars or drove us down unwelcome channels of slack water. In violent gales we were often actually held against the bank, all movement in advance being effectually checked. A mild wind was always welcome, for in the absence of a breeze when approaching the shore the mosquitoes made existence burdensome.

During hot days on the wide open river—singular as it may seem so near the Arctic Circle—the sun would strike down from overhead with a blistering effect and a bronzing effect from its reflection in the dancing waters that made one feel as though he were floating on the Nile, Congo or Amazon, or any where except in the very shadow of the Arctic Circle. Roughly improvised tent flies and flaps helped us to screen ourselves to a limited extent from the tropical torment, but if hung too high, the stern oarsman, who had charge of the "ship," could see nothing ahead on his course, and the curtain would have to come down. No annoyance could seem more singular in the Arctic and sub-Arctic zones than a blistering sun or a swarm of mosquitoes, and yet I believe my greatest discomforts in those regions came from these same causes, certainly from the latter. Several times our thermometer registered but little below 100° Fahrenheit in the shade, and the weather seemed much warmer even than that, owing to the bright reflections that gleamed from the water upon our faces.

"Cut-offs" through channels that led straight across were often most deceptive affairs, the swifter currents nearly always swinging around the great bends of the river. Especially bad was a peculiarly seductive "cut off" with a tempting by swift current as you entered it, caused by its flowing over a shallow bar, whereupon the current would rapidly and almost immediately deepen and would consequently slow down to a rate that was provoking beyond measure, especially as one saw one's self overtaken by piece after piece of drift-timber that by keeping to the main channel had "taken the longest way around as the shortest way home," and beaten us by long odds in the race. And worse than all it was not always possible to avoid getting in these side "sloughs of despond," even when we had learned their tempting little tricks of offering us a swifter current at the entrance, for this very swiftness produced a sort of suction on the surface water that drew in every thing that passed within a distance of the width of its entrance.

Of submerged obstructions, snags were of little account, for the great ponderous craft would go plowing through and casting aside some of the most formidable of them. I doubt very much if snags did us as much harm as benefit, for as they always indicated shoal water, and were easily visible, especially with glasses, they often served us as beacons. I saw very few of the huge snags which have received the appellation of "sawyers" on the Mississippi and Missouri, and are so much dreaded by the navigators of those waters.

Sand, mud and gravel bars were by far the worst obstruction we had to contend with, and I think I have given them in the order of their general perversity in raft navigation, sand being certainly the worst and gravel the slightest.

Sand bars and splits were particularly aggravating, and when the great gridiron of logs ran up on one of them in a swift current there was "fun ahead," to use a western expression of negation. Sometimes the mere jumping overboard of all the crew would lighten the craft so that she would float forward a few yards, and in lucky instances might clear the obstruction; but this was not often the case, and those who made preparations for hard work were seldom disappointed. In a swift current the running water would sweep out the sand around the logs of the raft until its buoyancy would prevent its sinking any deeper, and out of this rut the great bulky thing would have to be lifted before it would budge an inch in a lateral direction, and when this was accomplished, and, completely fagged out, we would stop to take a breath or two, we would often be gratified by seeing our noble craft sink down again, necessitating a repetition of the process. The simplest way to get off a sand bar was to find (by sounding with a stick or simply wading around), the point nearest to a deep navigable channel and then to swing the raft, end for end, up stream, even against the swiftest current that might come boiling over the upper logs, until that channel was reached. There was no more happy moment in a day's history than when, after an hour or so had been spent in prying the vessel inch by inch against the current, we could finally see the current catch it on the same side upon which we were working and perform the last half of our task in a few seconds, where perhaps we had spent as many hours upon our portion of the work. At one bad place, on the upper end of an island, we had to swing our forty-two foot corvette around four times. Our longest detention by a sand bar was three hours and fifty minutes.

Mud bars were not nearly so bad, unless the materials was of a clayey consistency, when a little adhesiveness would be added to the other impediments, and again, as we always endeavored to keep in the swift water we seldom encountered a mud bar. But when one occurred near to a camping place, it materially interfered with our wading ashore with our heavy camping effects on our backs, and would reduce our rubber boots to a deplorable looking condition. Elsewhere, it was possible to pry the raft right through the mud bank, by dint of muscle and patience, and then we could sit down on the outer logs of the deck and wash our boots in the water at leisure as we floated along. Our raft drew from twenty to twenty-two inches of water, and of course it could not ground in any thing deeper, so that good rubber boots coming up over the thighs kept our feet comparatively dry when overboard; but there were times when we were compelled to get in almost to our middle; and when the water was so swift that it boiled up over their tops and filled them they were about as useless an article as can be imagined, so that we went into all such places barefooted.

The best of all the bars were those of gravel, and the larger and coarser the pebbles the better. When the pebbles were well cemented into a firm bed by a binding of clay almost as solid and unyielding as rock, we could ask nothing better, and in such cases we always went to work with cheerful prospects of a speedy release. By simply lifting the raft with pries the swift current throws it forward, and since it does not settle as in sand, every exertion tells. By turning the raft broadside to the current and prying or "biting" at each end of the "boat" alternately, with our whole force of pries, leaving the swift water to throw her forward, we passed over gravel bars on which I do not think the water was over ten or eleven inches deep, although the raft drew twice as much. One of the gravel bars over which we passed in this manner was fully thirty or forty yards in length.

In aggravated cases of whatever nature the load would have to be taken off, carried on our backs through the water and placed on the shore, and when the raft was cleared or freed from the obstruction it would be brought alongside the bank at the very first favorable spot for reloading. Such cases occurred fully a score of times during our voyage. When the raft stranded on a bar with the water on each side so deep that we could not wade ashore, the canoe was used for "lightering the load," an extremely slow process which, fortunately, we were obliged to employ only once on the whole raft journey, although several times in wading the water came up to our waists before we could get to shore. In fact, with a heavy load on one's back or shoulders, it is evidently much easier to wade through water of that depth and proportional current than through very swift water over shallow bars.

Looking back, it seems almost miraculous that a raft could make a voyage of over thirteen hundred miles, the most difficult part of which was unknown, starting at the very head where the stream was so narrow that the raft would have been brought at a standstill if it swung out of a straight course end on (as it did in the Payer Rapids), and covering nearly two months of daily encounters with snags and bowlders, sticking on bars and shooting rapids, and yet get through almost unscathed. When I started to build this one on Lake Lindeman I had anticipated constructing two or three of these primitive craft before I could exchange to good and sufficient native or civilized transportation.

The raft is undoubtedly the oldest form of navigation extant, and undoubtedly the worst; it is interesting to know just how useful the raft can be as an auxiliary to geographical exploration, and certainly my raft journey was long enough to test it in this respect.

River Songs
collected by Mason Williams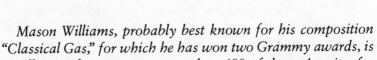

Mason Williams, probably best known for his composition "Classical Gas," for which he has won two Grammy awards, is a collector of river songs, more than 400 of them. A writer for the Smothers Brothers Comedy Hour and a number of specials for major TV networks, he has also produced and performed concerts of river songs, in some cases to raise funds for river protection.

Williams says that an important aspect of his collecting these songs is to give the river a voice . . . that voice being in the form of the songs and music it has inspired over the years. The result is that the concert reminds us of how much the river runs through our lives, both literally and metaphorically. And, Mason says, the concert shows us that we have a long-term relationship of great importance that is essential to maintain.

Williams' concerts, entitled "Of Time & Rivers Flowing," currently contain the following songs:

Water Music, (George Frederick Handel, 1717)

The Banks of the Dee (c 1767–1775, considered to be the first popular song in America)

Shenandoah (Traditional—1830s)

Dance Boatman Dance (Daniel Emmett—1843)

Old Folks at Home (Stephen Foster—1851)

Deep River (Negro spiritual—mid-nineteenth century)

Shall We Gather at the River (Religious hymn—Post Civil War)

On the Banks of the Wabash (Paul Dresser—1897)

Down by the Old Mill Stream (1910)

Beautiful Ohio (1918—became Ohio State Song in 1969)

Mississippi Mud (James Cavanaugh & Harry Barris—1927)

Ol' Man River (Jerome Kern—1929)

Miss the Mississippi and You (recorded by Jimmie Rogers—1931)

Cool Water (Bob Nolan—1936)

Roll on Columbia (Woody Guthrie)

Moon River (Johnny Mercer & Henry Mancini)

Burn On (Randy Newman—1970, about Cleveland's Cuyahoga River)

Of Time & Rivers Flowing (Pete Seeger, words to an ancient tune)

Part II

The Adventurers,
the Seekers,
the Observers

Life on the Mississippi
Mark Twain

Mark Twain (Samuel Langhorne Clemens), America's best-known writer of the late nineteenth century, grew up on the Mississippi. For a number of years he served as a steamboat pilot, learning to read the river and its rhythms. His best-known book, Huckleberry Finn, *includes a delightful account of an adventurous journey down the Mississippi by log raft. That famous book could no doubt be represented here, but it has been so often quoted and anthologized that I have selected a lesser-known passage from* Life on the Mississippi *that tells us of the changes Clemens observes when he returns to the river after an absence of many years.*

All day we swung along down the river, and had the stream almost wholly to ourselves. Formerly, at such a stage of the water, we should have passed acres of lumber-rafts and dozens of big coal-barges; also occasional little trading-scows, peddling along from farm to farm, with the peddler's family on board; possibly a random scow, bearing a humble Hamlet & Co. on an itinerant dramatic trip. But these were all absent. Far along in the day we saw one steamboat; just one, and no more. She was lying at rest in the shade, within the wooded mouth of the Obion River. The spy-glass revealed the fact that she was named for me—or *he* was named for me, whichever you prefer. As this was the first time I had ever encountered this species of honor, it seems excusable to mention it, and at the same time call the attention of the authorities to the tardiness of my recognition of it.

Noted a big change in the river at Island 21. It was a very large island, and used to lie out toward midstream; but it is joined fast to the main shore now, and has retired from business as an island.

As we approached famous and formidable Plum Point darkness fell, but that was nothing to shudder about—in these modern times. For now the national government has turned the Mississippi into a sort of two-thousand-mile torchlight procession. In the head of every crossing, and in the foot of every crossing, the government has set up a clear-burning lamp. You are never entirely in the dark, now; there is always a beacon in sight, either before you, or behind you, or abreast. One might almost say that lamps have been squandered there. Dozens of crossings are lighted which were not shoal when they were created, and have never been shoal since; crossings so plain, too, and also so straight, that a steamboat can take herself through them without any help, after she has been through once. Lamps in such places are of course not wasted; it is much more convenient and comfortable for a pilot to hold on them than on a spread of formless blackness that won't stay still; and money is saved to the boat, at the same time, for she can of course make more miles with her rudder amidships than she can with it squared across her stern and holding her back.

But this thing has knocked the romance out of piloting, to a large extent. It and some other things together have knocked all the romance out of it. For instance, the peril from snags is not now what it once was. The government's snag-boats go patrolling up and down, in these matter-of-fact days, pulling the river's teeth; they have rooted out all the old clusters which made many localities so formidable; and they allow no new ones to collect. Formerly, if your boat got away from you, on a black night, and broke for the woods, it was an anxious time with you; so was it, also, when you were groping your way through solidified darkness in a narrow chute, but all that is changed now—you flash out your electric light, transform night into day in the twinkling of an eye, and your perils and anxieties are at an end. Horace Bixby and George Ritchie have charted the crossings and laid out the courses by compass; they have invented a lamp to go with the chart, and have patented the whole. With these helps, one may run in the fog now, with considerable security, and with a confidence unknown in the old days.

With these abundant beacons, and the banishment of snags, plenty of daylight in a box and ready to be turned on whenever needed, and a chart compass to fight the fog with, piloting, at a good stage of water, is now nearly as safe and simple as driving stage, and is hardly more than three times as romantic.

And now, in these new days of infinite change, the Anchor Line have raised the captain above the pilot by giving him the bigger wages of the two. This was going far, but they have not stopped there. They have decreed that the pilot shall remain at his post, and stand his watch clear through, whether the boat be under way or tied up to the shore. We, that were once the aristocrats of the river, can't go to bed now, as we used to do, and sleep while a hundred tons of freight are lugged aboard; no, we must sit in the pilot-house; and keep awake, too. Verily we are being treated like a parcel of mates and engineers. The government has taken away the romance of our calling; the Company has taken away its state and dignity.

Plum Point looked as it had always looked by night, with the exception that now there were beacons to mark the crossings, and also a lot of other lights on the point and along its shore; these latter glinting from the fleet of the United States River Commission, and from a village which the officials have built on the land for offices and for the employees of the service. The military engineers of the Commission have taken upon their shoulders the job of making the Mississippi over again—a job transcended in size by only the original job of creating it. They are building wing-dams here and there to deflect the current; and dikes to confine it in narrower bounds; and other dikes to make it stay there; and for unnumbered miles along the Mississippi they are felling the timber-front for fifty yards back, with the purpose of shaving the bank down to low-water mark with the slant of a house-roof, and ballasting it with stones; and in many places they have protected the wasting shores with rows of piles. One who knows the Mississippi will promptly aver—not aloud but to himself—that ten thousand River Commissions, with the mines of the world at their back, cannot tame that lawless stream, cannot curb it or confine it, cannot say to it, "Go here," or "Go there," and make it obey; cannot save a shore which it has sentenced; cannot bar its path with an obstruction which it will not tear down, dance over, and laugh at. But a discreet man will not put these things into spoken words; for the West Point engineers have not their superiors anywhere; they know all that can be known of their abstruse science; and so, since they conceive that they can fetter and handcuff that river and boss him, it is but wisdom for the unscientific man to keep still, lie low, and wait till they do it. Captain Eads, with his jetties, has done a work at the mouth of the Mississippi which seemed clearly impossible; so we do not feel full confidence now to prophesy against like impossibilities. Otherwise one would pipe out and say the Commission might as well bully the comets in their courses and undertake to make them behave, as try to bully the Mississippi into right and reasonable conduct.

Exploring the Yukon River
Archie Satterfield

Archie Satterfield may have been born in Missouri, but he is a Northwest writer and editor of Alaska Northwest Publishing Company's new magazine, Northwest Edition. *A journalist by trade, he has worked for the Longview (WA)* Daily News, *the* Seattle Times *and the* Seattle Post-Intelligence. *He has also written 20 books, mostly about the Northwest. These include* Moods of the Columbia, Exploring the Yukon River, *and* The Lewis and Clark Trail.

In this excerpt, which constitutes the final pages of Exploring the Yukon River, *Satterfield tells us what the steamboat days were like on the upper Yukon. It was the building of the Alaskan Highway during World War II that finally ended the use of steamboats in Alaska. Until the highway was constructed, travel by boat was the way to get around during the summer months.*

The gold rush and steady ore shipments that followed it brought dozens of old-time rivermen to the Yukon to ply their trade. At the height of the stampede, shipyards in Seattle built boats "by the mile and cut them off when necessary." The rivermen took them up to the Yukon across the Gulf of Alaska and around through the Aleutians and into the estuary near St. Michael.

The Yukon taught them new tricks. Since the river is noted for its shallows and shifting sandbars, the sidewheelers and deep-draft ships that would work on the Mississippi and the Columbia were of no use. New boats had to be built for the river, and this meant big ships that virtually sat on top of the water with paddle wheels that barely skimmed the surface. Since a very shallow draft was required, regular keels would not work and each Yukon paddlewheeler was trussed up and braced along its bottom to keep it from becoming sway-backed.

Each was equipped with a winch on the bow and it wasn't unusual for one to run aground on a bar, then pull itself over it with the winch pulling and the paddle wheel slapping and pawing its way through the gravel. The paddles were adjustable and could be raised or lowered according to the depth of the water.

A complete transportation system was soon established by White Pass & Yukon Route using the railroad that was punched through the Coast Range over White Pass to Whitehorse, at the downstream end of Miles Canyon and the rapids. From there, cargo and passengers went by steamboat down to Dawson City. A few, but very few, steamboats ran on downriver from Dawson City to St. Michael and back.

However, in 1901 a steamboat named the *Lavelle Young* played an important, if accidental, role in establishing one of Alaska's major cities. A trader named Captain E. T. Barnett chartered the *Lavelle Young* to take him down the Yukon to the Tanana River, then up it some four hundred miles to establish a trading post for Indians. But only halfway up the river the paddlewheeler "ran out of water" as the saying went, and Barnett had to unload in the middle of the wilderness. He was furious and his wife was terrified and crying because they were faced with the prospect of wintering over with no shelter built. He had 125 tons of trade goods for the Indians, and there wasn't one in sight.

However, two prospectors saw the smoke of the paddlewheeler and came out of the subarctic bush to investigate. One of them was named Felix Pedro, who a year later discovered gold on a nearby stream. The two prospectors soon began to spread the word of Barnett's supplies and an improvised trading post was established. When the rush began, Barnett renamed his trading post Fairbanks and he grew rich. The town became the largest along the Yukon system and the terminus during World War II of both the Alaska Highway and the Alaska Railroad, which had been completed in 1923.

The steamboats created communities all along the river between Whitehorse and Dawson City, and people depended on them as much as they do trucks, buses, and airplanes today. Stationed at roughly thirty-mile intervals were the woodcutter camps where the boats stopped to take on cord after cord of four-foot-long spruce that had been dried a year before use. Many of these woodcutters were remnants of the Klondike stampede, men who failed to strike it rich but became either enamored with the Yukon or simply didn't know what else to do with themselves. They lived lives almost as monastic as monks and some went for years without seeing a town. They usually had one or two horses for snaking trees out of the timber and into camp, and some kept a small dog team for both companionship and for running trap lines during the winter. When they cut over one area, the company would move them to another, and before the wood supply was depleted and White Pass & Yukon Route converted to oil, the woodcutters had supplied some 300,000 cord of wood.

The steamboat season was about four months long in that northern latitude. Often the first trip of the season was delayed by ice in Lake Laberge, just below Whitehorse, so a dam was built on the river above Miles Canyon to store water in the spring. When the river ice cleared above and below Lake Laberge, the dam's floodgates would be opened to send a wall of water rushing downstream past Whitehorse and into the lake to flush out the ice. Then the armada of paddlewheelers loaded with passengers and freight would make a grand journey downriver, passing hundreds of small boats and rafts of logs bound for the sawmills at Dawson City, called "float-me-downs," and each town along the route and each woodcutter's camp would celebrate the day as though it were New Year's Eve.

The following September or October, the procedure would be reversed as the last steamboats left Dawson City headed upriver on the low water. Big parties would be held that last night in Dawson City, but it was a sad time because it meant the town was going into the isolation and almost hibernation of the long, dark winter. The residents knew they would be alone until the following May or June, when they would gather at the top of a high hill above town, called Midnight Dome, and watch for the first steamboat around the bend.

Some of the paddlewheelers were pulled up onto banks during the winter for overhauls and to protect them from the dangerous spring breakup when anything could happen. Sometimes ice jams created vast lakes, and if the steamboats were frozen to the bottom—a common occurrence—they would become inept submarines. Sometimes the ice rushing downriver would tear holes in them, or rip out an entire side. Some genius came up with the idea of partially flooding the steamboats just before breakup and shooting steam into the water to thaw the water around the boat and to free it from the bottom if it were touching. If it was not on the bottom, the crews would chop the ice loose around it so it could float free when the ice began moving.

The steamboat era lasted just over half a century on the Yukon, but everyone knew its days were numbered when the Alaska Highway was punched through the wilderness during World War II. The highway ran across the bottom of the Yukon Territory through Whitehorse on its way to Alaska, but the spur highways weren't far behind. Finally, the highway was completed from Whitehorse to Dawson City with others making crooked lines on the map to Ross River, Keno Hill, Mayo, and other towns which were built around new mines.

Where there once were more than two hundred steamboats on the river, suddenly, it seemed, there were none. What few were left sat high and dry on the banks. A few were accorded museum status— The *Keno* in Dawson City, the *Klondike* in Whitehorse, and the *Tutshi* in Carcross. Two others, the *Whitehorse* and *Casca*, were on the bank at Whitehorse for a quarter of a century, always just a step ahead of the demolition crew. When at last it was decided to make them into museum pieces too, an arsonist climbed the high fence surrounding them and turned them into a bonfire. Sadly, the old-timers of the river gathered to watch as the tinder-dry wooden vessels became ash heaps. Ironically, photos of the fire show smoke billowing from the stacks for the final time.

After the early 1950s, the river was virtually abandoned. The towns became ghost towns overnight, and cabins were left unlocked, with stoves, cupboards filled with dishes, beds and books. It simply was too expensive to ship the material out. Little Salmon, Big Salmon, Yukon Crossing, Fort Selkirk, Thistle Creek, and the other towns remained but they were ghost towns. Only a handful of trappers stayed on, still using the river as their highway.

Thus the river remained until the late 1960s when the wilderness became an "in" place for people to go on vacations, and the Yukon River was discovered all over again. Now, each summer a parade of canoes, inflatable boats, flat-bottomed riverboats, and rafts make the trip between Whitehorse and Dawson City. The river in Alaska isn't used much by vacationers, except an occasional hardy soul who intends to follow the whole river system to the ocean. Few make it because the two-thousand-mile course is simply too much wilderness for one summer. Those few who do complete it usually sell or give away their boat to the Indians near the estuary and fly out, wondering if the trip was worth the effort.

More dams on the Yukon seem inevitable, although it seems unlikely that the Ramparts Dam project will be revived for some time to come by Alaskan power officials. There is constant talk of building more hydroelectric dams in the Canadian Yukon, but this scheme has vocal opponents. And there is also talk of building a steel-hulled paddlewheeler to run between Whitehorse and Dawson City each summer for tourists, and pulling it up on the bank at Whitehorse during the winter for use as a restaurant.

Whatever happens to transportation on the Yukon River, nothing is likely ever to replace the romance of those old paddlewheelers. Now that it is no longer a transportation corridor other less colorful uses will be found for it.

Journeys to the Far North

Olaus J. Murie

Olaus J. Murie (1889–1963) was a field biologist for more than 30 years, much of which was spent in northern Canada and Alaska studying caribou, banding birds, sketching them, taking careful notes and collecting study skins. He wrote A Field Guide to Animal Tracks *in the Peterson Field Guide Series and illustrated J. Frank Dobie's book* Voice of the Coyote. *His book,* Elk of North America, *is the classic study of the wapiti.*

In 1914, as a young naturalist, he accompanied W. E. Clyde Todd, ornithologist with the Carnegie Museum of Pittsburgh, on an expedition to Hudson Bay. This began a life-long love of the arctic. A few years later he again accompanied a Todd canoe expedition, this time to the interior of Labrador. This excerpt from the account of that trip paints an appealing picture of the young biologist who spent the last 15 years of his life in the service of The Wilderness Society.

Two years later I was once more going north, into the unknown, this time farther east. That persistent ornithologist, Mr. Todd, wanted to learn what birds lived in interior Labrador, and I was again privileged to go with him. We were to enhance the collections and the knowledge residing in Carnegie Museum in Pittsburgh.

This time it was a bigger expedition. We had three nineteen-foot Peterborough freight canoes, all well loaded, and five Indians. Mr. Todd was, of course, to lead the expedition; I was to be his assistant, collecting specimens and taking scientific notes. The third white man of our party was Mr. Alfred Marshall, a retired businessman of Chicago who was paying half the expense of the trip in order to fish and enjoy wild country. He was an athletic, cheerful person, enjoying to the full the superb fishing he found all across Labrador. And he joyfully helped us collect certain specimens also.

There were three big canoes and the five experienced Indians. But it takes two to handle a canoe—one in the bow and one in the stern.

Since I was the youngest of the party, I became the sixth Indian, much to my satisfaction.

We did have some language barriers. Three of the Indians were tall and vigorous Ojibways, who spoke their own tongue, French, and English. The tallest one was named Mose Odjik; the other two, Jocko and Paul Commanda, had been with us two years before on Hudson Bay. Then there were two Cree Indians of Labrador, Charles and Philip, who knew something about the country we were entering. They were slighter in build, but how they could handle a canoe! They spoke French, but very little English. They would speak French to the Ojibways, who in turn spoke English to us—and thus we managed!

On May 26, 1917, we started up the Ste. Marguerite River from our camp near Clarke City, in the St. Lawrence gulf region. Our destination was away up north—across Labrador to Hudson Strait. Paul Commanda, the veteran canoe guide, was in the bow of one canoe and Mose Odjik in the stern, with Todd and Marshall in the middle. It was fitting that Charles and Philip, who both knew Cree and French, should have one canoe together. So Jocko was in the stern of the third canoe, with me as his bowsman. How would we do, with all the languages and personalities involved?

This time we were faced with going upstream much of the time, and had to use poles instead of paddles. Day after day, headed for the unknown interior of Labrador, we labored along with poles against the current. I, of course, became intimate with Jocko, who was teaching me so much about handling our canoe.

We had not gone many days on our way when it was brought forcibly to me how important little things can be in the wilderness. It was a very swift river we were going up; naturally, we were going along close to shore, both of us standing. Farther out, the river was too deep for our poles. Jocko in the stern would shove the canoe forward, the bow tending to turn toward shore as he shoved. I, in the bow, also pushed forward, but my effort shoved the bow out. Thus we corrected each other as we went along.

Ahead of us I saw a huge rock a little way out from the bank. The water rushing by on the outside was too deep, and between the rock and the bank the water came boiling through at a steeply slanting, fast pace. We headed up into this fast water near shore.

Halfway through, I was as usual pushing the bow away from shore. Suddenly an urgent command came from the stern: "Shove in to shore, *Bateese!*" (The Indians had nicknamed me "Baptiste.")

I suddenly realized that the rock prevented Jocko from shoving the stern out to correct my shove. We could have gone crosswise to the rock, and the canoe and all its contents would have been dumped over in the swift current. But we made it, thanks to Jocko's quick command. And thus, each day, the youngest member of the party was learning!

We helped each other as we went along. Mr. Todd and I were of course responsible for collecting specimens. Each night I put out some mouse traps to gather information on the extent of small mammal species across Labrador. But everyone in the party got specimens of birds and helped in every way they could. Marshall was happy to help in this way when he wasn't busy fishing.

Once, later in the season, when geese were flightless, we captured a goose out on a lake. I had with me some aluminum bands. When I had banded the bird and turned it loose, Charles cried out in a surprised voice, "No!" He could not understand anyone turning loose a captured bird.

Paul was the cook, but all the Indians helped in setting up camp each night, building a fire, and attending to other camp chores. They had full control of the canoes, afloat or ashore. While they were doing all these things, I would put out my traps. Marshall often went fishing and we had all the fish we needed in camp. While all this was going on, Mr. Todd was taking care of specimens and writing detailed notes.

So it went, day after day, as we traveled into the heart of Labrador. I cannot begin to tell of all our little adventures, but a few stand out in memory. I was impressed with the song of the winter wren—trilling, happy music. It was so lively that I attempted to write it, somehow, in my journal:

rrrrrr   se   se   serrrrrrr   sie   [trill]
se   se   se   [trill]   rrrr   sie   [low]

Jocko was teaching me some Ojibway words, but it took me days to learn his word for this tiny winter wren. Finally I got it written down to his satisfaction: *Ka-wi-miti-go-zhi-que-na-ga-mooch.* Such a long name for a tiny bird! He said the name meant "little French woman singer." This Indian name is surely evidence of the white man's influence.

Jocko and I became intimate enough that we could kid each other. As we poled along, he would say to me: "*Kawin nishishin shogenosh!* ('No good white man!')." To show off my meager knowledge of his language, I would reply, "*Kawin nishishin ishenabe!* ('No good Indian!')." And so we got along fine.

One day, on a slope high above us, we saw a black bear followed by a cub. We watched them crossing through an open place into trees beyond. A black bear is a common sight for many people today along certain roads, but I shall never forget that view from a canoe, up there in primitive, seldom-visited surroundings. Also, it was the first bear I had seen, and the only one I saw on that trip.

On another day, while we were resting on a portage, other inhabitants of this northern wilderness came into view. An Indian came walking along the portage, carrying a canoe. Behind him came his wife with a big pack on her back, and on top of the pack a small child. They stopped to pass the time of day with our two Cree Indians. While the woman stood there, not saying much, her child suddenly tumbled off the pack to the ground. Calmly the mother picked the youngster up and tossed him back onto the pack as though he were just another piece of dunnage. Presently they both went on, headed the way we had come.

These were the only human beings we met until we reached northern Labrador later in the summer. But someone had been up here. One day we were struggling against a strong current past some large rocks. There, in a crack in one of the rocks, was a canoe paddle! What catastrophe had happened here in the rapids? We never knew.

No scientific expedition had been all the way across Labrador, seven hundred miles south to north. Ours was to be the first. Very few Indians had been across, but Philip knew some of the geography of the southern area. One evening, when we had studied again our incomplete map, we all suddenly agreed that we were not on the best route—that instead of going up the Ste. Marguerite River, we should have gone up the Moisie. Paul was disgruntled and a bit sarcastic; the other Indians were somber and didn't say much. Apparently we were on the wrong track. What should we do?

We finally decided to cross over to the Moisie River system. We found out how spotted with lakes, ponds, and streams interior Labrador is—and how big! With much poling, paddling, and portaging, while still in the Ste. Marguerite watershed, almost to its head, we finally made it over to the Moisie River headwaters on July 15.

Interior Labrador is substantially a high, irregular plateau, about 4,000 feet in elevation, dotted with lakes and forested low hills between the many streams. We also saw many burned-over areas—cause unknown. There were many rainy days all summer long.

I tried to express in my diary the effect this big country had upon me. On May 27 I wrote, "I came up on a ridge and stood still there a while. The wind was cold; there were patches of snow, down logs and brush heaps. At first sight an uninteresting place. All at once I found the place alive with birds. A ruby-crowned kinglet appeared, seeking among the balsam twigs. He came up close, showing his ruby crown and his bright white-ringed eye. At intervals he sang and I could see his throat vibrate, but meanwhile he kept on seeking industriously. Flit-flip he went, from twig to twig, glancing this way and that in his everlasting search. Once he reached up and picked a tiny morsel from the branch overhead. He made a little swoop out in the air, and I heard his beak snap as he caught a little insect, then went on to the next twig.

"Another one came along, his ruby crown gleaming. Hopping, seeking, he passed on into the distance.

"A downy woodpecker then lit on a small limb near me and I heard him scraping his way up over the tree's bark. He came up closer onto a small birch sapling. Here he tapped away as he hitched upward, stopping in one spot to peck quite a while. Suddenly he dropped to a dry limb below. He gave a sharp "*spik*," and kept on, craned his head and looked around once, then flew up to another dry limb. From there to another, and another, then suddenly dived down the hill to another dry sapling. The downy is a busy fellow, only taking time to give you a mere glance and perhaps an exclamatory "*spik*," and then goes on with his business.

"A winter wren was singing in the distance somewhere."

Common birds these, and well-known. But to me, up there in the Labrador northland, the occasion was unique. The place itself and the circumstances meant as much to me as the birds.

Thus we observed, recorded, and enjoyed the bird life through Labrador—thrushes, warblers, sparrows, flycatchers, grouse—so many kinds in this north country. Waterfowl were on the lakes, shore birds along the borders, hawks overhead, and owls in the forest. We found a nest of the bald eagle, saw the kingfisher, and watched the nighthawk swooping in the evening sky.

It was surprising how well the Indians knew the lives of the birds. When Charles, Philip, and I went off to look for caribou, the day was made memorable for me by all the bird life we saw. We did not even see a caribou, but I was impressed by how carefully Philip examined tracks to see how recent they were. We came on one very clear track in the earth. "*Loup!*" Charles exlaimed. (He pronounced it"lo.") It was the only sign of a wolf we saw on that whole trip.

On this day we reached a point where the forest seemed to indicate the Hudsonian Life Zone. In the lower areas, we had been in the Canadian Life Zone. The forest intrigued me. I could not help wondering about life in various forms up here. On June 7, out from camp on field day, I entered this soliloquy in my journal:

"Now all is still. The farther shore is dark and indistinct. Flecks of foam float silently along and the woods life goes on as it has for ages. The little dead tamarack by me must be at least 30 years old, and the birch sapling ten or fifteen—all that time they have stood in this spot. Winters have come and gone. Summer, rain, sunshine and wind, Indian hunters—all have passed here. Beavers have lived in the pond, birds have sung and nested here—it is wonderful to think of all that has happened in the lifetime of these trees, and in the ages before. Tonight it is growing dark once more—not a bird note now, only the steady droning of the rapid at the foot of the pond—a wonderful, peaceful place."

How did all this appeal to the others? I don't know, but it seems significant to me that one evening I found Marshall stooping at the side of a pond, feeding a frog, giving it flies and bits of meat. The frog was blind in one eye.

Again on June 17 I went up over the hills at dusk and was moved to try to express what I felt in the journal:

"There was a delicate purple sunset, tall dead trees silhouetted against it. As I came to the top, I had a view of the rolling hills, bare except for the grove of trees here and there in the distance. Clumps of wild cherry shrubs in bloom dotted the slopes, and bumblebees were still buzzing about among them. From a clump of spruce over against the sunset came the songs of olive-backed thrushes. Occasionally a white-throated sparrow piped up, while behind me, over the river, two night hawks were swooping and calling. Labrador may be a barren, desolate land, but at moments like this there is the charm of nature at her best."

There were other such beautiful moments as we crossed Labrador. Then came a crisis, man-made. We were far into the wilderness but had not yet reached the height of land. The Indians now asked for a raise in wages—up to $95 a month. My interpretation of the situation was that we were in unknown, unmapped country, and the Indians were hesitant about going on. But I had nothing to do with it; the decision was up to our leader, Mr. Todd. Alfred Marshall, with his businessman's acumen, privately advised him that they were not really asking a great deal and that their demands should be met. This was done.

Then they came up with another objection: our outfit was too heavy. The upshot of this argument was that we left behind, in the middle of Labrador, one canoe, fully loaded! Each of us donated to the discard anything we thought we could get along without. But we kept all the food—bacon, beans, flour, dried fruit, and all the rest.

One of these items bothered Mose Odjik and me—a case of condensed milk. It was heavy, and we thought of the many portages still lying ahead. We could surely get along without that milk!

I smiled at him and asked, "Mose, do you like milk?"

He smiled broadly and replied: "Yes, *Bateese*, I like it very much!" At every meal thereafter Mose and I were mixing and drinking milk, and in just a few days we had no case of milk to carry over the portages. No one said anything.

For a while I hardly knew where we were. We had to assume that the two Cree Indians knew what they were doing. At times we poled upstream, crossed a lake, and went downstream again. But we were going somewhere!

One day we saw a letter on a piece of birchbark, fastened to a tree. Charles went ashore and read it. An Indian mailman had gone through here and cached his gun and other supplies—a mailman in the center of Ungava! The Indians went everywhere, sooner or later.

Two in the Far North

Margaret E. Murie

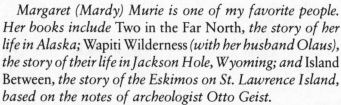

Margaret (Mardy) Murie is one of my favorite people. Her books include Two in the Far North, *the story of her life in Alaska;* Wapiti Wilderness *(with her husband Olaus), the story of their life in Jackson Hole, Wyoming; and* Island Between, *the story of the Eskimos on St. Lawrence Island, based on the notes of archeologist Otto Geist.*

When we discussed what passages from Two in the Far North *I might use in this anthology, we considered several: her wedding at Anvik, her travels by boat on several Alaskan rivers, often with her young children, dogsledding on the river ice, backpacking to the head of the Sheenjek. She said to me, "You know, I never realized how important rivers have been in my life."*

Mardy grew up in Alaska, married Olaus Murie shortly after becoming the first woman to graduate from the University of Alaska, and traveled with him on his biological assignments. In 1927 the Muries moved to Jackson Hole, where Olaus studied the elk. Mardy lives in active retirement at their ranch at the foot of the Teton Range.

The passage I have selected tells of the wedding of Mardy to Olaus, who had been studying birds all summer at the mouth of the Yukon River. They had planned to rendezvous for their wedding at Anvik and honeymoon on their way up the Koyuku River, where he had further work to do.

Five days later, on the afternoon of August 18, the *General Jacobs* was tied up at the end of her downriver run, in front of the Catholic mission village of Holy Cross, a good many miles down the Yukon from the Episcopal mission at Anvik mentioned in the wedding announcements. Mother, outwardly serene as always, was sitting up in the pilothouse, hemming wedding-gift napkins. Elizabeth and handsome Captain Looney were promenading through the Indian village playing with all the Malemute pups. Harry was on the beach teasing the trader's pet bear cubs with a can of milk.

I had hoped to escape all the joking sympathy over the gas boat

Tanana's failure to arrive from St. Michael, by retreating into my stateroom—I was beginning to feel a good cry coming on. But the Norwegian steward poked his head in the door to ask if he could give the wedding cake to a young Indian bride he knew of on shore, and the charming, irrepressible chief engineer called through the window wanting to know how it felt to have so much faith in one man that you would travel eight hundred miles with a whole wedding party when you had hardly heard from the man in three months.

They did all this, I knew, to hide their deep friendly concern, to help me pretend that waiting was bearable, to reassure me that that gas boat from St. Michael had not hit a snag, that it would come, that there would be a bridegroom on it. We sat at Holy Cross for twenty-four hours. Harry and Captain Looney had been talking, in whispers loud enough for me to hear, about the fact that by law they were supposed to wait only twenty-four hours for the connecting mail boat and then turn and go back upriver to keep on schedule!

At eight o'clock that evening, my birthday, we were all in the pilothouse as usual, everyone making forced, unconcerned remarks, when in the middle of a sentence the captain yelled: "Gas boat *Tanana!* " and pulled the whistle cord, which hung over the wheel. And the tension snapped. I fell on the captain's neck, and Mother on Harry's, and everyone hugged Elizabeth of course, but she reached for my hand and began pulling me out of the pilothouse and down the companionway. "Come on, get into your room. I'll tell Olaus where you are."

Behind us I heard Harry cry: "There's Olaus! I see him!"

Alone inside the stateroom, I listened to the shouts of greeting, and the bumpings and chuggings as that clumsy craft came alongside the *General Jacobs*, and tried to make myself realize what this moment was, but all I could think of was how loud my heart was pounding. Then the door opened quietly, and we were together and there was no thinking.

Suddenly, over our heads, we heard a loud thump, and then the *General Jacobs*'s whistle, the fifteen-minute whistle, and Olaus said: "Gee whiz, I've got to get out there, I guess, and get my stuff loaded!"

We went out on deck into the happiest, noisiest excitement—greetings and explanations, people rushing back and forth above and below deck, the luggage and mail being unloaded. The Indian deckhands were moving from the scow to the steamer with the speed and grace of cats, but managed to look over their shoulders to grin at us. The captain leaned from the pilothouse window—"Get that stuff over here now; step on it!"—and looked down at me with a wonderful smile. From his bedlam down below the engineer shouted up that he didn't blame me for coming all the way down the Yukon. In the midst of all this confusion we met Mr. Henderson and knew at once how fine he was.

So at last the party was complete, as we steamed back up the river in the deepening dusk of arctic August toward Anvik.

Olaus and his suitcase disappeared for a time, and when an absolutely jubilant group gathered for "midnight lunch" at ten o'clock, the bridegroom really looked like one. Mr. Henderson looked all round the table as we finished eating and said in his deep, authoritative voice: "Now, we're going to have a rehearsal. Elizabeth, go get your prayer book; you told me you had it with you."

We had a rehearsal, and it was then we discovered that everyone in the wedding party, including the captain and the chief engineer and the purser, was a member of the Episcopal Church—except the bride and groom and the bride's mother!

After that Harry sent us all away for a rest, assuring us that the cabin boy would wake us in plenty of time. I fell at once into a deep sleep, and it seemed only moments before there came a rap-tapping at the door: "Anvik in half an hour! " and Mother, leaning over me: "Are you ready for your wedding? It's half past two." [AM]

I suppose the most unusual thing about this wedding was the hour at which it was held. I felt a great wave of gratitude when Mother and I stepped out on deck and found all the rest of the party waiting, perfectly groomed, at that hour, and for us! Under the deck lights stood Elizabeth, in cream lace and a flowery cloche, the light glinted on the captain's gold buttons; the engineer was startlingly handsome, having scrubbed away the engine-room grease and sporting gray suede gloves and a fedora. The whole crew too was ready for the occasion. And the bride, in seal-brown crepe touched here and there with blue and orange, and a brown straw cloche trimmed with orange silk flowers. As the *General Jacobs* blew the landing blast and the gangplank swung out, I turned to catch a happy reassuring smile from Mother, and saw that she was wearing a big pink rose Mrs. Webster had given us from her hothouse at Tanana on our way downriver. Roses were rare, precious gems in Alaska, and yet here was one at our wedding far down the Yukon.

In the beam of the ship's light on the black shore stood the minister, dear Dr. Chapman, and all the mission family, six of them, up at this hour to welcome us. So we knew that our Signal Corps friend at Holy Cross had been able to get through to Dr. Chapman. How fortunate that this clergyman was a ham radio operator also!

We walked up the bank under the glow of lights strung miraculously from ship to shore, in those few minutes of landing, by that same teasing engineer and his crew, and we came to the little log church. The lights showed us its sturdy outline, low and square, its rustic bell tower, its tiny windows. What a comfortable quiet there was about it. Willows crowded thick beside it, and beyond them at this most silent hour of morning there spoke the voice of the great river flowing by.

Here Mr. Henderson took my arm, and we stepped over the threshold and into soft yellow light from the many tall candles shining on the brown log walls and the hand-made benches and chancel carved of tawny birch. From two large candelabra at the altar, candles shone also on bowls of ferns and pale-gold arctic poppies. This was like a dream—pausing but an hour in the night and finding all this beauty prepared for us.

Now came Dr. Chapman, in gown and stole, and while I was trying hard to realize the perfection of this hour, we were going on: "Dearly beloved, we are gathered together . . ."

What greater joy could life ever hold than to be able to repeat those words—"I Margaret, take thee, Olaus"—with a sure heart?

Then there was Elizabeth, clinging to me and weeping, and the captain with tears in his eyes, and Mother, not crying, but with shining eyes: "Oh, I'm so glad, and I can tell Daddy all about it!"

We went almost reluctantly out from that gracious candle-lit place; some happy tears were dropping upon the mass of ferns and arctic poppies that Dr. Chapman's daughter Ada had put into my arms, but there was someone to guide my steps, and we were saying "Thank you," not knowing how to say it enough, and "Good-by," and the *General Jacobs* was blowing a salute as we went up the gangplank.

As we slid away from the shore Dr. Chapman shouted up to the captain: "Four o'clock. Just one hour. And there's the sun!"

Out across the wide gray river, over the low willows, there was a bright splash of rose and molten gold. Mother and Olaus and I stood in the bow and watched a sunrise of promise. A beautiful world was waking to light here on the Yukon.

Dangerous River
Raymond M. Patterson

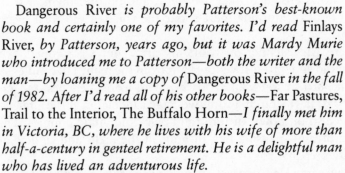

> Dangerous River *is probably Patterson's best-known*
> *book and certainly one of my favorites. I'd read* Finlays
> River, *by Patterson, years ago, but it was Mardy Murie*
> *who introduced me to Patterson—both the writer and the*
> *man—by loaning me a copy of* Dangerous River *in the fall*
> *of 1982. After I'd read all of his other books—*Far Pastures,
> Trail to the Interior, The Buffalo Horn—*I finally met him*
> *in Victoria, BC, where he lives with his wife of more than*
> *half-a-century in genteel retirement. He is a delightful man*
> *who has lived an adventurous life.*
>
> *In the mid-1920s he left a position with the Bank of*
> *England to homestead in the Peace River Country, where*
> *he became known through his adventures on the rivers of*
> *western Canada. An Oxford history scholar, he weaves a*
> *fabric of his experiences against a backdrop of history.*
> *He became a river man by running rivers, reading about*
> *them, experiencing them, and living on them in the wilds,*
> *where he was totally dependent upon his own resources to*
> *survive. He fished, hunted, trapped and prospected mostly*
> *along the South Nahanni.*
>
> *He is one of my heroes and one of my favorite writers.*
> *These three exerpts are all taken from Part Two.*

The storm broke with a blaze of lightning on the summit of the
Butte. Down came the rain, whole water, and by morning it
had set in for a day's downpour. The mosquitoes were drowned, most
of them, or frozen by the torrents of icy rain and we were never again
seriously bothered with them. All day it poured and we stayed in the
little cabin, cleaning up, cooking, reading and swapping the various
yarns we had heard about the Nahanni. We put markers in the sand
at the edge of the river to gauge its rise after this heavy rain: by evening
the Nahanni was on the climb and we eyed it sourly; every fresh inch
of height meant so much more weight of water against us. We talked
as we watched the rising flood: he was headed for the Flat River, Faille
told me. He would be the first white man to winter up the Nahanni

for seven years, he said, and we were the first ones to tackle the river alone in that time.

Next morning it was cold and misty and we loaded up and waited for it to clear. I drew my canoe tarp over the load and tucked it in, and adjusted the trackline in an insane kind of fixed "bridle" that somebody had shown me down by the lower rapids of the Liard. Fortunately Faille saw it.

"What's that rigging you've got on your canoe?" he asked.

"The way the line's fixed? That's the bridle for tracking."

"Well, whoever showed you that must be crazy. Keep that rigging the way it is and in two day's time you'll be walking out of here without your canoe, talking to yourself. How much line have you got?"

"A bit over eighty feet."

"That'll do. Let me have it and I'll show you—"

He undid the bridle, took off some kind of a jockey stick that was lashed across the forward thwart and chucked it into the river. Then he tied one end of the eighty-foot line to the ring in the nose of the canoe and the other end to the rear seat.

"That's all you need," he said. "Now watch me."

He pushed the canoe into the river and started to walk up the shore with the bight of the line in his left hand. The canoe wasn't far enough out, it was heading for a rock, so Faille passed the line through his hand in a forward direction: this let the nose of the canoe fall away from shore and drew the tail in: the current did the rest and the canoe swung outside the rock, avoiding it, and was straightened again by a pull on the forward end of the line: it was brought in close to shore, as Faille walked, by a jerk on the canoe's nose and then sent flying out into the stream again by a pull on the rear end. It was one of those beautifully simple things that any fool can understand—and it was flexible and perfect. With that and a strong hand on the paddle and the ability to use a pole a man can go anywhere.

Faille was letting the canoe drop downstream again.

"You can line down with that rigging, too," he said, "but it's not so easy as going up. You can make time up river that way, with a light load, just as fast as you can walk, as long as you've got a good tracking beach. But don't be afraid to let the canoe right out into the current, outside the shore eddies and into deep water whenever you can. Try to track her in shallow water and she'll suck down to the bottom and pull like a lump of lead."

Patches of blue sky were appearing. Then the sun broke through, the mist rolled away from the river and at noon we started. The canoes were hitched together as before, since the first eight miles of the

Nahanni, where it winds like a serpent in two tremendous oxbows at the foot of the Butte, is all quiet water. A couple of hours later the first swirl of fast water hit us and Faille pulled into a shelving bank of gravel. As we unhitched we looked at the prospect ahead: the wooded banks and quiet, sheltered water had given place to a wide-open flood plain strewn with sand-bars, shingle islands, wooded islands, huge driftpiles, and queer, dead-looking forests of snags where uprooted trees had lodged and settled on the river bottom and now, swept clean by ice and floods of all their branches, projected bleakly from the water, their broken tops pointing down river. Through this desolation rushed the Nahanni in, perhaps, two main channels and a maze of smaller ones. From a wooded bank nearby came the thudding lash of "sweepers"—trees that have been undercut by the floods into the river, but which still cling with their roots to the bank, lashing and beating at the water which drives through their branches. From all sides in this wasteland of the river came the noise of rushing water—it was the foot of the Splits.

Faille held out his hand. "Well friend," he said, "here's where we part. Good luck to you." We shook hands and he shoved out into the current, pulling on the kicker's starting cord.

I arranged the pole and paddle so that they were handy for quick action. The spare paddle was lightly tied to a thwart in a position where it could be quickly freed and grabbed in the event of the other one being broken or lost: there was a split second once, in the Lower Canyon when I almost lost a paddle—fending the canoe off the canyon wall I thrust hard at the rock and the blade of the paddle slipped neatly into a crevice and jammed there. The instinctive wrench brought it straight out again: had it stuck it would have been a case of hold on and be pulled out of the canoe, or let go and be whirled down the river plucking hurriedly at the ties that held the spare paddle. So it had to be handy. The sling straps of the rifle, a .303 Lee-Enfield sporting model, were fastened round the rear thwart, and the rifle itself was tucked in under the big canoe tarp, easy to get at quickly. A +8 Zeiss monocular in its leather case was strapped to the rear seat of the canoe. All seemed to be in order, so I flicked the canoe out into the current on the trackline and started upstream, wading in the shallows. I travelled for two or three miles and then made camp on a wooded island: the canoe was a bit too much down in the nose for this swift water and tended to sheer more than need be when coming out of an eddy—I could easily fix that by repacking and shifting the weight farther back. Later on I found that, on a long stretch of tracking, it paid to put a sizable rock in the canoe just forward of the rear seat to replace some of my own weight, and so to hold the nose well up and out of the grip of the eddies.

A little after seven I hit the river and poled on up the reach that I had seen the night before from the hill. Where the caribou had swum the river there was a tangle of tracks, some moose but mostly caribou: it was evidently a regular crossing place—there was probably a lick, not too far away, that attracted all the game. Shortly after that the walls of a low canyon closed in and I became busy, dealing with the hazards of the river.

About ten I came to a little bay, beyond which the canyon walls went on again, thirty to forty foot sheer on either side, with no beach and with a swift current between them. At the far end of this canyon reach I could hear the roar and see the boiling white water of a bad rapid.

The only thing to do was to beach the canoe and walk ahead some five or six hundred yards along the cliff to a rock point from which it looked as if one could see down on to the rapid. There were faint signs of an old trail: it took the easiest way through the bush, back from the cliff edge, and then dipped down to a great, sandy bay above the rapid; no doubt it was the old portage trail. I turned aside from it and pushed through the screen of trees on to the point. I stood still there for quite a time, just looking—and then I sat down and looked some more. It was an amazing sight, though by no means designed to make the voyageur burst into any hymn of thanksgiving: it was the Rapid-that-Runs-Both-Ways, the most dangerous bit of water on the lower river—now known as Hell's Gate.

The Nahanni swept downhill here, at great speed, round a righthand bend: suddenly, at the foot of the bend, the river made a right angle turn to the left, entering the low-walled canyon. But the current and the whole volume of the Nahanni could not make that sharp turn: the mass of water was hurled clean across the river in a ridge of foaming six-foot waves, to split on this point of rock on the right bank, thus forming two whirlpools, the upper and the lower. It would be almost equally difficult, one could see, to run this rapid either upstream or downstream: the only way would be to climb on to this surging hill of water at a fine angle, and to drop off it on the far side in the same way and as soon as possible. The trouble was that if the canoe was driven up too soon on to this "ridge of the white waters" it would be swamped by the big waves—and if it climbed on to it too late or stayed on it too long it would be hurled across the river and smashed, with its occupant, on to this rock point on which I was sitting. I looked down at the boiling water beneath: if one looked long enough, straight down, it seemed that the water stood still and that it was the point itself that was moving, surging upstream like the bow of a destroyer.

I walked back to the canoe and took out my axe and rifle, my packsack and some food and clothes, and laid them on the beach in case I lost the whole outfit but managed to get ashore myself: then I started up into the canyon.

I tried that rapid three times, but the current in the canyon was stronger than I had thought and I was not able to get speed enough on the canoe to drive it up on to the crest of the riffle that barred the way. Twice the canoe climbed the ridge, close under the big waves, only to be flung across the river and driven down the canyon, almost touching the cliff on the portage side. At the third and last attempt the eddies worked in my favour: the canoe was climbing the hill of racing water with speed enough (I thought) to take it on and over, when suddenly a gust of wind blew down the river, the nose swung off course and the canoe slid down into the lower whirlpool. It started to spin—and then was lifted on the upsurge of a huge boil from below. It was like the heave of one's cabin bunk at night in some great Atlantic storm. Then the water fell away from beneath the canoe and I caught a glimpse of the white waves of the rapid, a long way above, it seemed. The canoe rose once more and spun again, and then at last the paddle bit into solid water and drove the outfit out of the whirlpool and down the canyon for the last time, taking a sideways slap, in passing, from a stray eddy and shipping it green as a parting souvenir of a memorable visit.

Persistence is one thing and plain obstinacy is another. That last frolic with the rapid had set my mind at rest: some other fool could try his luck at running the thing in a light canoe—I would portage. And I put into the bay, beached the canoe, took the axe and started to cut out the portage trail.

Loading up next morning, with the canoe rocking and slapping about in the waves, was not easy in spite of a log skidway that I had made. The sheep head and meat I laid in the canoe, well forward, but the cape was left on its paddle and the paddle was lashed, upended like a mast, in the nose: that, I hoped, would keep the cape above the waves and dry. It was not early: I had let the sun climb high and swing out of the east before loading so as to avoid the blinding glare on the water as I ran southeast and down river. Then I shoved the canoe out from the rocks, jumped in and let drive with the paddle—and in two hours furious run downstream I undid the work of two toiling days.

It was all new to me, this downstream work on a fast river. One thing I noticed in particular was that all movement was relative— patches of white water foamed upstream towards one like the moving waves of the sea instead of the stationary waves of a river, while the scattered rocks in midstream drove towards the canoe with a foaming wake behind them like that of a speedboat. However, the little canoe rode down safely, swaying and pitching through this mad world of racing water, with every movement exaggerated by the insane-looking figurehead in the nose. I had tried to memorize each reach as I came up, but that soon faded out in the excitement of running downstream, and the best thing seemed to be to stand up in the canoe and size up each riffle as it came along: then, with the course picked out and the decision made, sit down and paddle like fury: get the canoe travelling faster than the river and go flat out, on the course planned, avoiding the big waves in the lashing tail of every riffle, dodging the eddies and following the leaping sheep-cape banner through into the quiet water.

Lunch was eaten at the head of the Hell's Gate portage, and by late afternoon the canoe, sheep and outfit had been carried through the woods and laid on the sands of the bay below the rapid. It was a lovely spot, especially after the jagged rockpile by the Falls, so I camped there overnight for the sheer joy of walking like a man again instead of hobbling over the pointed rocks like a wounded beast, and ran on down to the Flat River in the morning.

I avoided the difficult mouth of the river by making use of an offshoot of the Nahanni that cut through the point between the two rivers: it wound through thickets of willow and poplar and trickled over gravelly shallows, but in the end it ran out into the Flat River about half a mile above its mouth. There were no tracks to be seen but, a little way downstream, there were two poplars with long, white, fresh blazes on them. I walked down to see if there was a message there for me, but there was nothing but some fairly recent chips on the ground below the blazes, so I tracked on upstream and came, in about a mile, to Faille's landing.

The Wild Palms

William Faulkner

William Faulkner (1897–1962) was awarded the Nobel Prize for Literature in 1949. His picture of the South is gone forever except in Faulkner's characters, who peopled his imaginary Yoknapatawpha County. Rivers are part of Faulkner's works because they were part of the land about which he wrote; they flooded the land, marked boundaries, provided transportation, a place to fish and a backdrop for hunting.

The Mississippi in flood forms the setting for "Old Man," indeed is the old man that just keeps rollin' along. Two convicts in a rowboat try to save people who have been flooded out.

As the short convict had testified, the tall one, when he returned to the surface, still retained what the short one called the paddle. He clung to it, not instinctively against the time when he would be back inside the boat and would need it, because for a time he did not believe he would ever regain the skiff or anything else that would support him, but because he did not have time to think about turning it loose. Things had moved too fast for him. He had not been warned, he had felt the first snatching tug of the current, he had seen the skiff begin to spin and his companion vanish violently upward like in a translation out of Isaiah, then he himself was in the water, struggling against the drag of the paddle which he did not know he still held each time he fought back to the surface and grasped at the spinning skiff which at one instant was ten feet away and the next poised above his head as though about to brain him, until at last he grasped the stern, the drag of his body becoming a rudder to the skiff, the two of them, man and boat and with the paddle perpendicular above them like a jackstaff, vanishing from the view of the short convict (who had vanished from that of the tall one with the same celerity though in a vertical direction) like a tableau snatched offstage intact with violent and incredible speed.

He was now in the channel of a slough, a bayou, in which until today no current had run probably since the old subterranean outrage which had created the country. There was plenty of current in it now though; from his trough behind the stern he seemed to see the trees and sky rushing past with vertiginous speed, looking down at him between the gouts of cold yellow in lugubrious and mournful amazement. But they were fixed and secure in something; he thought of that, he remembered in an instant of despairing rage the firm earth fixed and founded strong and cemented fast and stable forever by the generations of laborious sweat, somewhere beneath him, beyond the reach of his feet, when, and again without warning, the stern of the skiff struck him a stunning blow across the bridge of his nose. The instinct which had caused him to cling to it now caused him to fling the paddle into the boat in order to grasp the gunwale with both hands just as the skiff pivoted and spun away again. With both hands free he now dragged himself over the stern and lay prone on his face, streaming with blood and water and panting, not with exhaustion but with that furious rage which is terror's aftermath.

But he had to get up at once because he believed he had come much faster (and so farther) than he had. So he rose, out of the watery scarlet puddle in which he had lain, streaming, the soaked denim heavy as iron on his limbs, the black hair plastered to his skull, the blood-infused water streaking his jumper, and dragged his forearm gingerly and hurriedly across his lower face and glanced at it, then grasped the paddle and began to try to swing the skiff back upstream. It did not even occur to him that he did not know where his companion was, in which tree among all which he had passed or might pass. He did not even speculate on that for the reason that he knew so incontestably that the other was upstream from him, and after his recent experience the mere connotation of the term upstream carried a sense of such violence and force and speed that the conception of it as other than a straight line was something which the intelligence, reason, simply refused to harbor, like the notion of a rifle bullet the width of a cotton field.

The bow began to swing back upstream. It turned readily, it outpaced the aghast and outraged instant in which he realised it was swinging far too easily, it had swung on over the arc and lay broadside to the current and began again that vicious spinning while he sat, his teeth bared in his bloody streaming face while his spent arms flailed the impotent paddle at the water, that innocent-appearing medium which at one time had held him in iron-like and shifting convolutions like an anaconda yet which now seemed to offer no more resistance to the thrust of his urge and need than so much air, like air; the boat which had threatened him and at last actually struck him in the face with the shocking violence of a mule's hoof now seemed to poise weightless upon it like a thistle bloom, spinning like a wind vane while he flailed at the water and thought of, envisioned, his companion safe, inactive and at ease in the tree with nothing to do but wait, musing with impotent and terrified fury upon that arbitrariness of human affairs which had abrogated to the one the secure tree and to the other the hysterical and unmanageable boat for the very reason that it knew that he alone of the two of them would make any attempt to return and rescue his companion.

The skiff had paid off and now ran with the current again. It seemed again to spring from immobility into incredible speed, and he thought he must already be miles away from where his companion had quitted him, though actually he had merely described a big circle since getting back into the skiff, and the object (a clump of cypress trees choked by floating logs and debris) which the skiff was now about to strike was the same one it had careened into before when the stern had struck him. He didn't know this because he had not yet ever looked higher than the bow of the boat. He didn't look higher now, he just saw that he was going to strike; he seemed to feel run through the very insentient fabric of the skiff a current of eager gleeful vicious incorrigible wilfulness; and he who had never ceased to flail at the bland treacherous water with what he had believed to be the limit of his strength now from somewhere, some ultimate absolute reserve, produced a final measure of endurance, will to endure which adumbrated mere muscle and nerves, continuing to flail the paddle right up to the instant of striking, completing one last reach thrust and recover out of pure desperate reflex, as a man slipping on ice reaches for his hat and money-pocket, as the skiff struck and hurled him once more flat on his face in the bottom of it.

This time he did not get up at once. He lay flat on his face, slightly spread-eagled and in an attitude almost peaceful, a kind of abject meditation. He would have to get up sometime, he knew that, just as all life consists of having to get up sooner or later and then having to lie down again sooner or later after a while. And he was not exactly exhausted and he was not particularly without hope and he did not especially dread getting up. It merely seemed to him that he had accidentally been caught in a situation in which time and environment, not himself, was mesmerised; he was being toyed with by a current of water going nowhere, beneath a day which would wane toward no evening; when it was done with him it would spew him back into the comparatively safe world he had been snatched violently out of and in the meantime it did not much matter just what he did or did not do. So he lay on his face, now not only feeling but hearing the strong quiet rustling of the current on the underside of the planks, for a while longer. Then he raised his head and this time touched his palm gingerly to his face and looked at the blood again, then he sat up onto his heels and leaning over the gunwale he pinched his nostrils between thumb and finger and expelled a gout of blood and was in the act of wiping his fingers on his thigh when a voice slightly above his line of sight said quietly, "It's taken you a while," and he who up to this moment had had neither reason nor time to raise his eyes higher than the bows looked up and saw, sitting in a tree and looking at him, a woman. She was not ten feet away. She sat on the lowest limb of one of the trees holding the jam he had grounded on, in a calico wrapper and an army private's tunic and a sunbonnet, a woman whom he did not even bother to examine since that first startled glance had been ample to reveal to him all the generations of her life and background, who could have been his sister if he had a sister, his wife if he had not entered the penitentiary at an age scarcely out of adolescence and some years younger than that at which even his prolific and monogamous kind married—a woman who sat clutching the trunk of the tree, her stockingless feet in a pair of man's unlaced brogans less than a yard from the water, who was very probably somebody's sister and quite certainly (or certainly should have been) somebody's wife, though this too he had entered the penitentiary too young to have had more than mere theoretical female experience to discover yet. "I thought for a minute you wasn't aiming to come back."

"Come back?"

"After the first time. After you run into this brush pile the first time and got into the boat and went on." He looked about, touching his face tenderly again; it could very well be the same place where the boat had hit him in the face.

"Yah," he said. "I'm here now though."

"Could you maybe get the boat a little closer? I taken a right sharp strain getting up here; maybe I better . . ." He was not listening; he had just discovered that the paddle was gone; this time when the skiff hurled him forward he had flung the paddle not into it but beyond it. "It's right there in them brush tops," the woman said. "You can get it. Here. Catch a holt of this." It was a grapevine. It had grown up into the tree and the flood had torn the roots loose. She had taken a turn with it about her upper body; she now loosed it and swung it out until he could grasp it. Holding to the end of the vine he warped the skiff around the end of the jam, picking up the paddle, and warped the skiff on beneath the limb and held it and now he watched her move, gather herself heavily and carefully to descend—that heaviness which was not painful but just excruciatingly careful, that profound and almost lethargic awkwardness which added nothing to the sum of that first aghast amazement which had served already for the catafalque of invincible dream since even in durance he had continued (and even with the old avidity, even though they had caused his downfall) to consume the impossible pulp-printed fables carefully censored and as carefully smuggled into the penitentiary; and who to say what Helen, what living Garbo, he had not dreamed of rescuing from what craggy pinnacle or dragoned keep when he and his companion embarked in the skiff. He watched her, he made no further effort to help her beyond holding the skiff savagely steady while she lowered herself from the limb—the entire body, the deformed swell of belly bulging the calico, suspended by its arms, thinking, *And this is what I get. This, out of all the female meat that walks, is what I have to be caught in a runaway boat with.*

"Where's that cottonhouse?" he said.

"Cottonhouse?"

"With that fellow on it. The other one."

"I don't know. It's a right smart of cottonhouses around here. With folks on them too, I reckon." She was examining him. "You're bloody as a hog," she said. "You look like a convict."

"Yah," he said snarled. "I feel like I done already been hung. Well, I got to pick up my pardner and then find that cottonhouse." He cast off. That is, he released his hold on the vine. That was all he had to do, for even while the bow of the skiff hung high on the log jam and even while he held it by the vine in the comparatively dead water behind the jam, he felt steadily and constantly the whisper, the strong purring power of the water just one inch beyond the frail planks on which he squatted and which, as soon as he realeased the vine, took charge of the skiff not with one powerful clutch but in a series of touches light, tentative, and catlike; he realised now that he had entertained a sort of foundationless hope that the added weight might make the skiff more controllable. During the first moment or two he had a wild (and still foundationless) belief that it had; he had got the head upstream and managed to hold it so by terrific exertion continued even after he discovered that they were travelling straight enough but stern-first and continued somehow even after the bow began to wear away and swing: the old irresistible movement which he knew well by now, too well to fight against it, so that he let the bow swing on downstream with the hope of utilising the skiff's own momentum to bring it through the full circle and so upstream again, the skiff travelling broadside then bow-first then broadside again, diagonally across the channel, toward the other wall of submerged trees; it began to flee beneath him with terrific speed, they were in an eddy but did not know it; he had no time to draw conclusions or even wonder; he crouched, his teeth bared in his blood-caked and swollen face, his lungs bursting, flailing at the water while the trees stooped hugely down at him. The skiff struck, spun, struck again; the woman half lay in the bow, clutching the gunwales, as if she were trying to crouch behind her own pregnancy; he banged now not at the water but at the living sap-blooded wood with the paddle, his desire now not to go anywhere, reach any destination, but just to keep the skiff from beating itself to fragments against the tree trunks. Then something exploded, this time against the back of his head, and stooping trees and dizzy water, the woman's face and all, fled together and vanished in bright soundless flash and glare.

The Pearl
John Steinbeck

John Steinbeck (1902–1968) is one of the more "teachable" writers. When I taught high school English, most of my students read his works: "The Red Pony" and "Flight," The Grapes of Wrath and Of Mice and Men. He was awarded a Pulitzer Prize in 1940 and the Nobel Prize for Literature in 1962.

I know the setting of so many of his short stories, the long valley of the Salinas River through which I have traveled numerous times during my ten years in California. I have seen that river flood, seen it nearly run dry and seen the irrigation operations. I also know the Carmel Valley, in which "The Frog Hunt" from Cannery Row is set, one of the funniest pieces I have ever read. Steinbeck was a naturalist, and rivers play a key role in several of his stories.

The tiny stream described in this short passage from The Pearl is perhaps typical of Steinbeck's descriptive genius and naturalist tendencies.

High in the gray stone mountains, under a frowning peak, a little spring bubbled out of a rupture in the stone. It was fed by shade-preserved snow in the summer, and now and then it died completely and bare rocks and dry algae were on its bottom. But nearly always it gushed out, cold and clean and lovely. In the time when the quick rains fell, it might become a freshet and send its column of white water crashing down the mountain cleft, but nearly always it was a lean little spring. It bubbled out into a pool and then fell a hundred feet to another pool, and this one, overflowing, dropped again, so that it continued, down and down, until it came to the rubble of the upland, and there it disappeared altogether. There wasn't much left of it then anyway, for every time it fell over an escarpment the thirsty air drank it, and it splashed from the pools to the dry vegetation. The animals from miles around came to drink from the little pools, and the wild sheep and the deer, the pumas and raccoons, and the mice—all came to drink. And the birds which spent the day in the brushland came at night to the little pools that were like steps in the mountain cleft. Beside this tiny stream, wherever enough earth collected for root-hold, colonies of plants grew, wild grape and little palms, maidenhair fern, hibiscus, and tall pampas grass with feathery rods raised above the spike leaves. And in the pool lived frogs and water-skaters, and waterworms crawled on the bottom of the pool. Everything that loved water came to these few shallow places. The cats took their prey there, and strewed feathers and lapped water through their bloody teeth. The little pools were places of life because of the water, and places of killing because of the water, too.

The lowest step, where the stream collected before it tumbled down a hundred feet and disappeared into the rubbly desert, was a little platform of stone and sand. Only a pencil of water fell into the pool, but it was enough to keep the pool full and to keep the ferns green in the underhang of the cliff, and wild grape climbed the stone mountain and all manner of little plants found comfort here. The freshets had made a small sandy beach through which the pool flowed, and bright green watercress grew in the damp sand. The beach was cut and scarred and padded by the feet of animals that had come to drink and to hunt.

Notes from the Century Before

Edward Hoagland

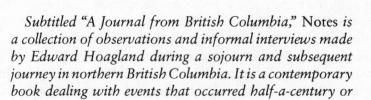

*Subtitled "A Journal from British Columbia," Notes is
a collection of observations and informal interviews made
by Edward Hoagland during a sojourn and subsequent
journey in northern British Columbia. It is a contemporary
book dealing with events that occurred half-a-century or
more ago. Most of Hoagland's interviews are with old
timers, largely natives and others who go native. In this
book Hoagland translates oral history into the written
word.*

*Several passages deal directly with rivers: traveling on
the rivers by boat, flying through storms by following rivers,
even using roads and railroads as they follow river routes.
The passage I have selected, however, deals with fish
migrating on rivers to their spawning streams.*

*Hoagland is a writer and teacher, author of novels and
collected essays, a traveler and a keen observer of nature
and human nature.*

A ugust 2, Tuesday:
Was lifted today by my fisheries friends to the slide on the
Tahltan River where the salmon are blocked. The Tahltan is the main
spawning tributary of the Stikine, which is naturally why the tribe
gave it their name. Lately, most of the fish are being harvested by
Alaskan boats on the coast and therefore the Americans are footing
part of the bill. The operation has been a fiasco so far. The first plan
was to have the men on the ground scoop the fish into barrels of
water that the helicopter simply lifted upriver. The fish were trauma-
tized by this, however, and the water in the barrels became toxic to
them. At present, the helicopter only ferries the men back and forth
and takes the foreman on tours. His dilemma is that if he blows a
passage with dynamite he will kill all the fish who are waiting and
perhaps precipitate a worse slide.

The canyon is a rudimentary steep V, the walls clay and silt. The
river within looks slender and white from the air, but the damaged

area is like an artillery range, pitted with boulders, heaped with khaki-colored debris. Our arrival sent up legions of birds—eagles, crows, gulls from the sea. Being left to my own devices, I explored gingerly, completely alone once the pilot dropped me. It's only a little neighborhood river but it moves with violent velocity. The *water* gets through, all right; it has blasted a zigzag chute for itself with the force of a fire hose. Just to sit in the thunder and watch is awesome. There were so many fish waiting in the slower water below the chute that half an hour must have gone by before I was even aware of them. I listened and looked at the gulls who had gotten the word and had traveled so far. I thought the actual fish were thickets of driftwood that the river had smashed together and submerged; their fins stuck out like a welter of branches. I was astonished instead at the carnage on shore, the bear-chewed or beak-bitten bodies scattered about everywhere. When I did see the living fish I gaped because there were many thousands. The Tahltan was jammed with them, flank to flank and atop one another, seldom moving, just holding whatever position they'd gained, though that took continual swimming. Hundreds of them were in water which scarcely covered their backs. I thought of shark fins, except that there was a capitulation to it, a stockade stillness, as if they were prisoners of war waiting in huddled silence under the river's bombarding roar. The pity I felt was so strong that I did everything I could not to alarm the ones nearest me. They were in an eddy behind a boulder a few feet away, and I wouldn't have dreamed of touching one of them. Each had fought to attain that eddy, and at any confusion or weakening of resolve he lost his hold and was washed downstream. Like mountain climbers, the most active fish would wiggle twenty yards further on and gain a new cranny. It might require a number of tries, but they were the freshest fish, unscarred, and occasionally one would get into some partially sheltered corner of the chute itself, in one of the zigs or zags. These dozen desperate niches were so packed that they were like boxfuls of crated fish set into the bullet-gray water. The salmon who were able to battle upcurrent did so by shimmying and thrusting more than by leaping, although they did leap now and again. This was the cruelest sight of all, because they were like paper airplanes thrown into the hydrant blast. The water shattered and obliterated the leap and then banged the limp, tender body down the same stretch of rapids that it had been fighting its way up for perhaps the past day and a half.

Most of the salmon were quite catatonic by now. They just held their own in whichever clump or eddy they'd reached, unless some pathetic impulse moved them again. They might try to better themselves, only to be dislodged and lose fifteen yards. For me, walking back and forth on the bank with absolute freedom, it was eerie to watch a spectacle of death that was measured in feet and yards. I could lift a fly out of a spider's web but I couldn't assist these salmon. The swimmer who drowns is surrounded by fish who scull at their ease, and I suppose there was something in it about spheres of existence and the difference between being on water and land. But I felt like a witness at a slow massacre. Thirty thousand fish, each as long as my arm, stymied and dying in the droning roar.

These were sockeyes. Their bodies have a carroty tint on top of the back at spawning time, often quite bright, and their heads turn a garish green. They wear a lurid, mascaraed look, a tragedian's look, as if they were dressed for an *auto-da-fé*. I could tell how long a fish had been waiting by the color he'd turned and also, especially, by the length of his nose. This was another delayed discovery. All of them were gashed from being battered on the rocks, but some, I realized in horror, had practically no nose left, as though a fishmonger had amputated it, as though he had thrown the poor fish on his chopping block and cut off the front end right by the eyes.

The Stikine is a very rough river. Permanent canyons shut off its upper tributaries to the salmon entirely. The Spatsizi, the Pitman, the Klappan have none. Tahltan Lake happens to be ideal for spawning, but this year only two individuals out of the umpteen thousands who've tried have been seen by the fisheries counters to have reached the lake. Salmon live in the ocean for four years or so before they return, by the grace of some unexplained recording device, to the fresh-water source where they were born. They lay their eggs, languish genteelly and die. Thus four generations are in the sea at a time, and when a rock slide occurs, three years can go by before the blockage *has* to be cleared. If the fourth generation is equally foiled when it tries to spawn, then the river ceases to be a salmon river because no other salmon are living with memories of how to swim there. Given that much time, the Tahltan itself, fire hose that it is, might manage to clear its bed of the debris of the slide, but in the meantime a lot of commercial fishermen will be going broke.

Home Country
Ernie Pyle

Ernie Pyle (1900–1945) is remembered as a war corre-
spondent, for he was killed by Japanese gunfire on the tiny
island of Iwo Jima in the Ryukyus near Okinawa only a
few months before the end of World War II. While it is
true that his wartime writing made his name a household
word, he had been a columnist for many years in the 1930s.
During the Depression he and his wife made 35 cross-
country trips, and Pyle wrote about the American heart-
land in his column. One of those trips included a short
run down the San Juan River in southeastern Utah, with
Norman Nevills, one of the earliest of the commercial river
guides. [It is interesting to note that Wallace Stegner also
ran the San Juan with Nevilles, a story told in The Sound
of Mountain Waters, *but I have elected to use a different*
piece from Stegner's book rather than duplicate Pyle's San
Juan venture.]
Pyle won a Pulitzer Prize for distinguished writing about
the Second World War, but some of his finest work appeared
in Home Country, *a collection of his pre-war writing*
published after his death.

I n each of the little settlements of the Navajo country there is
usually one white family that stands out. One such family was
the Nevills, of Mexican Hat, Utah. It was Norman Nevills who kept
the newspapers in hot water for more than a month in the summer
of 1938, with his expedition down the treacherous Colorado River.
The party was forty-two days making the six hundred sixty miles from
Green River, Utah, to Boulder Dam; for weeks they were supposedly
"lost." But they came through, and if you've ever shot a rapids with
Norman Nevills you'll understand why.

There were two families of Nevills at Mexican Hat—Norman and
his wife and little girl in one house, and his parents in another. The
elder Nevills was a California oil engineer. He had arrived in this
majestically bare part of Utah in 1920, and had been there ever since.

He was in poor health; he said that even to say a few words exhausted him.

Norman and his mother ran the Indian trading post, and a tasteful little lodge where they put up occasional wayfarers. But to Norman, those things were sidelines. The river was his main life. He was a college graduate from California, and had studied engineering. They'd had a lot of money at one time, but shot it all in oil, and didn't get it back. Norman was glad, now, for otherwise he might never have stayed at Mexican Hat so long, and today he loved it there above any other place in the world.

He was, I would say, not much over thirty. He spoke some Navajo, and dickered impatiently with the Indians who brought in rugs to trade for supplies. His mother said he offered the Indians too little. He said she offered them too much. But the Indians must have liked it, for they were always hanging around.

Norman had been playing with the rapids of the San Juan River for years. But it was the expedition of 1938 that was likely to provide him a livelihood for many years. It publicized him as a river guide, and it was from the river, mainly, that he made his living. His schedule was full for the summer, and far into the fall.

What he did was take summer parties on an eight-day boat ride from Mexican Hat, on the San Juan, clean down to Lee's Ferry, on the Colorado. He charged sixty-two dollars and a half a person for the eight-day trip, and that included grub, a cook, sleeping bags, a long taste of the simple outdoor life, much scenery, and many thrills. On the ninth day he pulled his boats from the water, loaded them on trailers, and in one hard day's driving over rough Navajo roads was back again at Mexican Hat. And on the tenth day he would be headed downriver again with a new party. "See the desert by water" was his slogan.

Norman told some whoppers about the force of the rapids, and I believed them all. For instance, he used to wear a stocking cap on the river to keep his hair from flying. But once, in particularly bad rapids, the water came over the whole boat with such terrific force that it pulled the stocking cap right down over his face, clear to his neck, and he couldn't see a thing.

He said he had never overturned a boat. In all these years the river had never nicked him, but he had an intensely respectful fear of it.

The greatest aviators I know are those who are always a little afraid; they're the ones I like to fly with. And so it was with Nevills, and the river he loved and feared. We were a little skittish about riding with Nevills. "I wonder if this guy can really row a boat?" my traveling friend asked, the night before. Before another twenty-four hours we knew damn well he could row a boat—and how!

We were up early. Nevills was up ahead of us, overalled and dirty, smearing black tar on the boat bottom with his hands. "I don't think it will leak much," he said. It was a fifteen-foot plywood rowboat, very thin. We lifted it onto a trailer, and drove twenty miles north, to where the road crossed Comb Wash. Then we headed the car right down the dry stream bed, dodging rocks, until at last we bumped up the shore of the San Juan River. We put the boat in the water, and we two passengers put on life jackets. By river, it was nineteen and a half miles back to Mexican Hat. Nevills said we would make it in five to six hours.

There are many odd things about boating on a river full of rapids. This very first is that you float down backwards—in other words, stern-to. This is so the oarsman can sit facing forward and see where he's going. Also, the boat takes it better.

Nevills took off his shirt before we started. He was a smallish man, but his muscles were powerful and steely, from much rowing. The first thing I knew, we were floating sideways. And, although the waves were a couple of feet high, we seemed to rock across them like a blob of oil. "In small waves, we always go sideways," Nevills said. "That way we don't smack the waves, and don't get so much water aboard. But when they get bigger, we have to switch around stern-to, or the boat would swamp."

For the first couple of hours the rapids we went through were small. To be sure, they looked bad enough to a novice. But we handled them so simply that my friend and I were disappointed.

It was beautiful to watch Nevills handle the boat—just fishing around, easing the boat through the big waves like an eel. Often we would go into a rapids stern-to, switch sideways in the middle, and come out into smooth water bow-to. Water oozed in through the seams of the boat, and soon we were wet. Every fifteen minutes or so one of us would bail with a tin can. "This boat can't leak," Nevills said, "but it's sure doing a good job of going through the motions, isn't it?" On dry land, that would have been a swell joke.

The hours went on. Nevills told us river tales. And always, as he gracefully oared that little boat through the rushing waves and around hidden rocks, he would sing or whistle. I think he must have made up his songs as he went along, for I'd never heard any of them before.

The riverbank rose gradually, and before long we were riding along between canyon walls a quarter of a mile high—frightening, forbidding cliffs of solid rock that would have been impossible to climb. Eating lunch on a rock ledge in those narrows, we were a little apprehensive, and kept our eyes on the boat. It was tied to a small jutting rock of the canyon wall. If it had broken loose, we sure would have been in a pickle. The ledge was cut off by canyon wall behind, and deep, rushing river in front.

It was just a little after noon when Nevills rowed over to a sandy beach, jumped out, and tied it up. "This is Eight-Foot Rapids around the bend," he said. "Hear it? It's bad. We'll walk down and see how it looks today." The personality of rapids changes from day to day, it seems.

It developed that Nevills didn't expect to take us through this rapids with him; we'd have to walk around, and he'd pick us up farther along. We walked down. The rapids didn't look bad to me. Nevills studied them, and finally said, "I guess maybe I could take one of you." I wanted the experience, and since I was the smaller of the two passengers, it was agreed that I could go. We left my friend alongside the rapids, and Nevills and I walked back to the boat. He really did a build-up on Eight-Foot Rapids. He said lots of boats had been lost there. He put on his own life jacket, for the first time. He told me just how to sit.

We got all ready to go. And then I learned something else—that it's a custom and a tradition among rivermen, just before shooting a big rapids, to—how shall I put it?—go to the gentlemen's room. We honored the tradition.

I was excited and eager as our little boat eased off from shore and the swift current caught it. We were around the bend in a few seconds. Going through was just like having an automobile accident. It was a blur—over so quickly I never caught any details at all. I only know that even right in the middle of it, I was let down, for it wasn't bad at all.

Our friend walked on down to us, and we started on. I'm afraid we disappointed Nevills, for two or three times he said, "I'm telling you, twenty-five per cent of the people who make this trip are scared speechless." And later he said, "You two are the only newspapermen who have ever shot rapids on either the San Juan or the Colorado. The rest are scared." Maybe I'm making this sound as if we were too brave. Just wait.

The afternoon was tame. The sun grew hotter, and the rapids down below were milder. For long stretches we floated on smooth water. We all got sleepy. Finally we came to the bluff above which sits Mexican Hat. Nevills started calling, hoping his family would hear and send the car and trailer down for us to the landing, another mile downstream. He yelled a weird, half-musical "Moo-hoo!" over and over again. And then he sang little nautical chanteys, made up as he went along. "Three men in a boat, yo ho. Sailors three. Ahoy, we're home. Come and get us."

"We're almost there," he said to us. "Just one more little rapids, if you want to call it a rapids. Gyp Creek. Doesn't amount to anything."

We were bored with small rapids by now. We hardly paid any attention. We hurt from five hours of sitting on a board seat. It had been a swell day, buy we were ready to quit.

And suddenly we saw what we were in for. Nevills saw it at the same time, but it was too late. Gyp Creek rapids, usually placid, had turned into a maelstrom. We were caught, and going like the wind. The roar ahead of us was terrifying. The sand-laden waves reared up ahead of us like a painting of a furious sea. Nevills was magnificent. He didn't sing this time—he was working too fast. He turned us, switched us, played the boat through those waves as though he was fingering piano keys. But we hit a hole. It was a terrific smack, like dropping down a roller-coaster and then ramming a blank wall. The water came over our heads in a great swoop. Boy, it was cold! It knocked off the dashboard in front of us, which was fastened on with long screws. It threw us off balance, but we held on.

The boat came up a third full of water, and logy. We grabbed the cans and started bailing. Nevills jerked off his sun helmet and bailed with it, a gallon at a time. We were soaked to our ears. But we were joyous, elated. We felt as though someone had handed us a million dollars. What a dramatic surprise! And what an end to a perfect day!

Within two minutes we were at the little landing. The water squished deliciously in our shoes as we stepped onto the safe white sand.

Wonder if that guy can really row a boat? We had thought the night before. Haw, haw, haw! Could he row a boat? By the Horny-handed Oarsman on the River known as Styx, that guy could row a boat!

Love Affair with a River

John W. Malo

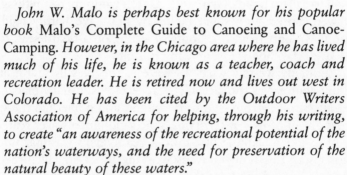

John W. Malo is perhaps best known for his popular book Malo's Complete Guide to Canoeing and Canoe-Camping. *However, in the Chicago area where he has lived much of his life, he is known as a teacher, coach and recreation leader. He is retired now and lives out west in Colorado. He has been cited by the Outdoor Writers Association of America for helping, through his writing, to create "an awareness of the recreational potential of the nation's waterways, and the need for preservation of the natural beauty of these waters."*

I first met Malo at a meeting of the Rocky Mountain Outdoor Writers Association in Jackson Hole. While we didn't get around to paddling the Snake together then, we did do a bit of canoeing at the 1983 annual meeting of the OWAA in Wichita, Kansas, on a little pond in Beech Craft Park. We are planning to tackle the Upper Missouri one of these years, following the route of Lewis and Clark and of that later explorer John Madson, whose "Where the River Fits the Song" deserves a place in these pages.

The how and why were providential, but exactly when it happened is vague; love affairs are that way. Perhaps a Kansas Jayhawker childhood with the Neosha River many miles from home was the puppy love stage. The pre-adolescent experiences were fleeting and unfulfilled; they did not satiate the hunger of river adventure, the lore and romance of eternal water, splashing it, wiping a summer brow with it, swimming in it and boating its back. Sauntering the ever-changing shorelines and observing its seasonal moods represent the byplay that further excited a budding suitor to the charms of a river mistress.

The coal mines where dad and older brothers, Tony, Ramage and Bill, toiled relinquished their non-renewable resources, and the mines closed for good. We had to give up our ten-acre mini-farm, selling, but mostly giving away to friends, the livestock of Jersey cows, hogs, chickens, geese, a greyhound dog, cats and household items. In 1923 our family of seven children left the land once the Pawnee Indian hunting grounds, the gently rolling hills and the Neosha River of southeastern Ringo, Kansas. Earlier the brothers during slowdowns at the mines, or just raccoon curiosity about a more stimulating world, had visited Chicago and realized its advantages, particularly the potential for work. My older brothers and dad immediately got jobs, while Matilda, Helen, Christy and I enrolled at James Otis Elementary School.

With the unfolding of exciting weeks and months, family members sensed that although we were economically viable and happy in Chicago, the hard smooth surfaces, crowds, hustle and bustle had to be tempered in keeping with rooted needs. At every opportunity we retreated to Humboldt Park, Lincoln Park, Lake Michigan, the soft green fields and vegetable farms that flourished beyond the end of the Milwaukee Avenue street car line. Then Tony bought a Model A Ford which immediately extended our range of experiences as it rattled us to the Cook County Forest Preserve and especially the DesPlaines River.

Summer vacations led to wider horizons: fields and farms, lakes and forests in Wisconsin, Michigan and later, Minnesota and Canada. The wanderings very often included mother, who loved every living thing; human and subhuman, plant and animal. She was as excited as we at the prospect of discovering a new piece of exciting geography; the mother hen, as it were, taking her brood to distant fields, to feed their varied and individual hungers. These were soft interludes that sustained us, long before the traffic dragon grew ferocious, the air hazard and newly-adopted brothers became suspect.

As in most families, older brothers are not known to recruit younger ones for companionship on outdoor trips. Thus, Christy and I had to suffer it out, wait for the dynamic of hierarchy to moderate . . . which of course it did many years later, after we learned the necessary camping and fishing skills. In the meantime we asked questions and listened, eyes wide open, mouths agape as the brothers recounted their adventures afield; seasonal hunting of rabbits, quail, squirrel, pheasant and duck, fishing far-away waters, picking mushrooms and walnuts, picnicking in the Forest Preserve with their friends and sweethearts, many from Kansas. Their sport clothes included white trousers and shirt, a straw hat, and Tony always included his banjo or ukelele. The brothers seemed compatible in either Daniel Boone or troubadour roles, extracting much from life, exhibiting a zest for the activity at hand, whether it be practicing the violin or piano, repairing a piece of furniture or dancing wildly with the short-skirted flappers.

A few times the brothers did, however, take us to the DesPlaines River, the Forest Preserve between Grand Ave. and Irving Park Road, for overnight fishing trips. (Camping was legal then.) The overnighters to this nearby semi-wild area required the planning and logistics of an extensive trip; firewood, pots, pans, utensils, food, axe, rope, tent and the mattress of hay that we picked from a nearby field.

After camp was set up we cast throw lines, anchored bank poles, and sometimes the experts would set out trot lines across a shallow part of the river and tend them all night. Once, cousin John caught a strange fish; it was a northern pike, and Kansas-style, he stringered the 19-inch prize through the gills and mouth. The Jayhawker technique was remiss, for in the morning when we went to inspect the fish, found but a limp stringer. None of us realized that during the night the sharp teeth of the pike would fray the line and give the fish its freedom.

How slow the youthful years pass. High school years according to mother gave the maturity and permission to roam without family supervision. I was fortunate in finding glowingly-active, outdoor-oriented and adventure-seeking friends, mostly from Lane Tech High School. Our daily habit, from September to June, was to hike to and from school over two miles away.

The passions of puppy love led us more and more to the trails and river. On our own we went pup tent camping to the Che-che-pin-qua Woods, playing touch football in the field, taking sides in crabapple fights, drinking water from a river bank spring, calling a barred owl to our night campfire, and sleeping in the warmth of smoldering coals.

The East Lake Ave. Woods offered a high bank campsite, which Al baptized "Camp Snorker." It gave a view of lots of river, and westward an open view of the sun's sweep all the way to the horizon. Nearby, two tall trees became initimate landmarks: the "Five-Fingered Tree" with massive branches flaring from a single trunk, the thumb position one sheared and stubbed by a storm to suggest a giant hand reaching out of the soil. A short distance downstream some love-struck canoeist, probably, resting on the grass, found time to carve in deeply precise letters, "Tree of Romance" in the large, dead and bleached cottonwood. I hope that his romance outlived the tree; it was blown over a few years laters.

We dated the DesPlaines in the winter too, its current seemingly stilled, but peering through the crystalline surface the water could be seen; moving, alive and clean. The muskrat leaving his cupcake-domed house of sticks and mud in the connecting slough to swim under the ice in search of plant food was a common sight. If you were willing to wait over its well-defined route you gained a nature observation for your collection.

Many times we skated the meandering river for miles and miles, the body generating welcome heat in the low temperatures. Periodically we sat on the fallen trees that extended over the water and experienced a bird's roosting perch on a frozen river. At day's end we continued to enjoy the ice by playing shinny, sometimes till the moon came out.

Always contriving new activities, we cut the thick ice in a series of rectangular slabs, and left them free-floating in place. Then walking across the five or six unstable stepping stones we dared not tarry on any one slab that would sink your weight. With practice, you learned the proper speed to negotiate the erratic ice; tarrying too long on a single square would sink it and result in wet shoes, and running too fast would result in taking a spill.

Ed was an engineering student and to temper the confinement of the study desk and drafting board he, too, became an aficionado of the river. Once, in his need for the long view, he roused and prodded me, and we went via the Grand Ave. street car line to its terminus. We hiked past a few homes, through open fields, along the railroad track, and finally to the Indian Boundary Preserve and along the banks of the river . . . all this, in the middle of winter when eight inches of snow covered the countryside.

Continued dalliance with a river inexorably deepens to a stronger and grander relationship. For the young that relationship can be nourished by buying a used wood-canvas canoe in Willow Springs and with a pal, Yam, paddling it for over 35 miles up the DesPlaines to Allison Woods. This was the site of the "House in the Wood," (today the site of River Trail Nature Center), that served as the Northwestern University Settlement summer camp, where we were to work through high school and college years.

As counselors we enjoyed our summer setting. The camp was situated on a bend of the DesPlaines River, the kitchen an original farm house, dining hall and dorms beautifully set off by tall oaks, maples, and hickories, and beyond, the low-growing hawthorn and crabapple. From the dining hall an open field sloped gently to the river.

A few of us worked the entire summer; a four-week period with the girls and four with the boys. During the depression years we had little in the way of budget, equipment or craft supplies, thus we had to use our own resources to evolve an interesting program. We did it with nature study, swimming, dramatics, sports, extended hikes and simple hammer and saw maintenance projects. Stimulation came from each other's company and the rousing activities that challenged the counselors as well as the inner-city campers. There was a verve to the daily program, the recurring adventures representing for many, the high point of their, and our, year.

Our swimming hole was the DesPlaines River at Dam #2, which held the water to about four feet; it was over a mile away, and the 40 to 50 campers hiked the distance every day. The swimming facility was well appointed and supervised: upriver restraining rope, diving board, slide, refreshment stand, and lifeguards in boats who regularly applied chlorine to the water. The swim period over, campers would dry off, then hike wearily to camp, sometimes munching a candy bar for an energy lift.

One day Yam and I planned a swim upstream to camp. We stroked and kicked, floated on our backs periodically for a rest, reached the camp objective, but decided to continue. We eventually finished at the Milwaukee Ave. bridge, a distance judged at over three miles.

How placid and tranquil the DesPlaines looked under the summer sun, but on occasion she could become capricious, even burst out in tantrum. After a copious rain on Saturday, the river became a surging, undisciplined force, racing over its banks, its fingers probing new places, grasping all in its wake, and evoking a dirge. On the following day during a picnic a teenage boy went swimming alone and, in the maelstrom, drowned. His body was recovered many miles downstream and several days later.

On occasion, after a hectic day, we paddled upstream at night to Villa Venice, a plush road house where gondolas were rented by couples and poled upriver that was over-hung with willows. We became acquainted with the gondolier, a Canadian canoeist, and when there was a lull in action he borrowed our canoe. Kneeling in the bottom, our exciting new-found friend paddled solo in powerful and graceful strokes, then burst into a voyageur song, his booming voice projecting to the tree-tops. Our craft never knew such expert handling, paddling and skimming so beautifully over the water.

We didn't tarry on the dock; instead, we crept to the back windows near the floor show stage and peeked through the curtained windows. Thus, in return for a loaned canoe we were treated to Papa Bouche's expensive entertainment. The band beat out the routine cues for thinly-clad chorus girls and, for some of us, we saw in public for the first time a bare female navel.

One makes love best by moonlight ... even to a river. After taps and our charges asleep the counselors convened at the river bank. On sweltering nights the talk sessions gave way to a nighttime swim. In the nude, surface diving and swimming underwater, opening the eyes to ink-black water gave an eerie feeling. The experience offered a fleeting apprehension, and we didn't stay underwater very long.

Some nights we launched the canoe and floated the calm current in total darkness. There was little concern about safety as we were expert swimmers and knew every foot of the shorelines. In the middle of the river we just laid back, paddles at rest, drifting with the current, time and history . . . akin to the aboriginal Indians, Marquette, Jolliet, LaSalle and Tonti, intrepid voyageurs who cruised the earlier river. In kinship with these explorer-patriots we listened to the same night sounds: the plop of a rising fish, the squawk of a night bird, the pee-yeeps of tree frogs, the compulsive droning of insects, the soft swirl of a paddle.

Periodically, our nighttime freedom turned to gustatory treats; Louis Shaw, the patron saint of camp directors, surprised us with an ice cream and cookie party . . . when he sensed that a boost in morale was necessary.

There were some attractions that took us from the river, but the DesPlaines was not jealous. She understood the temporary flirtations of capricious youth.

The twilight treasure hunt (for watermelons) became traditional. The quest took the entire group on a meandering path through the woods that ended in a clearing, then the easily-found melons were sliced, served and devoured. To the rising campfire flames stories were told and songs were sung. Ed and Frank with their trained voices led the group in community singing, and we never knew if the squawk of a disturbed great blue heron was a bravo or a bronx cheer.

One twilight hike with over forty boys we spotted a barred owl sitting high on à dead cottonwood tree, silhouetted against the light sky in hallowe'en glory. So orderly and silent were the group that all were able to observe the legendary oracle of the forest.

Chuck, today a noted Chicagoland ornithologist, made his first bird list observations at camp, and his recurring and exciting reports inspired most of us to keep faithful bird lists, which we do to this day.

The DesPlaines River today remains a slim thread of nature winding through rural woods and pastoral vistas. Much of her heritage survives, the riverine eco-systems cuffed a bit but not destroyed. It still proclaims a vestige of ancient wildness and freedom that must be loved and cherished. As R. L. Stevenson indicated,

"There's no music like a little river's . . . It takes the mind out of doors . . . and . . . sir, it quiets a man down like saying his prayers."

A River Never Sleeps
Roderick Haig-Brown

Roderick Haig-Brown (1908–1976), you know without asking, was an Englishman who loved fishing more than anything else—or so it seems to read his accounts. He migrated to North America and eventually settled on Vancouver Island's Campbell River, not far from where Raymond Patterson retired (they knew each other but rarely met).

Haig-Brown was at various times a logger and a trapper, but he was always a writer and a fisherman. His writing about fishing—all kinds of fishing in all kinds of weather at all seasons of the year in several countries—is simply superb. He captures the essence of the fly cast, the steelhead's leap, the tug of the river on wader-bound legs, the flow of the current. He is a fine river writer, one who died too early.

It is easy to forget about the river in winter, particularly if you are a trout fisherman and live in town. Even when you live in the country, close beside it, a river seems to hold you off a little in winter, closing itself into the murky opacity of freshet or slipping past ice-fringed banks in shrunken, silent flow. The weather and the season have their effect on the observer too, closing him into himself, allowing him to glance only quickly with a careless, almost hostile, eye at the runs and pools that give summer delight. And probably his eyes are on the sky for flight of ducks or geese or turned landward on the work of his dogs. Unless he is a winter fisherman, he is not likely to feel the intimate, probing, summer concern with what is happening below the surface.

It was January when I came with a rod to my first river in North America—the Pilchuck near Snohomish in Washington. My good friend Ed Dunn took me there, and we caught nothing, at least partly because neither of us knew very much about the fish we were after; but I cannot forget the day, because it was the first day and it started me thinking of steelhead—a habit I haven't grown out of yet. Two or three days later we went to the Stillaguamish, and I remember that day too, though the river was roaring down in tawny flood and I suppose we hadn't a chance of a fish even if we had known all there was to know. But there were dead salmon along the banks, and I saw and loved a fine Pacific coast river, so that day also is remembered.

And now, if all goes well and the Campbell, on whose bank I live, does not rise in full freshet, I know January for the best of all winter steelhead months. The fish have come in in good numbers by that time, but they are still fresh and silver and clean. There may be snow on the ground, two feet of it or more; and if so, the river will be flowing darkly and slowly, the running water below freezing but not ice, just flowing more slowly, as though it meant to thicken into ice—which it never does. Steelhead fishing can be good then, and there is a strange satisfaction in the life of the river flowing through the quiet, dead world. On the bank the maples and alders are stark and bare, drawn into themselves against the cold. The swamp robin moves among them, tame and almost bold for once, and perhaps an arctic owl hunts through them in heavy flight whose softness presses the air until the ear almost feels it. On the open water of the river are mergansers and mallards, bluebills, butterballs, perhaps even geese and teal. Under it and under the gravel, the eggs of the salmon are eyed now; the earliest of the cutthroat trout are beginning their spawning, and the lives of a thousand other creatures—May flies, stone flies, deer flies, dragonflies, sedges, gnats, water snails and all the myriad forms of plankton—are slowly stirring and growing and multiplying. But the steelhead, with the brightness of the sea still on him, is livliest of all the river's life. When you have made your cast for him, you are no longer a careless observer. As you mend the cast and work your fly well down to him through the cold water, your whole mind is with it, picturing its drift, guiding its swing, holding it where you know he will be. And when the shock of his take jars through to your forearms and you lift the rod to its bend, you know that in a moment the strength of his leaping body will shatter the water to brilliance, however dark the day.

I came to Deer Creek at a fine pool above a log jam. Upstream the river swung over to the foot of a round timber-covered hill about two thousand feet high; downstream, below the jam, it twisted its way between heavy green timber on the left and a slope of alders on the right. The river was a lot bigger than the word "creek" had led me to expect, and it was beautiful, clear and bright and fast, tumbled on rocks and gravel bars. I was standing on a wide gravel bar which gave me every chance to cast and fish as I wished, and my heart beat hard and my fingers trembled as I dumped my pack and began to put my rod up—they do that even today when I come to the bank of a river I have not fished before and find the reality of it better than anything I had dared hope.

I had brought in with me a nine-foot casting rod, a silex reel and a boxful of the spoons and devon minnows and phantoms we had used for salmon on the Dorsetshire Frome. As soon as the rod was up and the line was threaded, I went up to the head of the pool and began to fish. I made cast after cast across the swift water, working down a step or two at each cast, swinging the minnow across as slow and deep as I could. The pool became slower and deeper, and I really began to expect a fish. The minnow touched bottom several times among the big round rocks, and I knew I was deep enough. I made a cast whose swing carried the minnow almost under the log jam and felt a sharp, heavy strike. This was it, I told myself, a steelhead at last. The fish ran almost instantly from the strike, and I held hard to turn him from the log jam. It was a strong run, clear across the river; then he came back a little, and I began to think of the stories. In spite of anything I could do, he would run again under the log jam and break me there. He ought to jump soon; all the stories said they jumped like mad things. I began to walk him upstream, away from the jam, and at first he came quietly enough. Then he seemed to decide that he wanted to go that way anyhow, and he ran steadily and smoothly right up to the head of the pool. Still there was no jumping and no sign of the fierce strength of a good fish that raps the handle of the reel against your knuckles and makes you think you really have lost control this time.

I put pressure on him, and he came into the shallow water at the foot of the gravel bar steadily and quietly. I walked close and lifted him to the surface; he struggled and bored away once, came back and was finished, quiet on his side on top of the water. I ran him up on the beach without difficulty and stooped down to look him over. He was a fish of about four pounds, silver gray all over, very little darker on the back than on the belly; he was thick and fat, and along his sides there were pale lemon-colored spots.

I didn't think he was a steelhead. I almost hoped he wasn't, because he was so far from what I had looked forward to, in strength, size, fighting quality, beauty, everything. Yet no one had warned me to expect any other fish but steelhead in Deer Creek, and it was hard to believe that such a good-sized, handsome fish as this certainly was could be overlooked. Doubtfully I went back to my fishing.

I caught three more fish that evening, all almost exactly like the first one. Not one of them had jumped; but all had fought well enough for their size, and at least they made something to take back to camp. I went up from the creek a little before dark and made camp beside a small stream that ran down to it. About fifty feet below my camp the stream ran shallow under a big log, and I threw the fish down there, thinking it was cool and shaded and they would keep well through the heat of the next day. Then I made supper and rolled happily into my single blanket, tired, thoroughly contented, in love with Deer Creek and fully determined that it should show me a steelhead the next day.

I woke in the quiet dim light before sunrise. For once I didn't want to go on sleeping. There was a whole day of Deer Creek ahead, and I sat straight up in my blanket. Below me, near the log where my fish were, I saw a movement. It was a bear, a fine, handsome black bear who hadn't the slightest idea I was within a hundred miles of him. For a moment I was more pleased than scared; then I realized he was eating my good fish. I yelled in fury. He looked up at me, and I thought he looked calm and contented, as he very well may have. I reached for my boots and yelled again, and he turned round then, lifting his forepaws from the ground in that lovely liquid movement bears have. I drew back a boot to throw at him—a logger's calked boot at fifty feet is something of a weapon—but he didn't wait for that. I pulled on my boots and went down to look at the wreck of my fish. His meal had not really been disturbed; my first yell had come merely as a grace at the end of it.

January, 1929, was a cold month on Vancouver Island, and my partners and I were busy with a series of trap lines. Since there was the perfectly legitimate argument that we needed fresh fish for trap bait, I took a day out every once in a while to work the river. One cold, windy Sunday I took the skiff and poled up into the Canyon Pool. We knew steelhead were running to the river because we had found them trapped by the falling tide in the pool behind the Indian Island, but I was not feeling optimistic. Snow began drifting in coldly from the north, and the line kept freezing in the rings of the rod. After half an hour of it my fingers were so cold and stiff that I could hardly turn the reel to bring the bait in. I thought of going home but made another cast instead and hunched down into my mackinaw to watch the swing of the ice-hung line as the rod top followed the bait around. The fish took with a jolt that snapped the ice fragments yards away. He ran straight upstream, deep down, jumped as he was opposite me and fell back on his tail. My stiff fingers fumbled wildly to recover line and failed miserably—only the drag of the current on the belly of the line kept a strain on him. A moment later I was trying as frantically to find the drum of the reel and check his heavy run to the tail of the pool. I had the feeling that a big fish in his first runs should give one—a feeling of temporary helplessness, of being a little late for every move he makes, dependent on a break of luck to reduce his strength until it is evenly matched to the strength of the tackle. This fish seemed determined to run right on out of the pool and down the rapid, and my only hope was to follow him in the skiff. I began to run and stumble toward it over the difficult, icy footing. Then he jumped again, just above the rapid. Without help from me he turned and held almost still in five or six feet of heavy water. I tightened on him gently and began to walk slowly backward to where I had hooked him. He came, slowly and quietly, and from then on I had a measure of control.

He kept me busy for ten or fifteen minutes after that. I filled my boots with ice water, stumbled after him, checked his rushes, watched his jumps and at last brought him close enough to set the gaff. He was clean and beautiful, so strongly marked with deep-water colors that he might have been caught in salt water. And he weighed twenty-two pounds, the only steelhead of over twenty pounds that I have yet caught.

He doesn't know how close he is to being taken up. I reflect on those scientific friends of mine at M.I.T. and Harvard who are quite seriously stocking their Vermont farms against Armageddon, and it is a temptation to imagine that there might be sanctuary in this remote and beautiful canyon. But that lasts only thirty seconds. Out in the flood-swollen stream, snags and logs and drift go by, rocking in the swift water, circling with corpselike dignity in eddies and whirlpools, and as we watch we see a dead deer or sheep, its four stiff hooves in the air, go floating by in mid-river. We abandon the notion of sanctuary; even here, the world would drive its dead sheep and driftwood by the door.

But we can forget that at least another day, until we hit Lee's Ferry. At the mouth of Forbidden Canyon, after we return from the fourteen-mile hike to the Rainbow Bridge and back, we discover that the catfish will bite on anything or nothing, they will rise and gobble cigarette butts, or eat empty hooks as fast as we can drop them in. *This is the way things were when the world was young; we had better enjoy them while we can.*

River World: Wildlife of the Mississippi

Virginia S. Eifert

Virginia S. Eifert (1911–1966) was a naturalist, writer and artist who has been called "the most popular and articulate writer on the natural world of Illinois in the state's history." She initiated The Living Museum, *a publication of the Illinois State Museum, in 1939, and edited it until her death in 1966. An excerpt from one of her books, "The Rainy Day" from* Land of the Snowshoe Hare *appears in Hal Borland's* Our Natural World *(1965), which includes a number of excerpts on rivers by authors represented in this anthology.*

Several of her books are about rivers: Three Rivers South *is about Abe Lincoln's travels to New Orleans on the Sanhamon, Illinois and Mississippi;* Delta Queen *is the story of a steamboat;* Louis Jolliet, *is about the "Explorer of Rivers;"* George Shannon *concerns a member of the Lewis and Clark expedition; and* Of Men and Rivers *is a series of adventures and discoveries along American waterways. She also wrote* Wonders of the Rivers.

But it is from her book River World: Wildlife of the Mississippi *that I have selected the Introduction. It tells of her experiences aboard Mississippi River towboats, traveling from Minnesota to New Orleans, and about nature along the way. If only there were room to use more of her book!*

Fog enfolded the river. Mist among the willows decorated every spider web with droplets which softened and blurred the outlines of bleached driftwood and exposed tree roots. Webs and fog interlaced mud and crayfish chimneys near the water, connected willow with willow, joined boat with shore. Only the restless brown water of the Mississippi flowing closest to the banks was visible in the drifting, pallid murk of the morning.

On the wet deck of a white and blue steel towboat 115 feet long, the Diesel-driven *Cape Zephyr* tied up to the bank, I stood shivering as fog wraiths, endlessly in motion, brushed veils of dampness across my face. The river lapped with a fog-subdued air at the quiescent hull and along the red-brown sides of four barges loaded with eight thousand tons of gasoline.

Even before the sun was visible, a pearly illumination came into the upper levels of fog, gilding the water particles with unseen light. As if this were a signal, birds promptly awoke in the willows and burst into song. They were surely some of the loudest mockingbirds, brown thrashers, catbirds, yellow-breasted chats, orchard orioles, cardinals and Carolina wrens to be heard anywhere on a morning in spring. Their music, besides, had something of the magnified quality which sounds assume in a woods full of newly-fallen fluffy snow. I couldn't remember having ever heard such a strong morning chorus before nor, perhaps, had I ever been so close to it, so much a part of willows and birds and river and fog.

Meanwhile, a suffusion of glorious golden-pink light was dyeing the upper levels of mist with an other-worldly glow. The fog was lifting from the hurrying brown water, higher and higher, now drifting in great, loose, smoky swaths across the river and over the yellow sand bars.

And then the sun climbed over the willows and burst full upon the fog-blurred river, the blanket broke, the veils vanished, the whiteness dissolved or rose as clouds into an April sky drenched in sunshine. The boat was quickly underway up the glittering Mississippi River with a load destined for a port in Wisconsin.

For years, I had roamed the shores of the river, had explored woods and weedy bottomlands, and waded swamp and marsh, had walked on sand bars, open shores and along rocky cliffs; but not until I rode the length of the navigable Mississippi did I get the true perspective of the river. For the river is a world apart. It is a liquid avenue endlessly in motion, a restless pathway which is never the same from one minute to the next or from one mile to another, uniting a stretch of the North American continent by means of 2,552 miles of running water.

To learn about it from the viewpoint of the river itself, I traveled more than six thousand miles on the towboats *Cape Zephyr* and *St. Louis Zephyr* and on the passenger steamboat *Delta Queen*, as well as on lesser craft. The slow pace of the big boats, seldom exceeding twelve miles an hour downstream and sometimes reduced, when heavily loaded and bucking a strong downbound current, to three to five miles an hour upstream, is excellent for watching the wild things of the river.

Unlike the harbor tugs along the seacoast, which pull their barges at the end of a long hawser, the towboats of the inland rivers push their barges as a single, immovable unit fastened tightly to the squared-off bow of the boat itself. Thus, I could step from boat to barge and, avoiding the taut wire rope, clamps, ratchets, expansion pipes, winches, hatches, manifolds and coils of massive manila line, could walk the length of the barges. These, each containing two thousand tons of gasoline, were fifty feet wide, eleven feet deep, and 295 feet long, forming a wide-open promenade obviously designed for the purpose of nature study and the placid contemplation of the river.

Far out at the end of the tow, often a thousand feet from the end of the boat itself, there were peace and stillness and sunshine, and a wind that was flavored with river water, willows and whatever was blossoming on the banks. The noise and vibration of diesel engines stayed far back in the boat. Out here was only the gentle swish of water curving in a satin comber past the rake of the fore-barge. With my back against a barrel-shaped hatch, I could sit for hours to watch the river go by and, with it, the wild things, the endlessly mobile surface pattern of eddies and boils and curvets and currents, and the ever-varying shores.

From the elevation of the pilothouse, with its chairs and leather bench for the comfort of visiting pilots, some twenty-five to thirty feet above the river, I found another excellent vantage point. At night, when the dim, deep fire of the stars was laid upon the black water, the sweeping white glare of the arc lights, searching out shore markers and the lay of the next bend, the next point, the location of levee or revetment, or the next sand bar or boat or buoy, also picked out in sudden notice many a quiet animal or night bird feeding on the shore.

There were the pairs of green sparks which were bullfrogs' eggs; the red neon of whip-poor-wills' eyes; the aquamarine lights in the eyes of muskrats crouched on a levee, eating clams, or the living glow in the eyes of a raccoon catching frogs; once, the large orbs of a deer swimming the river.

Black-crowned night herons often got up in the light and flew slowly, with guttural comments, upstream to another willow shore. Insects and bats cut parabolas through the white beam. Sometimes a mother bat, heavily loaded with a baby riding piggy-back, would become confused in that glare and propel herself down to a deck for recuperation and orientation.

Occasionally the passing boat and its restless searchlights startled birds spending the night on remote sand bars. In April, on the broad reaches of the Lower Mississippi, a flock of eighty-five migrant white pelicans, grounded by a storm, rose suddenly in confusion as the light swept mercilessly across them. One, separated from the others in wind, rain and lightning, swerved and came down on the first barge in the tow of the *Cape Zephyr*. Immense and strange and prehistoric-looking, it stood spotlighted by the purple-edged white beam against the black river and the beating rain.

A pair of eager deckhands went out cautiously to attempt to capture the visitor. The closer they came, the larger it looked; the bird stood four feet tall, and its pouched yellow beak had a most forbidding look of strength and sharpness. The young men were beginning to question themselves as to whether or not they really wanted a pet pelican after all, when the bird settled the matter. Suddenly unfolding an awe-inspiring nine-foot white wingspread tipped with black, it swirled off into the driving rain of the river night.

Although the day may be long gone since steamboats on the Upper Mississippi and the Missouri had to tie up while thousands of buffalo swam the river in front of them, wildlife of the Mississippi is always to be seen, forever and inescapably part of the river.

For the Mississippi is an avenue of wildlife extending from the northern coniferous forests of Minnesota to the sea marshes of the Louisiana Gulf coast. The Upper Mississippi at its source is Canadian in the nature of its plants, animals and climate, the Middle is midwestern and the Lower river is subtropical; the whole magnificent stream unites to become one complex Mississippi River. The much diluted, cold, clear waters of the North Country are indistinguishable from the waters, thick and yellow-brown, of the Missouri, or the gray-green Ohio or the turbulent Arkansas, once they mingle and become part of the whole.

But the wild creatures and plants living on, above, in or beside the river are distinct. It is they which give the river its true personality, characterizing it as much as the color, the clarity or the potent murkiness of the waters, or the shores of its several life zones.

The Sound of Mountain Waters

Wallace Stegner

Wallace Stegner is a scholar and a gentleman. Born in the Midwest, he grew to manhood in Mormon country (where I lived for awhile and where Ed Abbey still dwells) and has crossed the continent, teaching at the universities of Utah, Wisconsin, Harvard and Stanford. His Beyond the Hundredth Meridian *tells the story of the Powell Expedition perhaps better than Powell did himself, given the historical perspective and sound research Stegner devoted to that book.*

His essays and novels have made the world a better place, if only for the pleasure they give one in reading them. But they go beyond that kind of surface pleasure, demanding that one think about what he says, reflect upon his observations and even act—to save a Dinosaur National Monument, a desert wilderness, or even modern man. I never saw Glen Canyon as Stegner and Abbey did, before it was dammed, but I have seen grown men cry at the loss. This excerpt gives us, in Stegner's words, a look at that loss.

G len Canyon, once the most serenely beautiful of all the canyons of the Colorado River, is now Lake Powell, impounded by the Glen Canyon Dam. It is called a great recreational resource. The Bureau of Reclamation promotes its beauty in an attempt to counter continuing criticisms of the dam itself, and the National Park Service, which manages the Recreation Area, is installing or planning facilities for all the boating, water skiing, fishing, camping, swimming, and plain sightseeing that should now ensue.

But I come back to Lake Powell reluctantly and skeptically, for I remember Glen Canyon as it used to be.

Once the river ran through Glen's two hundred miles in a twisting, many-branched stone trough eight hundred to twelve hundred feet deep, just deep enough to be impressive without being overwhelming. Awe was never Glen Canyon's province. That is for the Grand Canyon. Glen Canyon was for delight. The river that used to run here cooper-ated with the scenery by flowing swift and smooth, without a major rapid. Any ordinary boatman could take anyone through it. Boy Scouts made annual pilgrimages on rubber rafts. In 1947 we went through with a party that contained an old lady of seventy and a girl of ten. There was superlative camping anywhere, on sandbars furred with tamarisk and willow, under cliffs that whispered with the sound of flowing water.

Through many of those two hundred idyllic miles the view was shut in by red walls, but down straight reaches or up side canyons there would be glimpses of noble towers and buttes lifting high beyond the canyon rims, and somewhat more than halfway down there was a major confrontation where the Kaiparowits Plateau, seventy-five hundred feet high, thrust its knife-blade cliff above the north rim to face the dome of Navajo Mountain, more than ten thousand feet high, on the south side. Those two uplifts, as strikingly different as if designed to dominate some gigantic world's fair, added magnificence to the intimate colored trough of the river.

Seen from the air, the Glen Canyon country reveals itself as a bare-stone, salmon-pink tableland whose surface is a chaos of domes, knobs, beehives, baldheads, hollows, and potholes, dissected by the deep corkscrew channels of streams. Out of the platform north of the main river rise the gray-green peaks of the Henry Mountains, the last-discovered mountains in the contiguous United States. West of them is the bloody welt of the Waterpocket Fold, whose westward creeks flow into the Escalante, the last-discovered river. Northward rise the cliffs of Utah's high plateaus. South of Glen Canyon, like a great period at the foot of the fifty-mile exclamation point of the Kaiparowits, is Navajo Mountain, whose slopes apron off on every side into the stone and sand of the reservation.

When cut by streams, the Navajo sandstone which is the country rock forms monolithic cliffs with rounded rims. In straight stretches the cliffs tend to be sheer, on the curves undercut, especially in the narrow side canyons. I have measured a six-hundred-foot wall that was undercut a good five hundred feet—not a cliff at all but a musical shell for the multiplication of echoes. Into these deep scoured amphitheaters on the outside of bends, the promontories on the inside fit like thighbones into a hip socket. Often, straightening bends, creeks have cut through promontories to form bridges, as at Rainbow Bridge National Monument, Gregory Bridge in Fiftymile Canyon, and dozens of other places. And systematically, when a river cleft has exposed the rock to the lateral thrust of its own weight, fracturing begins to peel great slabs from the cliff faces. The slabs are thinner at top than at bottom, and curve together so that great alcoves form in the walls. If they are near the rim, they may break through to let a window-wink of sky down on a canyon traveler, and always they make panels of fresh pink in weathered and stained and darkened red walls.

Floating down the river one passed, every mile or two on right or left, the mouth of some side canyon, narrow, shadowed, releasing a secret stream into the taffy-colored, whirlpooled Colorado. Between the mouth of the Dirty Devil and the dam, which is a few miles above the actual foot of the Glen Canyon, there are at least three dozen such gulches on the north side, including the major canyon of the Escalante; and on the south nearly that many more, including the major canyon of the San Juan. Every such gulch used to be a little wonder, each with its multiplying branches, each as deep at the mouth as its parent canyon. Hundreds of feet deep, sometimes only a few yards wide, they wove into the rock so sinuously that all sky was shut off. The floors were smooth sand or rounded stone pavement of stone pools linked by stone gutters, and nearly every gulch ran, except in flood season, a thin clear stream. Silt pockets out of reach of flood were gardens of fern and redbud; every talus and rockslide gave footing to cottonwood and willow and single-leafed ash; ponded places were solid with watercress; maidenhair hung from seepage cracks in the cliffs.

Often these canyons, pursued upward, ended in falls, and sometimes the falls came down through a slot or a skylight in the roof of a domed chamber, to trickle down the wall into a plunge pool that made a lyrical dunk bath on a hot day. In such chambers the light was dim, reflected, richly colored. The red rock was stained with the dark manganese exudations called desert varnish, striped black to green to yellow to white along horizontal lines of seepage, patched with the chemical, sunless green of moss. One such grotto was named Music Temple by Major John Wesley Powell on his first exploration, in 1869; another is the so-called Cathedral in the Desert, at the head of Clear Water Canyon off the Escalante.

That was what Glen Canyon was like before the closing of the dam in 1963. What was flooded here was potentially a superb national park. It had its history, too, sparse but significant. Exploring the gulches, one came upon ancient chiseled footholds leading up the slickrock to mortared dwellings or storage cysts of the Basket Makers and Pueblos who once inhabited these canyons. At the mouth of Padre Creek a line of chiseled steps marked where Fathers Escalante and Dominguez, groping back toward Santa Fe in 1776, got their animals down to the fjord that was afterward known as the Crossing of the Fathers. In Music Temple men from Powell's two river expeditions had scratched their names. Here and there on the walls near the river were names and initials of men from Robert Brewster Stanton's party that surveyed a water-level railroad down the canyon in 1889–90, and miners from the abortive goldrush of the 1890's. There were Mormon echoes at Lee's Ferry, below the dam, and at the slot canyon called Hole-in-the-Rock, where a Mormon colonizing party got their wagons down the cliffs on their way to the San Juan in 1880.

Some of this is now under Lake Powell. I am interested to know how much is gone, how much left. Because I don't much like the thought of power boats and water skiers in these canyons, I come in March, before the season has properly begun, and at a time when the lake (stabilized they say because of water shortages far downriver at Lake Mead) is as high as it has ever been, but is still more than two hundred feet below its capacity level of thirty-seven hundred feet. Not everything that may eventually be drowned will be drowned yet, and there will be none of the stained walls and exposed mudflats that make a drawdown reservoir ugly at low water.

Our boat is the Park Service patrol boat, a thirty-four-foot diesel workhorse. It has a voice like a bulldozer's. As we back away from the dock and head out deserted Wahweap Bay, conversing at the tops of our lungs with our noses a foot apart, we acknowledge that we needn't have worried about motor noises among the cliffs. We couldn't have heard a Chriscraft if it had passed us with its throttle wide open.

One thing is comfortingly clear from the moment we back away from the dock at Wahweap and start out between the low walls of what used to be Wahweap Creek toward the main channel. Though they have diminished it, they haven't utterly ruined it. Though these walls are lower and tamer than they used to be, and though the whole sensation is a little like looking at a picture of Miss America that doesn't show her legs, Lake Powell *is* beautiful. It isn't Glen Canyon, but it is something in itself. The contact of deep blue water and uncompromising stone is bizarre and somehow exciting. Enough of the canyon feeling is left so that traveling up-lake one watches with a sense of discovery as every bend rotates into view new colors, new forms, new vistas: a great glowing wall with the sun on it, a slot side canyon buried to the eyes in water and inviting exploration, a half-drowned cave on whose roof dance the little flames of reflected ripples.

Moreover, since we float three hundred feet or more above the old river, the views out are much wider, and where the lake broadens, as at Padre Creek, they are superb. From the river, Navajo Mountain used to be seen only in brief, distant glimpses. From the lake it is often visible for minutes, an hour, at a time—gray-green, snow-streaked, a high mysterious bubble rising above the red world, incontrovertibly the holy mountain. And the broken country around the Crossing of the Fathers was always wild and strange as a moon landscape, but you had to climb out to see it. Now, from the bay that covers the crossing and spreads into the mouths of tributary creeks, we see Gunsight Butte, Tower Butte, and the other fantastic pinnacles of the Entrada formation surging up a sheer thousand feet above the rounding platform of the Navajo. The horizon reels with surrealist forms, dark red at the base, gray from there to rimrock, the profiles rigid and angular and carved, as different as possible from the Navajo's filigreed, ripple-marked sandstone.

We find the larger side canyons, as well as the deeper reaches of the main canyon, almost as impressive as they used to be, especially after we get far enough up-lake so that the water is shallower and the cliffs less reduced in height. Navajo Canyon is splendid despite the flooding of its green bottom that used to provide pasture for the stolen horses of raiders. Forbidden Canyon that leads to Rainbow Bridge is lessened, but still marvelous: it is like going by boat to Petra. Rainbow Bridge itself is still the place of magic that it used to be when we walked the six miles up from the river, and turned a corner to see the great arch framing the dome of Navajo Mountain. The canyon of the Escalante, with all its tortuous side canyons, is one of the stunning scenic experiences of a lifetime, and far easier to reach by lake than it used to be by foot or horseback. And all up and down these canyons, big or little, is the constantly changing, nobly repetitive spectacle of the cliffs with their contrasts of rounding and sheer, their great blackboard faces and their amphitheaters. Streaked with desert varnish, weathered and lichened and shadowed, patched with clean pink fresh-broken stone, they are as magically colored as shot silk.

And there is God's plenty of it. This lake is already a hundred and fifty miles long, with scores of tributaries. If it ever fills—which its critics guess it will not—it will have eighteen hundred miles of shoreline. Its fishing is good and apparently getting better, not only catfish and perch but rainbow trout and largemouth black bass that are periodically sown broadcast from planes. At present its supply and access points are few and far apart—at Wahweap, Hall's Crossing, and Hite—but when floating facilities are anchored in the narrows below Rainbow Bridge and when boat ramps and supply stations are developed at Warm Creek, Hole-in-the-Rock, and Bullfrog Basin, this will draw people. The prediction of a million visitors in 1965 is probably enthusiastic, but there is no question that as developed facilities extend the range of boats and multiply places of access, this will become one of the great water playgrounds.

And yet, vast and beautiful as it is, open now to anyone with a boat or the money to rent one, available soon (one supposes) to the quickie tour by float-plane and hydrofoil, democratically accessible and with its most secret beauties captured on color transparencies at infallible exposures, it strikes me, even in my exhilaration, with the consciousness of loss. In gaining the lovely and the usable, we have given up the incomparable.

Goodbye to a River
John Graves

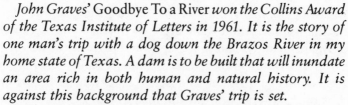

John Graves' Goodbye To a River won the Collins Award of the Texas Institute of Letters in 1961. It is the story of one man's trip with a dog down the Brazos River in my home state of Texas. A dam is to be built that will inundate an area rich in both human and natural history. It is against this background that Graves' trip is set.

Graves taught at the University of Texas while I was a student there, but we never met. A native Texan and a naturalist, he writes primarily about past and present Texas.

> *My heaven! cried my father, springing out of his chair, as he swore,—I have not one appointment belonging to me, which I set so much store by, as I do by these jack-boots,—they were our great-grandfather's, brother Toby,—they were hereditary.*

Usually the good time to go to the Brazos, and when you can choose, October is the best month—if, for that matter, you choose to go there at all, and most people don't. Snakes and mosquitoes and ticks are torpid then, maybe gone if frosts have come early, nights are cool and days blue and yellow and soft of air, and in the spread abundance of even a Texas autumn the shooting and the fishing overlap and are both likely to be good. Scores of kinds of birds, huntable or pleasant to see, pause there in their migrations before the later, bitterer northers push many of them farther south. Men and women are scarce.

Most autumns, the water is low from the long dry summer, and you have to get out from time to time and wade, leading or dragging your boat through trickling shallows from one pool to the long channel-twisted pool below, hanging up occasionally on shuddering bars of quicksand, making six or eight miles a day's lazy work, but if you go to the river at all, you tend not to mind. You are not in a hurry there; you learned long since not to be.

· October is the good month. . . .

I don't mean the whole Brazos, but a piece of it that has had meaning for me during a good part of my life in the way that pieces of rivers can have meaning. You can comprehend a piece of river. A whole river that is really a river is much to comprehend unless it is the Mississippi or the Danube or the Yangtze-Kiang and you spend a lifetime in its navigation; and even then what you comprehend, probably, are channels and topography and perhaps the honky-tonks in the river's towns. A whole river is mountain country and hill country and flat country and swamp and delta country, is rock bottom and sand bottom and weed bottom and mud bottom, is blue, green, red, clear, brown, wide, narrow, fast, slow, clean, and filthy water, is all the kinds of trees and grasses and all the breeds of animals and birds that men pertain and have ever pertained to its changing shores, is a thousand differing and not compatible things in-between that point where enough of the highland drainlets have trickled together to form it, and that wide, flat, probably desolate place where it discharges itself into the salt of the sea.

It is also an entity, one of the real wholes, but to feel the whole is hard because to know it is harder still. Feelings without knowledge— love, and hatred, too—seem to flow easily in any time, but they never worked well for me. . . .

The Brazos does not come from haunts of coot and hern, or even from mountains. It comes from West Texas, and in part from an equally stark stretch of New Mexico, and it runs for something over 800 miles down to the Gulf. On the high plains it is a gypsum-salty intermittent creek; down toward the coast it is a rolling Southern river, with levees and cotton fields and ancient hardwood bottoms. It slices across Texas history as it does across the map of the state; the Republic's first capitol stood by it, near the coast, and settlement flowed northwestward up its long trough as the water flowed down.

I have shot blue quail out by the salty trickles, and a long time ago hunted alligators at night with a jacklight on the sloughs the river makes in the swamplands near the Gulf, but I do not know those places. I don't have them in me. I like them as I have liked all kinds of country from Oahu to Castilla la Vieja, but they are a part of that whole which isn't, in the way I mean, comprehensible.

A piece, then . . . A hundred and fifty or 200 miles of the river toward its center on the fringe of West Texas, where it loops and coils snakishly from the Possum Kingdom dam down between the rough low mountains of the Palo Pinto country, into sandy peanut and

post-oak land, and through the cedar-dark limestone hills above a
new lake called Whitney. Not many highways cross that stretch. For
scores of years no boom has brought people to its banks; booms
elsewhere have sucked them thence. Old respect for the river's occasional violence makes farmers and ranchers build on high ground
away from the stream itself, which runs primitive and neglected. When
you paddle and pole along it, the things you see are much the same
things the Comanches and the Kiowas used to see, riding lean ponies
down it a hundred years ago to raid the new settlements in its valley.

Few people nowadays give much of a damn about what the
Comanches and the Kiowas saw. Those who don't, have good reason.
It is harsh country for the most part, and like most of West Texas
accords ill with the Saxon nostalgia for cool, green, dew-wet land-
scapes. Even to get into it is work. If you pick your time, the hunting
and the fishing are all right, but they too are work, and the Brazos is
treacherous for the sort of puttering around on water that most people
like. It snubs play. Its shoals shear the propeller pins of the big new
outboard motors, and quicksands and whirlpools occasionally swallow folks down, so that generally visitors go to the predictable
impounded lakes, leaving the river to the hardbitten yeomanry who
live along it, and to their kinsmen who gravitate back to it on weekends
away from the aircraft factories and automobile assembly plants of
Dallas and Fort Worth, and to those others of us for whom, in one
way or another, it has meaning which makes it worth the trouble.

Personal meaning, maybe, that includes trips when you were a kid
and, with the others like you, could devil the men away from their
fishing by trying to swim against orders where the deep swirls boiled,
and catfish on the trotlines in the mornings, sliced up then and there
for breakfast . . . And later trips when they let you go out with a friend
named Hale and a huge colored man Bill Briggs who could lift entire
tree trunks to lay across the fire where you camped under pecans by
a creek mouth, above the wide sand flats of the river, and who could
fry eggs, rounded and brown on the outside and soft within, in a way
you have never seen since . . . Later still, entrusted with your own
safety, you went out with homemade canvas canoes that were almost
coracles in their shapelessness, and wouldn't hold straight, and ripped
on the rocks of the rapids. Squirrel shooting on cold Sunday mornings,
and ducks, and skunk-squirted dogs, and deer watering while you
watched at dawn, and the slim river bass, and bird song of a hundred
kinds, and always the fly-fishing for fat bream and the feel of the
water on bare skin and its salty taste, and the changing shore. The

river's people, as distinct from one another as any other people anywhere, but all with a West Texas set to their frames and their faces which on occasion you have been able to recognize when you saw it in foreign countries ... Even first bottles of beer, bitter, drunk with two bawdy ranchers' daughters you and Hale ran across once, fishing ...

Enough meaning, enough comprehension ... Not the kind that might have ruined it for you, though. It had always the specialness of known good places where you had never actually lived, that you had never taken for granted, so that it was still special when in later years you would come back to it from six or eight years away to find it still running as it had run, changed a little but not much. After the dam was finished at Possum Kingdom near the beginning of the war, it began to filter out the West Texas drainings, and that piece of the Brazos ran clear for more of the year than it had before, and the old head rises no longer roared down, and the spring floods were gentler and the quicksands less quick. But it was there still, touchable in a way that other things of childhood were not.

The history was in it, too. When we were young we would beg tales from surviving old ones, obscure and petty and always violent tales, hearsay usually and as often as not untrue, and later we confirmed and partly straightened them in our minds by reading in the little county histories and the illiterate memoirs, and they were a part of the river. All the murdered, scalped, raped, tortured people, red and white, all the proud names that belonged with hills and valleys and bends and crossings or maybe just hovered over the whole—Bigfoot Wallace, Oliver Loving, Charles Goodnight, Cynthia Ann Parker and her Indian son Quanah, Peta Nocona, Satank, Satanta, Iron Shirt ... Few people outside of West Texas ever heard of most of them, and long ago I learned that the history of the upper-middle Brazos was not the pop of a cap gun in the big pageant, but that knowledge never stopped the old names from ringing like a bell in my head.

Meaning, yes.

To note that our present world is a strange one is tepid, and it is becoming a little untrue, for strangeness and change are so familiar to us now that they are getting to be normal. Most of us in one way or another count on them as strongly as other ages counted on the green shoots rising in the spring. We're dedicated to them; we have a hunger to believe that other sorts of beings are eyeing us from the portholes of Unidentified Flying Objects, that automobiles will glitter with yet more chromed facets next year than this, and that we shall shortly be privileged to carry our inadequacies with us to the stars. And furthermore that while all rivers may continue to flow to the sea, those who represent us in such matters will at least slow down the process by transforming them from rivers into bead strings of placid reservoirs behind concrete dams . . .

Bitterness? No, ma'am . . . In a region like the Southwest, scorched to begin with, alternating between floods and drouths, its absorbent cities quadrupling their censuses every few years, electrical power and flood control and moisture conservation and water skiing are praiseworthy projects. More than that, they are essential. We river-minded ones can't say much against them—nor, probably, should we want to. Nor, mostly, do we. . . .

But if you are built like me, neither the certainty of change, nor the need for any wry philosophy will keep you from feeling a certain enraged awe when you hear that a river that you've known always, and that all men of that place have known always back into the red dawn of men, will shortly not exist. A piece of river, anyhow, my piece . . . They had not yet done more than survey the sites for the new dams, five between those two that had already risen during my life. But the squabbling had begun between their proponents and those otherwise-minded types—bottomland farmers and ranchers whose holdings would be inundated, competitive utility companies shrilling "Socialism!" and big irrigationists downstream—who would make a noise before they lost, but who would lose. When someone official dreams up a dam, it generally goes in. Dams are ipso facto good all by themselves, like mothers and flags. Maybe you save a Dinosaur Monument from time to time, but in-between such salvations you lose ten Brazoses. . . .

It was not my fight. That was not even my part of the country any more; I had been living out of the state for years. I knew, though, that it might be years again before I got back with time enough on my hands to make the trip, and what I wanted to do was to wrap it up, the river, before what I and Hale and Satanta the White Bear and Mr. Charlie Goodnight had known ended up down yonder under all the Criss-Crafts and the tinkle of portable radios.

Or was that, maybe, an excuse for a childishness? What I wanted was to float my piece of the river again. All of it.

Cataract Canyon's Rockbound Riddle

Bill Belknap

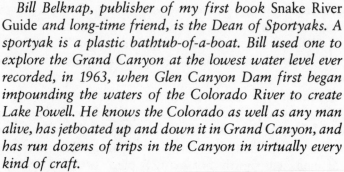

Bill Belknap, publisher of my first book Snake River Guide *and long-time friend, is the Dean of Sportyaks. A sportyak is a plastic bathtub-of-a-boat. Bill used one to explore the Grand Canyon at the lowest water level ever recorded, in 1963, when Glen Canyon Dam first began impounding the waters of the Colorado River to create Lake Powell. He knows the Colorado as well as any man alive, has jetboated up and down it in Grand Canyon, and has run dozens of trips in the Canyon in virtually every kind of craft.*

But here he writes of another canyon on the Colorado River, Cataract Canyon, which is now largely drowned by Lake Powell. And he writes of Dock Marston, the Grand Historian of the Colorado River, who wrote the article in the Utah Historical Quarterly *that featured the* Lost Journal of John Colton Sumner, *excerpts of which appear elsewhere in this anthology.*

He writes, too, of Dennis Julien, who left his mark at a number of points along the Green and Colorado rivers, way back in 1836, the year my home state of Texas won her independence. Bill knows rivers and river history, and he loves them as much as I do.

Was explorer John Wesley Powell the first man to navigate Cataract Canyon on the Colorado River? Evidence confirmed in Utah this spring by Otis (Dock) Marston, intrepid river historian, suggests that a lone French-Canadian trapper braved the swirling waters 33 years before Major Powell's famed expedition of 1869.

A water-worn inscription on the canyon wall, "1836 D. Julien"—lost for 43 years and possibly never before photographed—says he was there. But who was this mysterious Julien? Was he traveling up river or down, afoot or afloat?

First reported in 1889 by Robert Brewster Stanton, a railroad survey engineer, the name and date were later twice noted, the last time in

1921. Several parties had since searched in vain, and it was thought floods had eroded D. Julien's handiwork.

But according to Stanton the inscription had been deeply cut, and Dock Marston was never convinced that it had vanished. The riddle had nagged him for years.

When Lake Powell began forming behind Glen Canyon Dam, Dock realized that within months the rising water would drown "D. Julien." In March, 1964, he asked Jorgen Visbak, Buzz Belknap and me to join the search.

Sixty-five miles south of Moab, Utah, the Colorado River joins the Green, then plunges forty miles down Cataract Canyon. Much of this seldom-seen gorge lies in the proposed Canyonlands National Park*, adjoining Glen Canyon National Recreation Area. Our search centered in its depths.

Rubber rafts, wooden skiffs and even motor boats have run Cataract's thunderous rapids on high water. But with the river low many rapids are too rocky to run, and must be lined or portaged. As Dock had picked extreme low water—hoping to find "D. Julien" high and dry—we were in for some rugged boating.

We rowed tough little plastic skiffs called Sportyaks. Only seven feet long and weighing 38 pounds, each carried one man and his gear. Duffel, food and cameras we stowed in waterproof bags, with everything tied down in case of capsize. Diving suits of heavy black neoprene insulated us from the icy water.

Dock had planned a full week on the river. In order to spend as much of it as possible in Cataract, we chartered a jet boat to haul us from Moab down to the first rapid.

Good weather held for three days, then winter swept the canyon. Often we had to thaw out beside roaring driftwood fires. Some nights we found rock shelters; others we slept under Sportyaks propped against the wind.

By careful study of old journals and photographs Dock had selected a half-mile of shoreline near Cove Canyon for the search. Stanton's notebook had given him the key clues. Having worked as a surveyor, Dock knew the lingo and accurately converted Stanton's "stations" to miles, adjusting them to present-day maps.

But finding a 128-year-old name on a canyon wall—flooded countless times—still seemed unlikely when we beached the boats about mid-day April 3 and began looking.

"That stretch ahead of you should be hot," Dock said as I waded ashore.

Suddenly it was there. Twenty feet away the ancient letters

loomed: "1836 D. Julien." I could hardly believe my eyes.

Dock had felt sure we'd find it. But to zero in so precisely—without instruments of any kind—seemed fantastic to Buzz and Jorgen and me. Quickly, as though afraid the handwriting might disappear, we started photographing.

What more is known of D. Julien? Three other Utah rocks preserve his name. Two on the Green River dated "3 Mai" and "16 Mai, 1836"—one with a crude sketch of a boat—hint he was heading upstream. A third near Fort Robidoux, on the Uinta River, reads "Denis Julien 1831."

Painstaking research by historian Charles Kelly shows that Julien came west from St. Louis to trap beaver, and was connected with Antoine Robidoux who established Utah's first permanent trading post.

Dock Marston's confirmation of the Cataract carving fits one more piece into the puzzle, and suggests that trapper Julien may have navigated the Colorado even farther south.

*Canyonlands is now protected as a national park.

Snake River of Hells Canyon

Cort Conley

Cort Conley, publisher of Backeddy Books and one of the best river guides with whom I have had the pleasure of sharing a river experience, is the unquestionable historian of Idaho rivers: His recently-published Idaho for the Curious *is rapidly becoming a regional classic.*

His wit and knowledge, his concern for the land and its rivers, for the people who live along those rivers, his competence and care make every river trip with him a pleasure. We have run the Middle Fork of the Salmon together, as well as the Snake in both Hells Canyon and Jackson Hole. His knowledge of river history is displayed in his first three books: The Middle Fork & The Sheepeater War *(1977),* River of No Return *(1978) and* Snake River of Hells Canyon *(1979). The first of these has already been revised (1980) because he had found enough new material and the first edition had sold out.*

From his Hells Canyon book, these excerpts give thumbnail sketches of two pioneer river runners, Amos Burg and Buzz Holmstrom.

Amos Burg
1925

A young man beached his canoe at Homestead during the fall of 1925, looking for someone willing to accompany him through Hells Canyon. The voyageur had embarked on his journey the 9th of July at the source of the Snake, almost 9000-feet above sea level in the southern part of Yellowstone National Park. He had survived the loss of his first canoe, many difficult portages (once six in an afternoon), and intimidating rapids. He was no novice—the 24-year-old boatman had already spent years at sea, canoed Alaska's Inland Passage to the mouth of the Fraser, twice floated the Columbia from its Canadian source to the Pacific, and canoed the Yellowstone,

Missouri, and Mississippi from Livingston to New Orleans. In addition, he was a journalism student at Oregon State College. His name: Amos Burg—one of the intrepid pioneer boaters on western whitewater.

Burg found his companion in veteran riverman and prospector John Mullins. Mullins claimed to know the canyon and every rock in the river. They departed Homestead in the canoe *Song o' the Winds* on the morning of October 20. John sat in the stern with the steering paddle; Burg had a rowing arrangement midship. They fought the breakers in Kern Rapid, had a close call at Squaw Creek, capsized the canoe at Buck Creek when a tow line broke, shattered the stern at Thirtytwo Point (Sawpit Rapid), washed out of the craft at Steamboat, and nearly dumped at Copper Ledge Falls. John kept saying he "knew every rock in the river," and Burg allowed "that he ought to since he'd hit them all."

The difficult stretch of the trip behind them, John Mullins lassooed an old range horse above Johnson Bar. He said it belonged to Ralph Barton and he'd give him three dollars for it if they ever cut trails. Mullins rode back to Homestead, proud of having wielded a paddle on the first canoe through the canyon. Burg continued downriver to the Columbia confluence and paddled on to Portland.

Amos Burg made the Hells Canyon run three more times. He returned with a canoe in 1929, and ran the river again in 1946, with a 16-foot rubber raft called *Charlie*. That trip had a party of four: Doc Russ Frazier from Utah, Charles Wheeler, vice president of McCormack Steamship Company in San Francisco, and Alexander Paterson of Seattle. There were two other rubber boats along—six-foot *Junior* and 12-foot *Patches*. Junior flipped in the rapids at the foot of Eagle Island. Deciding they could use additional support, the men bought a 12-foot wooden boat for $15 from a ferryman they met below Homestead.

The group lined Squaw and Buck Rapids, then damaged the wooden craft while lining Thirtytwo Point. An impromptu bandage from socks and towels was fashioned for the leaking hull. They stopped to fish at Steamboat Creek and found it thick with trout. The smaller boats were lined through Wild Sheep and Granite Rapids. Nine days had been allowed for the trip, but their decision to take more time caused an Army search plane to come looking for them. Wheeler and Paterson flew out at Pittsburg Landing; Burg and Frazier floated down to Lewiston.

Burg's adventures had just begun in 1925. He canoed from Skagway, Alaska, to Portland the next year, ran the Yukon River for the *National*

Geographic, and descended the Athabaska, Slave, and McKenzie Rivers. The latter trip was completed alone, by packing a six-foot rubber raft five days across the Peel Portage, with the help of Indians and dogs, in order to float down the Bell and Porcupine Rivers to Old Crow.

Amos rafted 72 days down the Green and Colorado Rivers with Haldane "Buzz" Holmstrom in 1938—Burg's rubber raft was the first to be used in the Grand Canyon. The following summer he ran Idaho's Middle Fork with Doc Frazier. Later he sailed a 26-foot sloop around the southern tip of South America via the Strait of Magellan, and visited China, Europe, South America and Alaska, completing 25 educational films for the *Encyclopedia Britannica* and 12 articles for the *National Geographic*.

Amos settled in Juneau, Alaska, in 1952, where he served 20 years as education and information officer for the Alaska Department of Fish and Game. He retired in 1974.

In the summer of 1978, Burg returned to run Hells Canyon with his wife Carolyn, whom he married in 1958. The Burgs had their own 12-foot Avon raft, and were accompanied by friends in four additional boats. Amos discovered with dismay, in his words, "that dams had destroyed one of nature's most magnificent masterpieces."

Buzz Holmstrom
1939

"I'd have to say he was the best."
"If he'd been shootin folks instead of rapids
his light would shine with the cowboys."
"Always calm and cool, knowing what to do and
having the skill and power to do it."
"Best boatman of his time."

That's what those who knew him say about Haldane Buzz Holmstrom—extraordinary river runner during the brief, adventurous years that preceded the commercial whitewater business. For Buzz, river running was not an acquired taste—he took to it naturally. His handprint is in the boatman's annals and his fingerprint in Hells Canyon of the Snake.

This blonde, blue-eyed Swedish farm boy was born in Gardiner, Oregon, in 1909. Plowing, milking, and haying developed his powerful body: a cask of a chest, large hands, and arms of a blacksmith. All agreed he was strong as a jail.

From the time he was old enough to look over a hay bale, Holmstrom had seen loggers and boaters on the Umpqua and Coquille Rivers. Moving water captivated Haldane, hooked him with the magic of its challenge. In 1935 he ran the Rogue, then the "River of No Return" from Salmon to Lewiston in 1936. Between times he worked in a Coquille gas station. He read Kolb's *Down the Colorado*; it was the genesis of a dream that finally resolved itself in action. The Colorado would be his next dare.

Buzz went to the woods and selected a Port Orford cedar that he felled for its light, durable wood. Days laboring in the service station were followed by nights spent shaping a boat from the fragrant cedar. In his basement he fashioned a fifteen by five-foot hull with a center cockpit and water-tight compartments fore and aft. Preferring to enter rapids stern foremost (this reduced speed and increased control), he designed a stout, square stern. Handles were affixed to the bow in order to drag the 450-pound vessel around risky rapids. Then coats of lobster red paint brought the long task to completion.

Holmstrom loaded his craft on a rickety trailer, hitched it to his five-dollar Dodge, waved goodbye to his mother, and drove off to Green River, Utah. His friend Clarence Bean was expected to accompany him, but got sidetracked by an ocean voyage. So Haldane Holmstrom went alone. It was 1937, and he had a rendezvous with river history.

Over the next 52 days Buzz Holmstrom became the first person to make a solo transit of Grand Canyon of the Colorado. He portaged five rapids, realizing an accident could have fatal consequences. A year later he returned, and accompanied by Willis Johnson and Amos Burg, who ran a rubber raft, piloted his boat through all the rapids without mishap. It was a longer journey, begun near the Continental Divide and ending at Boulder Dam. A conversation on that trip gives insight into Holmstrom's values: Burg recalled that Buzz said he would "rather live on beans and bacon than kill a canyon deer." The gun they carried was never used.

An excerpt from a note to his mother, which he wrote on the shore of Lake Mead reveals more: "The last bad rapid is behind me. I had thought that once past that my reward would begin, but now everything ahead seems kind of empty, and I find I have already had my reward in the doing of the thing."

The publicity generated by the Coquille boatman's exploits spawned his next venture. He was contacted by Edith B. Clegg, a wealthy 53-year-widowed mother of four, and grandmother of nine. At a hundred pounds she was scarcely big enough to keep, but she possessed an admirable resilience in temperament and character. Her husband had been an English diplomat, but the couple had lived in Vancouver for years.

Mrs. Clegg presented Holmstrom with a startling proposition. She wanted to make a transcontinental water voyage to New York, where she would take in the World's Fair, before going on to visit her daughter in England. Buzz agreed.

He designed two 14-foot flat-bottomed spruce boats that were built by Art Ellingson, of Coquille: the *Mongoose* and the *St. George*. They had water-tight cargo holds fore and midship, with passenger wells fore and aft. Spare oars were lashed to the deck and a ten-horse Johnson outboard provided power. Crew consisted of Holmstrom, Earl C. Hamilton (a pre-med student) and Clarence Bean, all of Coquille, and Willis Johnson, Utah friend and boatman.

The party began their 4,000 mile expedition from Portland on April 14, 1939—120 years to the day since McKenzie and his voyageurs ·completed the first upstream passage of Hells Canyon.

Mrs. Clegg disdained publicity. Cornered by reporters, she always said the trip "was just a private venture, just for the interest" and she seems to have enjoyed each day. In a letter, Buzz wrote: "One good thing is that she doesn't want publicity . . . won't talk to a reporter . . . doesn't write."

Saint George and the *Mongoose* scudded up the Columbia and the Snake—sometimes fast as a dog could trot, 35 miles a day, other times slow as a long afternoon. They had no schedule. Gasoline was cached by the mail boat upriver to Johnson Bar. At that point they entered the fortress cliffs of the main canyon. They left behind skeptics on the shore who scoffed at their "mosquito fleet." "Somebody's going to get a dunking that will get his name in the obituary column", one of them sneered. Another remarked, "The state border is the only thing that runs through that gorge without getting drowned."

Yet with only three portages (Granite, Squaw and Buck), the group arrived at Kinney Creek May 30, taking 18 days from Lewiston. The skeptics could eat their words with knife and fork.

Willis Johnson left the trip at Weiser to run the Middle Fork with Frank Swain and Doc Frazier. Clarence Bean headed back to Coquille. It was at Weiser that Holmstrom made a surprising statement. He said he had found the uphill run through Hells Canyon four times more difficult than his 1938 trip down the Colorado. He had been fighting a 15,000 c.f.s. flow, had fallen out of the boat once, and the rapids must have tired him.

The expedition pressed on to the headwaters of the Snake, trailered across the divide to the Yellowstone River and reembarked a couple of miles below Gardiner, Montana, June 21. Earl Hamilton left with the *St. George* at the Yellowstone, as support was no longer considered necessary. Three motors had been exhausted at that point. The couple followed the Yellowstone to the Missouri. Buzz and Edith reached Kansas City in early August. They floated down the Mississippi to Cairo, turned northeast up the Ohio, then into the Alleghany, across the great Lakes to the barge canal and down the Hudson, arriving in New York the second week of September. The fair was an anti-climax.

World War II interrupted Holmstrom's river running. He joined the Navy and spent duty time in New Guinea as a carpenter's mate. "Boos" was such a favorite with some of the islanders in the South Pacific that they offered him a wife and land if only he would remain. But after three and a half years in the service, he returned to Coquille. He took a job with the Bureau of Reclamation on a core-drilling project at potential damsites on western rivers.

Then in May of 1946, Buzz was back on the river—happy as a lost soul with hell in flood. He had been hired to boat supplies on the Grande Ronde for a U.S. Coast and Geodetic Survey party, piloting an 18- by 6-foot craft. On that river his inexplicable death occurred. Surveyors said that he came into camp and borrowed a .22 rifle, saying he was "going to kill some chickens" (sage hens). His body was found with a fatal head wound. The crew said he was depressed about not being able to handle such a large boat on the Ronde. But 1946 was a high-water year. (The river is now run by commercial outfitters, sometimes with wooden boats.) Holmstrom's death was listed as suicide, and there is evidence of some problems which could have induced it. On the other hand, his many friends and the people of Coquille were never satisfied with that explanation. No autopsy or inquest was held.

Haldane "Buzz" Holmstrom's river accomplishments covered less than a decade, and like the streak of a falling star, have slipped from sight. He is buried in Coquille, beneath a granite gravestone that bears this epitaph: "Home is the Sailor, Home from the Sea."

Part III

Modern Times—The Past Fifteen Years

Must This Be Lost to the Sight of Man?

Michael Frome

> *Michael Frome is a travel writer who became so inter-*
> *ested in the conservation movement that many readers*
> *know him better as an outdoor writer who prods the*
> *conscience of individuals, organizations and agencies. He*
> *has served on the board of directors for the Outdoor Writers*
> *Association of America and for a number of environmental*
> *and conservation organizations. Among his best-known*
> *books are* Whose Woods These Are *and* Battle for the
> Wilderness. *We have been friends since he took a Snake*
> *River float trip with me in the mid-1960s.*

At the confluence of the Snake and Clearwater Rivers, where Lewis and Clark pitched camp in October 1805, and where the pioneers found shelter the following year enroute home, I arrived at the gateway to glad tidings, the kind we need in this age when emasculation of the landscape is almost a national psychosis.

It was not precisely the immediate setting that gave me the feeling of promise. The community of Lewiston, Idaho, seemed far from a fitting mirror of its heritage. An old logging mill town, rundown around the edges and bursting planlessly at the seams, with sulphurous pulp fumes drifting down the narrow canyon, Lewiston recalls a thousand other places that absolutely ignore the natural and historic endowments placed in their midst, and in their trust.

But the surrounding region, embracing portions of Idaho, Washington, and Oregon, is wide open country, the Northwest that Easterners dream about—uncrowded, uncluttered. Here one can go for endless miles without running out of pride in the native land. This is due largely to protection over more than half a century by the U.S. Forest Service—which began with the homesteaders, hard-rock miners, stockmen and loggers, and found itself growing up with hikers, hunters, fishermen, boatmen, scientists and scholars. Critics may feel that occasionally the Forest Service slips in its responsibility, but here it has clearly held firm. And of all the National Forestland in this tri-state area, Hells Canyon of the Snake River sums up our yesterdays, todays, and tomorrows with the special challenge, hope, and second chance for this generation of Americans.

The United States Supreme Court afforded the second chance for Hells Canyon in 1967 when it questioned the need of damming the last free-flowing stretch of the Snake River, thus reopening a case that seemed already signed and sealed. Aren't there other criteria than economics, the High Court asked, for determining the fate of wild land not specifically protected?

To put it another way, Hells Canyon may not be as renowned a phenomenon as the Grand Canyon of the Colorado, simply because it is more remote, but this doesn't mean that it is any less of a national treasure, or less worth saving in its natural state.

I had come to observe the river in question for *Field & Stream* and my own conscience, in company with Ernie Day, of Boise, Idaho, noted outdoorsman and photographer, and director of the National Wildlife Federation. We were joined by three men of the Forest Service. From the Idaho side was Everett Sanderson, supervisor of the Nez Perce National Forest, which embraces some of the finest wilderness and back-country recreation in America: the Selway-Bitterroot, Salmon River Breaks, Seven Devils Range, and a large portion of Hells Canyon. From Oregon we had Wade Hall, who has been on the staff of the Wallowa-Whitman National Forest, which borders the Snake, since 1926. He is almost part of the heritage of the river country because, as he explained, his mother had come to eastern Oregon in 1880 in a covered wagon at the age of 4. Then there was Alex Smith, a good friend of Ernie's and mine from the regional office at Ogden, Utah, and also a veteran of the Oregon forests.

It was a bright morning of last October when we started from the hotel (of course named Lewis and Clark) for Hells Canyon. At the river front we boarded the *Idaho Queen II*, whose owner and captain, Dick Rivers, holds the mail contract for delivery to isolated ranches over the 92-mile stretch of river from Lewiston to the head of navigation. Daring and dramatic riverboat trips started over this route a century ago, when sternwheelers clawed, rammed, and winched as far as they could to unload supplies for gold seekers and homesteaders, who had no other link with the outside world. The 48-foot *Queen*, powered by twin 260-horsepower diesel engines, was clearly a work boat, but not unattractive, nor unpleasant to be aboard. Nor were we alone. A snug cabin had accommodations for about forty passengers and every seat seemed filled. Many were older people, derived from the group of travelers sometimes called "the tennis-shoe set." And around us along the wharf were jet-powered boats of various sizes, which also carry sightseeing passengers and fishermen. I was reminded of the popular trip on the Rogue River from Gold Beach to Agness in western Oregon. Such excursions afford a great many people an exciting run, a glimpse into wilderness without depleting the resource or depriving others of enjoyment.

This was my first trip into Hells Canyon, though I had become acquainted over the years with the Snake River in other portions of its thousand-mile journey from the Rocky Mountains to its merger with the Columbia. The second longest river in the Northwest, the Snake rises in western Wyoming, motherland of glorious rivers— including the Green, which becomes the main stem of the Colorado; the Madison and Gallatin Forks of the Missouri; and the Yellowstone. After joining the waters of little streams from high lakes and forests in the Teton and Yellowstone country, the Snake flows through a beautiful forested canyon south of Jackson, then winds across the sagebrush plains of southern Idaho before turning sharply north along the Oregon border for its final journey. Captain William Clark named it the Lewis River, after his intrepid partner, and the tributary now known as the Salmon River, a great stream in its own right, he called the South Fork. But others insisted on using the Indian name of *Shoshoneah*, which translated into English as Snake, and Snake it is.

In recent years, the Snake has been plugged by twelve major dams and reservoirs of varying sizes, shapes, and purposes. In the lurid dam-building orgy of the past decade that destroyed beautiful stretches of river and canyon all over America, in the name of profit, politics, and progress, the Corps of Engineers imposed four impoundments downstream from Lewiston. And upstream, in the deep series of gorges along the Idaho-Oregon border, carved by the river in the last twenty-five million years, the Idaho Power Company added three more, named Brownlee, Oxbow, and Hells Canyon. Today, only a little more than one hundred miles remain of the native river, untamed, unspoiled, approaching the natural conditions in which man found it. This area is in the very middle and embraces the wildest stretches of white water, flowing through the deepest canyons. And even this is threatened, for still another dam, Asotin, has been authorized at the upstream edge of Lewiston, and that will reduce the free-flowing segment of the river to 75 miles.

Such is the tragedy of the Northwest. The mighty Columbia, once the proudest river on the continent, is only a shadow of itself, almost entirely bottled by eleven main dams. Stream habitat for game fish and wildlife has been consistently destroyed. Only fifty miles of the whole Columbia River above tidewater remains free-flowing, and proposals have been actively advanced to construct dam No. 12. Named generously for Ben Franklin, No. 12 would eliminate the last natural steelhead fishery, as well as wipe out a trout and whitefish fishery, plus spawning areas of summer-run steelhead. Turbulence, temperature changes, and oxygen-deficient releases from reservoirs are a constant threat. Fishermen may be promised tailrace fishing below such projects, but with pumped-storage peaking operations a fact of the future, these fishing areas will vanish also under violent water fluctuations. In the name of power production for industrial development, the Ben Franklin dam would also flood wildlife and waterfowl habitat, mule deer fawning areas, and nesting areas which produce 15 percent of Washington's Canada geese. No wonder the Washington Department of Game, sportsmen, and other conservationists are up in arms against this project of the Corps of Engineers.

The issues are parallel on the Snake River, which leads one to ask: Must the entire face of America be reshaped to look alike—overindustrialized, overpolluted, overpopulated?

The stubby *Idaho Queen II* headed upstream, for the first thirty miles between low hills on the flanking Idaho and Washington shores. A road paralleled our course on the Washington side to the Grande Ronde River, and then it stopped; I learned that other roads furnish access to points on both banks below the deepest part of the gorge, while hiking trails run forty or fifty miles along the river and numerous connecting trails feed in from side canyons.

At the mouth of the Grande Ronde, we saw fishermen casting from a gravel bar. Wade Hall mentioned that in summer water skiers come out in numbers. The hills grew higher as we continued upstream, with 3,000 foot cliffs rising from the water and white beaches.

It's the annual flooding action of the river that builds and refreshes these sand beaches and gravel bars, and that flushes the algae which accumulate during warm summer months. And it's the erosive power of the river in flood stage that sculptures and colors the striking canyon walls and midstream boulders. Such is life in a natural environment. Light-green broadleaf foliage growing on the beaches, bars, and at the mouths of tributary creeks contrasted softly with the walls of basalt and granite. On the warm canyon floor were white alder, wild cherry, and elderberry, while on the slopes were bitterbrush, serviceberry, blue bunch wheatgrass, western hackberry, mountain mahogany, and maple—the lower brushy draws furnishing ideal cover for game birds, as well as winter feed for the big game, with the timbered slopes as excellent deer country.

The canyon scene changed. Black rocks glistened beneath the sun. The scenery grew more towering. It changed with the hours as sunlight turned from one feature to another. It responded to clouds, shading first one, then another portion of the landscape. "It changes with the seasons, too," said Wade.

At Garden Creek Ranch on the Idaho side, facing the Washington-Oregon border, the *Queen* made her first stop, the first of about a dozen. The ports along the way are bits of beach into which a boat can ram its bow and back off again after letters, magazines and parcel post are put ashore. The schedule being purely flexible, we stopped to fish awhile. A few fish were caught at our several stops. I noted that periodically the canyon would relent and fall back, allowing a bench on which some pioneer once staked his future. The various ranches that now survive actually began as either mining claims or homesteads operated by hardy souls struggling to survive.

The voyage through the turbulent stream was an adventure. The boat crashed headlong through rapids and ripples, the skipper heading straight for one bank, cutting close to a jagged boulder, then whirling the wheel. Rivermen once had to learn and memorize the rapids and channels, but now they have target boards on shore, which they line up like gunsights, enabling them to work their way upriver in switchbacks.

In due course all of us were impressed by the depth of Hells Canyon. The maximum measurable depth is 6,550 feet. It is deeper than Yosemite, and more than a thousand feet deeper than the Grand Canyon. Kings Canyon in California is rated its equal, but the great gorge of the Snake River is considered by scientists as the deepest canyon formed by any major river in America.

Presently the boat came abreast of the most celebrated stretch in the river, the battleground, which engineers, lawyers, planners, profiteers, and politicians seem about to destroy.

In quick succession we passed the site of the proposed Nez Perce Dam, the confluence with the Salmon River on the Idaho side, marked by spectacular facing of metamorphic basalt; and, a half-mile above the confluence, the site of the proposed High Mountain Sheep Dam; followed by the Imnaha River, flowing in from the Oregon side down a steep narrow valley with rocky grandeur, and then Dug Bar, the point where Chief Joseph and his Nez Perce followers crossed the Snake on their historic flight for freedom.

A veritable concentration of treasures, indeed. The Salmon River flows from its source in the Sawtooth Mountains and Whiteclouds north across the heart of Idaho, then west through rocky canyons between North Fork and Riggins before turning north again, without a single dam to mar its way. The Salmon is noted for its recreational value, as well as for being a spawning ground of steelhead and salmon, important to fisheries in the Northwest, Canada and Alaska. Little wonder the Sport Fishing Institute proposed recently that the Salmon be designated as the first National Anadromous Fish Spawning Sanctuary, with restrictions on any diversions and downstream development that might adversely affect its natural function. The Imnaha is also a major migratory fish stream. In fact, half the steelhead still caught in the Columbia are produced in the Snake River system. Chief Joseph was of this country, born near the mouth of the Imnaha. He and his people wintered here. The Nez Perce came down the breaks and smooth benches of the Imnaha in 1877, then retreated over the river before the cavalry, without loss of a single human or animal. Archaeologists have reported that native Americans have lived along the Snake for 8,000 years. Rock shelters, caves, carvings, paintings in nearly 200 villages and campsites are available for investigation—one of the last opportunities for such studies in the entire Columbia Basin.

This section and the whole river have a magic fascination for scientists, boatmen, fishermen, hikers, hunters, photographers, botanists, and archaeologists, all who love the outdoors. The Middle Snake presents an array of free-flowing pure water, rivershore trails, campsites, and canyon scenery. The word "unique" is often overdone, but there is no doubt that in fisheries alone this river is superb, not only for its anadromous fish, but for the resident species of smallmouth bass, channel catfish, and the immense white sturgeon, the largest fresh-water fish in North America.

The trouble with such values is that you can't measure them in terms of economic profitability, or market them for the glory of the Gross National Product. Accordingly, for many years assorted boomers of Federal, private, and public power have been competing for the privilege of desecrating the scene on the theory that nature must be controlled, harnessed, distorted, but never left to God's own simple ways.

In 1964, a syndicate of four private utilities called Pacific Northwest Power Company (PNP) was awarded a license by the Federal Power Commission to construct the 670-foot High Mountain Sheep Dam. However, it was opposed in a legal dispute by a combine of eighteen public power utilities, the Washington Public Power System (WPPS), which placed its bets on the Nez Perce site for best hydropower development, although blocking access to the Salmon River fishery. The issue ultimately went to the Supreme Court, which in June 1967, handed down one of the most important resource-related decisions in its history. The Court directed the FPC to reconsider its license to PNP on the grounds that it had not adequately considered the feasibility of the Federal role, as provided by the Federal Power Act. Then the Court raised the question of whether any dam should be built on the Middle Snake. In a decision written by Justice William O. Douglas, a veteran Northwesterner, champion of law, human rights, and of the outdoors, the Court declared: "The test is whether the project will be in the public interest and that determination can be made only after an exploration of all issues relevant to the public interest. These include future power demand and supply in the area, alternate sources of power, and the public interest in preserving reaches of wild river in wilderness areas, and the preservation of anadromous fish for commercial and recreational purposes, and the protection of wildlife."

The Court decision gave heart to conservation groups, both local and national—the Idaho Wildlife Federation, Idaho Alpine Club, Federation of Western Outdoor Clubs, Sierra Club and Wilderness Society. The Hells Canyon Preservation Council was organized to fight any dams. It was the second chance come alive, after all had seemed lost.

The other side was not inactive. The old rivals, PNP and WPPS, patched up their differences. Deciding there would be enough to divide between them, they applied for a joint license to build the High Mountain Sheep Dam. Then in May 1968, the Federals jumped in. Secretary of the Interior Stewart L. Udall generously proposed instead that his outfit build and operate a dam at the Apaloosa site, about eight miles above the mouth of the Salmon, on grounds that it would afford better protection to the fishery resource and make more use of the Snake for recreation. And besides (as he might have mentioned), Interior's dam builders, having been frustrated at the Grand Canyon, were in need of work. Anybody who thinks of Interior as a "Department of Conservation" has another think coming. While a few of its bureaus truly endeavor to safeguard natural resources, other bureaus and many political appointees are devoted to the cause of everlasting construction, development, exploitation of oil, gas, metals, water, and land.

In building dams for power these days, the principal structure is often accompanied by a secondary, or reregulating, dam placed downstream in order to recycle water. Thus the Apaloosa dam would require a reregulating dam at the Low Mountain Sheep site, just above the mouth of the Imnaha. Another dam under consideration upstream at a site called Pleasant Valley also would need a reregulating dam. High Mountain Sheep dam would not only block the Imnaha itself, but require another dam at China Gardens, twenty miles below the mouth of the Salmon River, which would possibly have as much adverse affect as Nez Perce itself. And all kinds of complicated devices were offered with the competing designs in order to prove compliance with the Supreme Court order.

Hearings were held by the Federal Power Commission at Portland, Oregon, and Lewiston during 1968, but the dam proponents failed, and rather dismally, I think. They produced the usual assortment of economists, power technicians, and planners to warn gloomily that the Northwest must have every potential kilowatt of hydropower or face peril. Yet Northwest utilities and Bonneville Power have launched a multi-billion dollar nuclear power program for the next twenty years. As the Vice President of Portland General Electric admitted, "If High Mountain Sheep does not become available in any particular assumed year, it does not follow that the lights in the Northwest will be turned out, but merely that in the planning process we will advance an alternate nuclear plant by seven months to a year to fill the gap." The Assistant Administrator of the Bonneville Power Authority conceded further when he said, "Viewed as merely an additional 3 million kilowatts in the regional power growth, Apaloosa is hardly distinguishable from the approximately 25 million kilowatts of hydro and 16 million kilowatts of thermal that will be added by 1987." But the developers must have Apaloosa for other reasons, he insisted; like all dams, it is guaranteed to control floods, boost payrolls and taxes, expand recreation, and bring a flood of tourists. The Bureau of Outdoor Recreation obligingly produced a plan full of everything a chamber of commerce would dream of: picnicking, swimming, boating, water skiing, sightseeing, fishing, hunting, horseback riding, hiking, nature study—precisely what people can do at a thousand other places. The BOR failed to mention that water fluctuations of as much as 170 feet would leave Hells Canyon biologically barren and unsightly, with stained canyon walls and mudflats—degrading to recreational concepts, and equally degrading to a quality environment in which the natural river serves as an ecologic lifeline. It neglected to mention the superabundance of reservoir-type recreation already in the Northwest, including nearby Brownlee which is in sharp contrast with the critical shortage of recreation forms which only wilderness and wild rivers can fulfill.

The Supreme Court made such considerations important. It forced recognition of the natural environment, of the values of fish and wildlife. The Interior Department obliged by proposing expensive, complicated multi-level devices for the Apaloosa design in order to reintroduce oxygen and remove nitrogen, which it claimed would actually increase productivity. But a reading of the testimony indicates the Department's biologists did not have their hearts in it. They admitted that any dam would have harmful effects on fish production, that the whole project was an immense game of guesswork, without precedent, and certain to cost many millions of dollars. There might be an outside chance of saving part of the production for commercial fishing, but to maintain the sport fishery in a "pooled-up" river would be virtually impossible. The river would be changed to an impoundment and, quite apart from steelhead and salmon, the native sturgeon, small mouth, and catfish would be essentially lost—even though nowhere else does a fishery of such excellent quantity and quality exist for all three species in the same water. "The project would inundate and otherwise destroy about 11,900 acres of big-game habitat, 5,430 acres in Oregon and 6,480 acres in Idaho," one Federal official reported. "Any one of the three projects would cause substantial damage to wildlife resources, even if all apparent potential measures to reduce or offset detrimental effects were assured with the projects."

Professional experts of Oregon, Idaho, and Washington fish and game departments were unanimous in their testimony that no dam could possibly benefit the sports resources. After all, with the construction of each new project, additional habitat and spawning areas of Oregon, Idaho, and Washington have been wiped out. Despite the application of all known measures, and the expenditure of $250 million of anadromous fish passages in the Columbia Basin, the fishery resource has gone steadily downhill. Clearly, the perpetuation of salmon and steelhead doesn't rest in mechanics and machinations but in honoring the life-cycle of the fish as they travel thousands of miles from the mountains to the ocean and home again, and in respecting the natural laws. With more than 50 percent of the Snake no longer accessible to anadromous fish, the remaining areas are more important and more critical.

"If all the dam construction projects now under construction, authorized, or seriously considered are completed," John R. Woodworth, Idaho's Director of Fish and Game, declared at the Lewiston hearing last September, "it will not be very long until the entire Columbia River within the United States upstream from Bonneville Dam, the entire Snake River from its mouth upstream to

Weiser, Idaho, and major portions of the Clearwater and Grande Ronde River drainages will be impounded. It is our opinion that under the theory of true multiple-use development of water resources, maintenance of a stretch of the mid-Snake River in a free-flowing condition, coupled with its unique fishery and scenic attractions, would be in the best interest of the public and future generations hereafter."

Officials and the dam promoters were not alone at these hearings. The spokesmen for the people came, too, citing the interests and values of natural science, history, outdoor sports, the therapy of nature to man. It's tough to battle big industry and big government, with their resources and paid staffs, but at the Hells Canyon hearings the people were represented by their own technical experts, many with national reputations, who came to testify without pay.

Dr. William L. Blackadar, of Salmon, Idaho, was a star performer. He turned up after riding thirty-five miles in his kayak through huge waves and rapids from Hells Canyon to Pittsburgh Landing. "We do not realize the potential of this area," he testified. "Eight years ago the first fiber-glass slalom kayak was designed. At that time less than 500 people were rafting the Middle Fork of the Salmon River annually. Now over ten times that number run the river and for the first time sizable numbers of kayaks have appeared. This area will soon be alive with these 'banana' boats. Isn't it great that these challenges await us? Wouldn't it be sad to think that these bigger waves might be hidden under hundreds of feet of water? There are few areas left and these will become priceless."

I said earlier the dam builders had failed in their presentation. They made this plain last November, when the old enemies, PNP, WPPS, and the Interior Department, joined in a three-way bid to finance, build, and operate the Apaloosa Dam—rather ironic considering earlier complaints of the latter concerning the troubles with "intervening non-Federal ownerships" in Northwest power projects. Almost at once the new partners requested a delay in FPC proceedings, preferring to seek Congressional approval and avoiding the whole license question. Fortunately, the only conflict they resolved was the one among themselves, and not the issue of principle before the people.

"Any dam," said Wade Hall, "changes this river from a vibrant stream into a placid pond where water movement appears only vertical as elevation rises and falls. Gone forever are the camp spots where the visitor may enjoy isolation and which allow free choice as to length of journey each day." We had lately passed Dug Bar Ranch, a successful base for stock operations since the early 1880's. If the dam were built, it would be flooded out completely, along with the rest of the ranches.

In late afternoon we pulled in at Copper Creek, our home for the night, where Rivers operates a camp for use on the midweek scheduled run. It was a pleasant setting with several furnished cabins clustered in the meadow. After we were settled, we all fished a while and watched an osprey upstream diving for his dinner. The number and variety of birds along the river is amazing. Eagles and falcons use the high canyons for their necessary isolation in breeding. Herons soar high overhead and gather food along the riverbanks. Canada geese nest in the cliffs. Hungarian partridge, quail, and grouse are common. But if any one game bird stands out as numerous, it's the chukar. Apparently foodstuffs little utilized by other species make this an ideal habitat, for coveys of these rugged birds seemed to pop out everywhere, although the species was introduced only fifteen years ago.

The next morning we continued a little while with Rivers and the party on the boat, then were put ashore on the Oregon side where arrangements had been made for saddle horses. The horses were waiting. So were Jack Hooker, a well-known outfitter of northeast Oregon, and a wrangler. Continuing our journey in this way we'd be able to get another perspective of Hells Canyon and also to travel beyond the end of navigation.

We rode past the Circle C Ranch at Pittsburg Landing (the Pleasant Valley damsite) on the Idaho side which is an oasis of green alfalfa fields surrounded by dry hillsides. This is one of the main access points, reached by road from Riggins and Whitebird. A jet boat zipped upstream. It was named fittingly *Hell's Angel*, which Everett explained is the craft operated by Floyd Harvey between Lewiston and his fishing camp at Willow Creek, which we would reach soon. The feeling of wild places increased. Looking across into Idaho, for a time we saw little except sheer solid walls, rising almost vertically from the river bank. Then the dramatic topography yielded into stairsteps, great benches, and terraced cliffs. Snow-patched mountains towered against the sky. They were part of the Seven Devils, comprising a famous recreation area. "You can see the trails," said Everett, "that any ordinary citizen can use to hike or ride into the bottom of Hells Canyon within a day."

The river flowed swift and deep, winding through bend after bend of great gorges, with rapids seeming like boiling water. We passed a ranch on Kirkwood Creek, where Senator Len Jordan once lived, and then rested opposite the location of Harvey's tent camp. It was an ideal wilderness setting, sheltered beneath a cliffside. Our interest was in the stream, for here the sturgeon find a running-water habitat of deep holes, swift-flowing rapids and shallow riffles it needs for spawning and survival. We watched closely and spotted two sturgeon near the surface. They looked about 9-feet long. One came floating to the top, then both vanished.

The great white sturgeon once was common in the United States. Fish were caught commercially weighing a thousand pounds and more. Records indicate that fish 10- to 15-feet long were not uncommon before the dams were built on the Snake and Columbia. Now the sturgeon is reduced to its last stronghold in places like the Middle Snake, a fishery that technology cannot match.

Beyond Johnson Bar, the end of navigation, the river became much rougher, apparently too dangerous except for extraordinary boatmen. Our trail seemed to take full advantage of every possible break in topography, one moment at water level, almost within feel of the spray, then climbing hundreds of feet to skirt huge rims. We crossed a dramatic stretch aptly called Eagle's Nest, then another, Devil's Slide, where the trail was carved out of solid rock.

We rode through semi-desert and foothills covered with cactus, hackberry, grasses, juniper, and pinyon pine. A rattlesnake crossed our trail. I became more conscious of wildlife. A whitetail deer bounded through the timber, then a larger mule deer skirted over a dry open hillside. A coyote "topped out" over the crest. Because it is remote, Hells Canyon is blessed with a variety and abundance of wildlife. That night, while camping at a site where a person could enjoy the same atmosphere as the first white man to see the place, we talked about this point.

"I believe that hunter success is about as high here as anywhere in Oregon," the outfitter, Jack Hooker, said. "Sixty-six percent on deer, 25 percent on elk. I've had people hunt deer and upland birds and fish all on the same trip."

While we talked, an eagle rode the evening breeze, broad-winged, silent, patient.

It takes patience to shape the land, to balance the life forms, and to absorb the true meaning of life, and perhaps the appreciation of patience is God's gift to man at Hells Canyon. Such were my thoughts when we adjourned and I crawled under canvas flaps that night.

We rode out next morning into big country. The elevation changed rapidly—5,000 feet in five hours—as we rode through ponderosa pine and Douglas fir cloaking steep, narrow-sided valleys, high plateaus of spruce and fir, and finally topped out in a breezy world of alpine sedge and grass, before meeting our ride to the town of Imnaha and another world.

As for the future of Hells Canyon, the Department of Agriculture recently gave support to the Forest Service position against any dam on the Middle Snake. This is heartening. Both Idaho Senators, Frank Church and Len Jordan, have proposed the so-called Moratorium Bill, providing for a 10-year study period. Their reasons differ, Church hoping to save the anadromous fish runs and the recreational resource, Jordan apparently wanting time to decide whether Idaho should claim the water for downstate irrigation.

There is still another way. Conservationists now are pressing for establishment of a Hells Canyon-Snake National River. This would embrace 721,000 acres, including a quarter-mile shoreline along the Snake and Salmon, a Seven Devils Unit of 256,000 acres in Idaho, and an Imnaha Unit of 335,000 acres in Oregon. Existing activities, such as ranching and grazing, would be protected as part of the historic pioneer tableau, but no contrary developments would be allowed to compromise the scenic values of the rivers. Virtually all the land involved lies within National Forest boundaries and the Forest Service has for years recognized that the Snake merits special management consideration. In 1963, it designated the 130,000-acre Hells Canyon-Seven Devils Scenic Area, and judiciously administered it primarily for recreation, scenery, and scientific values. Under the National River plan, an enlarged system of trails, campsites, and boat ramps would make the area more usable, and would disperse use in order to eliminate concentrations and conserve the atmosphere. Some of the steep slopes, canyon breaks, and rugged terrain appear suitable to reintroduction of mountain sheep, which once ranged here and were observed as recently as fifteen years ago.

The price of all these would be minimal. Indeed, it costs virtually nothing but disciplined restraint to protect the vital, rich records of geology, archaeology, and ecology, as compared with a half a billion dollars or more for a scrubby dam and rancid reservoir that would submerge irreplaceable treasures under 500-feet of water. The boomers of power and concrete speak in almost lustful terms of Hells Canyon as "the last major hydroelectric site in the United States," as though it's indecent and sinful to leave alone the works that God hath wrought. But Americans with ethics, morality and good sense may build the monument of this age by preserving the wonders of nature— so that all this will not be lost to the sight of man!

'That River Swallows People. Some It Gives Up. Some It Don't.'

Tom Brokaw

The Middle Fork of the Salmon is the wildest river in Idaho. Designated in 1968 by Congress as part of the National Wild and Scenic River System, its raging rapids are among the last examples of untamed white water in the world. Shooting those rapids takes skill, strength, courage and careful strategy. But even on a beautiful day, sometimes you lose.

Tom Brokaw is the anchor of NBC's Nightly News. In the high-water summer of 1970, he and a few friends ran the Middle Fork of the Salmon River in the central Idaho wilderness. Brokaw's interest in the outdoors remains high, although he now spends more time rock climbing and backpacking than river running.

It was a rough, dusty ride across the scarred gravel road that clings to the north bank of the Salmon River, just east of its union with the Middle Fork.

Bill Guth, a veteran Idaho fishing and hunting guide was driving. "Yeah," he said, "when I saw Spaulding last night he told me 'I lost one of my dudes.' "

The word was an explosion.

DUDES!

"Dudes? No, dammit, that's not fair," I thought. "Ellis wasn't a dude. We're not dudes. Not after what we've been through." And there was also a missing guide.

But we were too tired to sustain an emotion as demanding as anger and it quickly subsided. We drifted back into the painful memories of the past 24 hours and tried to prepare for the painful moments yet to come. It was not the ending Harvey Karp had described in his first letter from New York.

"On the last day," he wrote, "we'll get out of the Middle Fork about noon. Someone will drive us to the little town of Salmon. There we'll have a final lunch with the guides and give them a tip."

Karp was organizing a five day float trip down the Middle Fork of the Salmon River in central Idaho. Last summer he had taken his family, but this year his boys were in camp and his wife said she preferred the canyons of Manhattan to those of Idaho.

So Karp turned to Martin Stone, his friend and business associate in Los Angeles. Together they had shaped Monogram Industries Incorporated into a successful conglomerate and had become millionaires in the process.

Two years ago, when he was 40, Karp decided to reduce his role in the company and return to New York City, his home, to live, as he put it, *la dolce vita*.

Marty Stone, who also is in his early forties, continues as board chairman of Monogram, and he is president of the Los Angeles Urban Coalition.

Stone was excited about Harvey's plans and quickly convinced me to sign on.

Karp also invited Dick Gold, the retired president of Barker Brothers Furniture Company who is now a 43-year-old bearded graduate student in economics at UCLA.

Two of my friends filled out the party: Ellis Harmon, a young Century City lawyer and militant Sierra Club member, and Roy Doumani, a bachelor and financial vice president of Alison Company, a mortgage banking firm.

We were scheduled to go onto the Middle Fork for five days the last week in June, but for a time there was a possibility the trip would be postponed or cancelled.

Everett Spaulding, our outfitter in Idaho, reported that late snows in the Salmon River Mountains were producing an unusually heavy runoff into streams and rivers, including the Middle Fork.

By early June, however, he was satisfied with the water level and the trip was on.

Designated by Congress in 1968 as part of the National Wild and Scenic River System, the Middle Fork of the Salmon begins life at the confluence of the Bear Valley and Marsh Creeks 20 miles northwest of Stanley, Idaho, and drops 1,600 feet in its 106 mile race to a union with the main Salmon.

Enroute it plunges through four National Forests, the Boise, Challis, Payette and Salmon, in Idaho's Primitive Area, more than a million acres of wilderness protected by federal laws designed to preserve its natural state.

The Middle Fork is the wildest river in Idaho. Even so, until this summer, there had been no fatalities on Middle Fork excursions headed by professional outfitters.

And our guide, Everett Spaulding, was an old hand on Idaho rivers. He's been guiding parties down the Middle Fork, the main Salmon and the Snake Rivers for more than 30 years.

He had a hand in the construction of the first McKenzie boats, lightweight, high-prowed, 16-foot rowboats designed specifically for running rapids on the McKenzie River in Oregon.

For our trip Spaulding chose two McKenzies and a 16-foot rubber raft. He'd man one of the boats and his friend, Gene Teague, would be in charge of the other.

Teague, who had known Spaulding since they were teenagers 40 years ago, was a Stayton, Oregon, auto dealer, but he spent his summers on Idaho and Oregon rivers.

For the raft Spaulding hired Ken Smith, a 26-year-old Marine veteran of Vietnam who was home from [sic] (for) the summer from his studies at San Jose State. Smith grew up on Idaho rivers, assisting his father and brother, two well known Salmon area outfitters.

Most Middle Fork trips begin at Dagger Falls, near the head of the river, or at Indian Creek Landing, a U.S. Forest Service Station about 30 miles downstream.

Spaulding picked Indian Creek, figuring that with the heavy runoff, the Dagger Falls leg would be too rough for a full party.

There are no roads into Indian Creek, only the river and an air strip, crude by urban standards, but routine for experienced bush pilots.

Still, getting there was a problem for Marty Stone who can't fly comfortably in a light airplane because of a sinus condition.

Spaulding agreed to let Stone and Harvey ride along in the McKenzies when he and Gene Teague brought them downstream from Dagger Falls.

The trip started on Sunday, June 21. Stone and Karp met Spaulding and Teague at Dagger Falls for the trip to Indian Creek.

It was a rough, exciting ride, especially for Stone who was experiencing wild water for the first time. Often they were forced to get out of the boats and, with a line attached, guide themselves over particularly hazardous rapids from shore.

Impressed by the seemingly routine maneuvers Spaulding and Teague performed with the boats, Stone was surprised when Spaulding confessed later that the trip from Dagger Falls had been rougher than he had anticipated.

And Karp confided to Stone that the Dagger Falls leg was much wilder than anything he'd experienced the year before.

However, Spaulding said nothing about possibly cancelling the trip.

After a commercial flight from Los Angeles, Gold, Harmon, Doumani, and I chartered a twin engine Aero Commander in Boise and flew into Indian Creek Sunday night.

As we stepped from the plane we were drawn to the Middle Fork, first by its ceaseless, full throated roar, demanding attention and then by its appearance: it was so full it bulged in the middle and there were a hundred different currents, each fighting the other in a test of strength.

In camp Spaulding made it clear that he was in charge. He issued blunt instructions to everyone.

"You sleep over there."

"Teague, get those potatoes on the fire."

Questions about the trip were barely tolerated.

"Everett, what can we expect in the way of fishing?"

"We'll talk about that tomorrow."

He not only talked tough, he looked tough. More than 30 years of fighting river currents left his hands and arms with a muscled tension that refuses to relax, even at his most leisurely moments.

His thatch of close-cropped, unruly white hair has a strength of its own atop his chiseled face, which is stained walnut brown after a lifetime of exposure to sun rays crashing off canyon walls and river waters.

With Daylight Savings Time and its proximity to the western edge of the Mountain Standard Time zone Idaho has daylight until 10 p.m. in the summer months. And so it had been a full day when we were ready for the fabled fellowship around a flickering campfire Sunday night.

I solemnly declared that sex and fishing would be the only acceptable topics on the trip. Everyone shot back that they didn't know anything about fishing. But that first night, the bond market won out over sex.

Monday. Our alarm was Gene Teague splitting logs for the breakfast fire which quickly brewed strong, black coffee in a scarred gray pot.

The Big Breakfast. Somewhere it must be written that it is the inalienable right of every man, woman and child on a river trip to eat a big breakfast.

Everett Spaulding was a strict constructionist. Each morning he prepared in an oversized skillet eggs, ham, sausage, fish or French toast to go with toast, cereal, coffee and juice.

During breakfast Monday we were joined by Ken Smith and a friend, Billy Maxwell.

Maxwell agreed to help out in the raft because Ken's left hand was in a cast to protect a broken finger, the consolation prize in a test of strength a few nights before. Smith explained that after one or two beers too many he'd been caught off guard by what he described as a "big farm kid."

It was difficult to imagine anyone besting Smith who at 6 feet 4 inches, 215 pounds, was in drill sergeant condition, and his bushy red hair and beard only heightened his image of strength.

By 10:30 we were ready to shove off. If Spaulding was concerned about the condition of the river he didn't express it, and he issued no special instructions.

"Do we wear life jackets?"

"No. Your guide will tell you when to put 'em on."

Harmon and Gold were with Spaulding in the lead boat. Doumani and I followed with Teague. Stone and Karp rode in the raft with Smith and Maxwell. In the McKenzies I was surprised by the gentle ride.

The current provided power, the oars direction. With a few choppy strokes Teague would turn us sideways for a graceful slide across small rapids and then pull quickly into position for the next watery slope. He apologized profusely if the slightest amount of water spilled over the side of the plywood bow.

In the raft that first day it was a different story. It was overloaded with food, cooking gear, our duffel bags and people. Smith and Maxwell were struggling to maintain control with the big sweep oars forward and aft. Soaked and cold, Stone and Karp spent most of their morning bailing the 40 degree water that crashed into the clumsy raft at every ripple.

After about an hour on the river Spaulding pulled everyone ashore to rearrange the raft, dry the gear and eat lunch.

Before returning to the river we took a short, fast hike to work off the effects of a big breakfast followed by a lunch of cold sausage, tuna salad, cheese, punch, peanuts and cookies.

Downstream we could see what appeared to be the first big set of rapids.

The white water stretched from bank to bank and dropped sharply, about eight feet. The only navigable passage was a narrow lip of water at the edge of a large hole created by conflicting currents.

Spaulding and Teague, in their light, maneuverable boats negotiated it easily, but Spaulding was worried about the raft. As it approached he repeatedly waved his big straw hat toward the north bank.

Ken Smith understood. Working his big sweep oars furiously he found the narrow passage and slipped the raft around the edge of the dangerous hole and through the rapids, emerging to the cheers of Stone and Karp, wet but upright.

After a brief stop at Middle Fork Lodge, an elaborate private fishing resort constructed before the Wilderness Act went into effect, we camped for the night at Jackass Flat, a few miles downstream. Normally, Jackass Flat has a wide, sandy beach, but during our stay much of it was submerged. The Middle Fork continued to run high and fast.

Before dinner Teague rigged a spin casting outfit with small silver and gold spoons and pointed Stone upstream toward a small eddy, a calm area bordered by the river's current.

Stone, an eager beginner, quickly landed two Dolly Varden trout, one a respectable 15 inches long. But generally fishing was poor because of the muddy conditions created by the high water.

After dinner, as we climbed out of the beach area for a hike across a nearby meadow, Spaulding muttered, "Well, there goes the thundering herd," a cynicism born of 30 years of watching city slickers crash through the underbrush.

We comforted ourselves with the thought that Spaulding wouldn't be much help in a television studio, courtroom or corporate merger.

It was a beautiful night.

One should leave the city from time to time to be reminded there still are stars in the sky, that pure, unfiltered moonlight on a meadow of sage and tall grass creates an excitement and beauty no neon sign artist will ever capture.

Along the trail Stone found a horseshoe, rusted and worn, but valuable as a souvenir. He'd have reason to value it as a symbol of good luck as well.

Tuesday. We were on the river for less than an hour; it was moving so fast we could have reached the mouth in two full days.

We stopped at Whity Cox Landing, a campsite named for a prospector killed in a rockslide. He's buried there, near some murky hot springs, his grave marked by a tangle of elk and deer antlers and a simple white stone.

Cox Landing was trout territory. Working steadily with spinning gear in a large eddy at a bend in the river we landed 10 Dolly Varden and cutthroat trout, pan size and larger.

Dick Gold was clearly the percentage leader. As he was studying the mechanics of a fly casting outfit the line with two dry flies attached fell into the water. Instantly and simultaneously two cutthroats struck. Dick reeled them in and retired on the spot. Undefeated.

At mid-afternoon Doumani, who was anxious for more physical activity, led a punishing 2,500-foot climb to the top of a steep, wooded ridge that hovered over the river.

It was at once a brutal and refreshing experience, the evils of city life draining from every pore as we struggled to the summit, the angle so steep that we could climb only a few hundred feet at a time without resting.

The descent was difficult as well, and when we returned to camp we were hot and tired.

Harmon quickly stripped and plunged into the frigid waters of the Middle Fork, thinking they might have a restorative effect. Always the experimenter, he tried to swim, but his efforts were soon reduced to a few wild strokes followed by a rapid exit.

Spaulding was concerned more about the water level than he was about the temperature and his concern for the level was prompted mostly by hopes for better fishing conditions. Just before dark Tuesday night he looked across at a shale wall at the river's edge and said, "I think she's dropping."

Wednesday. In the morning the shale wall had a new water mark, higher yet. The Middle Fork continued to rise.

After a breakfast of trout sauteed in butter, we found the river, although higher and faster, no rougher than the first two days.

Downstream we passed a rubber raft party that had passed us the day before, and exchanged fishing news.

"Any salmon?"

"No, some trout, but we had to work for them."

There were 13 people in two 25-foot rafts, one called Slo-mo-shun, and they were without a licensed guide.

Spaulding plainly didn't approve. He explained that he's lobbying for a law that will permit only licensed outfitters on the Snake, Middle Fork and Salmon rivers.

Traffic on those rivers is increasing. During the summer of 1970 an estimated 2,700 people floated the Middle Fork alone, compared with approximately 1,400 in 1966, an increase of nearly 100 percent in four years.

Most parties were accompanied by professionals, but increasingly amateurs are moving in. For amateurs there are no restrictions beyond good camping practices and a prohibition on motor driven boats or rafts on water under the Wild River System Act.

In a pamphlet devoted largely to promoting Middle Fork trips the U.S. Forest Service reports that float boating is hazardous and that in cases of an upset, chances of rescue are poor.

The warning is buried in a section entitled "Enjoy Safe Boating" which is preceded by another section under the title, "Points of Interest at Every Turn." More space is given to first aid kits and poison ivy. The Forest Service advises, "Avoid touching this three leaved plant."

Spaulding was convivial, recalling past trips, including one with George Romney, and the recent, well publicized Arthur Godfrey expedition. When we brought up Robert Kennedy's visits to the Snake and Middle Fork, he dismissed them as publicity stunts.

We moved into increasingly rugged terrain, as sheer granite and shale walls, a thousand feet high, replaced wooded slopes. There was a sharp contrast between the cool, wet movement of the river and the harsh, hot immobility of the cliffs.

We drifted wordlessly, our eyes riveted on rocky ledges, hoping to catch a glimpse of a bighorn sheep. It was not a good week for wildlife. We saw just one black bear and a deer.

When I told Spaulding I'd ship him some deer and rattle snake from Laurel Canyon he wasn't amused.

Karp pointed to a break in the mountains where the year before he was able to get radio reception and hear Neil Armstrong say, "One small step for man, a giant leap for mankind." The communication from the moon was simple enough. Getting it through the Middle Fork was another matter.

On the raft, Harmon and Doumani were enjoying a wild ride. With a lighter load more evenly distributed Smith was guiding it directly into the fiercest rapids.

From the boats, the raft resembled a mad, black bull, bucking and snorting, the rapids nipping at its heels.

At Tappen Falls, a half mile of white water deep within narrow canyons, the tempo and roar of the rapids increased, broken only by sharp whoops of joy from Harmon. He was ecstatic.

Early in the afternoon we drifted into a small, barren valley and stopped at the Flying B Ranch, a fishing and hunting resort attractive to river parties for its radio, should they want to get a message out, an air strip, should they want to get out themselves, and a well stocked cooler, should they be out of beer.

We were interested only in the latter.

Camp Wednesday night was at Rattlesnake Creek, a sandy beach punctuated by large boulders and inhabited by one bull snake and several million ants.

Thursday. As we broke camp Harmon wondered aloud whether he should protest Spaulding's furtive burial of bottles and cans, a cardinal sin in Harmon's eyes.

Remembering the occasions when Harmon had commanded complete strangers to recover litter I was surprised when he decided not
to confront Spaulding until after the trip. He was afraid it might be
uncomfortable for the rest of us.

Since we anticipated the roughest water of the trip on the leg ahead
we again casually discussed the possibility of capsizing.

Teague was firm in his guidelines; stay with the over-turned boat
or raft and let the current carry you to an eddy.

After a boyhood of swimming in the Missouri river, often at flood
stage, I had a slightly different theory: stay with the capsized boat or
raft only long enough to get your bearings and then strike out for
shore, letting the current do most of the work. I thought complete
submission to the whimsy of the current could be dangerous given
the cold, swift condition of the river.

Still, we thought the whole discussion was academic. In fact, we
were beginning to be bored by our mastery of the river.

Thursday we hoped for a little more excitement. There were 13
major rapids between us and the mouth of the Middle Fork and we
were due to hit more than half of them that day.

Doumani and Harmon reluctantly gave up their place in the raft to
Stone and me. They joined Teague in one of the boats. Gold and
Karp were with Spaulding in the lead.

In the raft, Smith was growing impatient with Spaulding's caution
in the rapids. He began to ignore instructions to run the raft close to
shore. As he'd done the day before, he nosed it into the middle of
the white water time after time, and successfully.

About 1:30 p.m. we stopped just above Redside Rapids, white water
from bank to bank for about 50 yards with a drop of at least 12 feet.

And 100 yards downstream there was another set of rapids, Webber
Falls, only slightly less forbidding in appearance.

After watching Redside, Spaulding outlined his plan: he would go
over Redside with Gold and Karp in his McKenzie. He instructed
Teague to line his boat over, that is, guide it from shore on a rope,
and then get back in for the trip through Webber Falls.

He ordered the rest of us to pull the raft about 50 yards back
upstream so it could have a longer run at the far bank, where he
decided the rapids were least hazardous.

Doumani leaped into the water to help Smith and Billy Maxwell
pull the raft into position. Once there, Stone yelled for Doumani to
stay with the raft. He'd go with Harmon in Teague's boat.

Meanwhile, our friends in the Slo-mo-shun raft party drifted by,
waved, and slipped over the middle of Redside with a few squeals

from the women, but no problems.

Smith, by now convinced that Spaulding was excessively cautious, muttered, "I think we've got a case of river paranoia on our hands."

While Teague, Stone and Harmon were lining their boat over the east bank, Spaulding rowed out into the current and, with a few short strokes, successfully negotiated the rapids.

In the small eddy between Redside and Webber Falls, he pulled ashore to watch for the rest of us.

In the raft, Billy Maxwell strapped on his life jacket and recommended that Doumani and I follow suit. Doumani was reluctant, but he slipped one over his head and hooked it loosely around his waist.

Working the front sweep with his good right hand, Smith steered the raft into the current and headed it for the middle of Redside, not the east bank as Everett had recommended.

With ever increasing speed we drifted to the lip of the rapids and plunged in.

Instantly, a wall of white water arose on three sides, several feet higher than the raft. Billy Maxwell released the rear sweep and dropped to the wooden deck to hang on. Smith remained on his feet, looking not unlike Captain Ahab, his wet, red beard glistening in the sun as he struck back at the angry wave with his long, powerful sweep oar. The raft creaked and groaned. For a moment, that wall of water was all there was to see and hear. In another instant, the wave retreated and we were safely through.

I looked up to see Teague, with Stone and Harmon as passengers, heading into Webber Falls. They were ahead of Spaulding who remained on the east bank, watching our progress.

Karp, who was in Spaulding's boat, said they turned their attention to us because they thought Teague was going to pull ashore, just downstream.

In the raft we were elated with our success at Redside and, thinking the worst was behind us, Doumani pulled the life jacket from around his neck and let it dangle in front of him.

Suddenly I noticed that Teague's boat appeared to be stalled in the middle of Webber Falls.

It was sinking.

Later, Stone described the scene. He said a huge wave broke over them and practically filled the right side of the boat. Teague yelled out, "Shift your weight, shift your weight," and he began frantically pulling on the oars, trying to move to calmer waters.

But it was too late. Another wave rolled over the other side. All three men were swept into the raging water.

On the raft, Smith shouted, "Those guys are swamping. Stand by, we'll be making some pickups."

Doumani turned to signal Spaulding and I began coiling a length of rope and assembling loose life jackets. Downstream I could see Stone and Harmon neck deep in the middle of the river, racing in tandem toward another set of rapids. Teague was off to the side and behind them heading for the same rapids.

Suddenly we had our own problems. The raft flipped over when hit by a powerful wave as it plunged into Webber Falls. As I tumbled into the water I was stunned by the ferocity of the current. In a lifetime of swimming I can't recall a greater struggle to break back through the surface, even with the assistance of a lifejacket.

When I did come up, I was swept under again, this time by Doumani who was imprisoned when the loose ends of his life jacket caught on the raft's frame.

He was able to break free quickly, however, and we grabbed onto the sides of the overturned raft with Billy Maxwell. Smith scrambled atop the raft and he was obviously relieved when he found us huddled together. As we climbed up to join him the raft drifted near the east bank and he yelled, "I think we'd better get out before we get into more trouble." Practically as one we leaped into the water and swam the short distance to shore.

Downstream there was no sign of Stone, Harmon or Teague, only Spaulding, Gold and Harvey in Spaulding's McKenzie in pursuit.

Gold and Harvey were unaware of the gravity of the situation. They weren't certain Teague's boat had swamped. Karp did think that without the provisions in the raft we'd be uncomfortable.

Gold thought it looked like fun.

It wasn't. For Stone, Harmon and Gene Teague, it was a battle for survival.

When they first were washed from the boat Stone knew they were in trouble. Even with a life jacket he could barely keep his head above water as strong, deep currents insisted he join them.

Harmon, recalling Spaulding's advice, pulled himself onto the hull of the overturned boat when it surfaced. He saw the bow line trailing in the water near Stone and yelled, "Grab the line, get the line."

By pulling himself up on the rope, Stone was able to look around. He saw a small eddy off to the right. His impulse was to swim for it and he shouted the question to Harmon, "Do you want to try for shore?"

"No," Harmon yelled back. "Hang onto the boat."

Stone's impulse continued.

"Let's swim for it."

This time, from behind him, Teague yelled, "No, stick with the boat, hang onto the boat."

Stone was impressed with Teague's calm. He was wearing a life jacket and holding a seat cushion, looking as serene as a Sunday stroller. That was the last Stone saw of Teague, ever. The water quickly became much rougher and although he couldn't see more than a few feet downstream, Stone was certain they were moving into rapids again.

He was right.

He started into the rapids trailing Harmon and the hull of the boat, straining to hang onto the rope as he was sucked under water, battered by currents on every side, fighting for the surface and another breath. When he did break free, Stone still had the rope, but he was a few feet in front of Harmon who was still on the battered hull. They didn't speak, concentrating only on their private struggles for air.

Harmon was taking wave after wave flush in the face as they washed over the hull, and the numbing effect of the 40 degree water was weakening his grip on the boat, as it was Stone's on the rope.

Stone's will also was beginning to weaken.

"This is a dream. I'm not even supposed to be here. I'm supposed to be on the raft. I'm gonna die," he thought.

Just then he was sucked under water again and the rope was torn from his hands.

When he struggled to the surface for what seemed like the hundredth time, Harmon and the boat were gone.

He had no choice. He had to swim for shore. Near death from exhaustion alone, Stone flailed against the surface currents, convinced that he was making no progress. And his tennis shoes, incredibly heavy, were dragging him down.

But gradually the water was less turbulent. Ahead of him he could make out the calm surface of an eddy.

Mustering his remaining strength, he churned out of the current and into the eddy. Totally spent, he draped himself over a boulder in shallow water, afraid he'd collapse and drown if he tried to make the final, few steps to shore.

It was there that Gold and Spaulding discovered him, less than a mile from the site of the swamping. Of course, Gold and Karp had no idea what their friend had been through. They were shocked by his condition. Stone cried out weakly, "Help me, please help me."

Meanwhile, those of us who had been in the raft moved as fast as we could along the rugged east bank.

Remembering Harmon's earlier attempts to swim in the frigid water and my own brief struggle when the raft went over, I was numb with fear.

Seeing Stone at a distance, sitting safely on the shore, raised new hopes, but as we approached, Dick Gold quietly signalled [sic] (signaled) that Harmon and Teague were still missing.

And there was no encouragement to be drawn from Stone. He sat in the hot sun, his head bowed, sobbing softly, "Ellis didn't have a chance. He didn't have a chance."

A few feet off shore the battered hull of Teague's boat floated motionlessly.

After comforting Stone briefly Doumani and I moved on downstream, certain that we'd find Spaulding with Harmon and Teague just around the next bend.

Progress was tortuous. Large, sharp rocks lined the water's edge. Higher up there were steep slopes and thick underbrush.

We were ill suited for that kind of terrain, dressed only in swimming trunks and sneakers.

Along the shore there were curious reminders of the accident; heads of lettuce, loaves of bread, plastic cups and smashed storage chests washed up on the rocks.

The raft itself was tied neatly to a tree. That raised a new, optimistic theory: Spaulding couldn't take the time to tie up the raft if Harmon and Teague were still missing. The next day we learned we were wrong. Spaulding stopped at the raft because he thought someone might be beneath it, he said.

Finally, we caught up with Smith and Maxwell and they reported the canyon ahead was impassible.

Gold, Karp and Stone were not far behind. With the exception of understandable fatigue and some water in his lungs, Stone was in remarkably good condition.

After agreeing to sit tight and wait for rescuers we stumbled onto a rocky ledge a few feet above the water. It was well protected by a towering ponderosa pine and a large boulder at the water's edge and a 100 foot granite wall on the backside.

It was about 4:30 p.m.

Karp and Gold suggested that we start making preparations to stay the night, but Smith was confident that wouldn't be necessary. He was certain jet powered boats, which drew little water, could soon be sent up after us.

That was encouraging; however, Gold and Karp continued to insist that we prepare for all contingencies. We began collecting firewood and drying out our several varieties of wet matches. Gold spread them out across the boulder, directly in the waning sunlight.

Karp went to work on the life jackets, removing the foam sections and spreading them across the sharpest rocks, distributing the tattered orange remains to the shirtless.

Shortly, Smith and Maxwell decided to try another route downstream to look for assistance. They spent the night on a rockslide about a mile away, cold and uncomfortable without a fire. By 8 p.m. a fire was our chief concern for chances of a rescue that night were diminishing.

Stone was eager to help, but he didn't care about the cold. He remembers thinking, "Hell, I'm just glad I'm able to feel the cold."

The supply of damp matches dwindled steadily as Gold, assisted by Karp, patiently and with great care scratched one after another across a well worn striking surface on a match book.

Doumani tried to heat up the blade of a butcher knife we recovered by rubbing it rapidly across the boulder. I searched my faded Boy Scout training and came up with a futile, clumsy attempt at the wood friction method, forgetting completely the static electricity system for drying matches by running them through your hair.

Finally, we were down to our last match, one with a misshapen head that Gold had picked up at the Flying B the day before. As he scratched that last match, Gold was reminded of Jack London's famous story. But this one had a happy ending. The match struck.

In turn, it quickly ignited a small arrangement of dry grass and twigs which before long was a roaring fire.

Just as darkness was closing in we heard the drone of a light airplane. It circled twice and then as it made a low pass over the canyon rim behind us it dropped a package which bounced down a cliff about a quarter mile upstream.

Scrambling across the cliff I found it perched precariously in a tree top leaning out over the water. It was a sleeping bag packed with tins of crackers, ham, beef, apricots, chocolate nut roll, coffee, tea, two spoons, a miniature can opener and white paper napkins.

But no matches or flashlight. We were furious at the oversight and doubly grateful our last match had ignited.

Karp and Doumani opened the tins, identified them and passed them on, each of us taking one bite until the contents were gone. It was a curious crowd: three millionaire Jewish businessmen, a wealthy young Arab bachelor (Doumani is Lebanese), and a WASP reporter. Brotherhood can be found in a shared can of apricots.

Before the trip none of us knew more than two members of the group well. Now we were bound together, not just by the apricots and the warmth of the fire, but by a common concern for each other's well being.

Stone spoke for each of us when he said, "If Ellis is alive this will have been a great adventure. If he isn't . . ." and his voice trailed off.

I was especially haunted by what I then regarded as the certainty of Harmon's death. I knew him best. I invited him on the trip.

Harmon was a son of the city, but his heart lay in the wilderness. I knew of no more dedicated or knowledgeable conservationist. During the trip he lectured us constantly on the necessity of preserving nature in its rawest form, undeterred by our reminders that he didn't have to convince us.

When we stopped at the Middle Fork Lodge, as a protest he refused to go inside, and his ire wasn't relieved when the manager gave us soft drinks in aluminum cans.

"Super camper," we called him. He also was a super lawyer, about to become a partner at Irell-Manella in Century City. He was the new breed: devoted to his assignment, tax law, but equally committed to public interest cases.

But most of that long night I thought of Harmon's family: his wife, Millie, and their three daughters, ages 4, 2 and 8 months, asleep in their Santa Monica home.

"God, how they'll miss him," I thought.

At 29 it was not enough to say that Ellis Harmon showed promise. He was a whole man. And he was dead.

We learned that shortly after dawn when two helicopters landed on a rock slide about a half mile upstream and stood by to lift us out. I charged up to meet one of the pilots and asked, "Did they find any bodies?" He said, "Yes, they've got a young man in the mortuary in Salmon."

His body had been recovered at the mouth of the Middle Fork about three hours after the accident. He'd suffered a sharp blow on the head.

Teague's body was not found, and as of this writing, he is still missing.

Spaulding would later say, "That river swallows people. Some it gives up. Some it don't."

If Harmon was a dude, Teague was a professional. He had been a founder of a river guide group in Oregon and was experienced with the Idaho rivers.

But at 58, the river had quickly taken him. He leaves his wife, Grace, two married daughters and five grandchildren. There are also five brothers and two sisters to mourn him. He had been looking forward to his retirement so he could devote more of his time to pollution and conservation work.

That week the Middle Fork and the main Salmon swallowed six people. On the main Salmon two U.S. Forest Service employees drowned when their pickup truck was forced off the road into the river, and a Detroit teenager was swept away when his kayak capsized. A Stanford professor drowned in the Middle Fork when he attempted to cross the river while attached to a rope.

At the time we were unaware of the deaths.

When word of our accident spread, two parties behind us which included Sir Edmund Hillary, the conqueror of Mt. Everest, and Frank Gifford, the sportscaster and former professional football star, got out of the river at the Flying B Ranch. Thus they avoided Webber Falls, the scene of our accident.

It turns out that Webber was especially wild because it was just below Big Creek which was draining the Payette National Forest that received the heaviest of the late spring snows.

Big Creek gave Webber a fury unlike any we had experienced, and it wasn't evident from shore. Once Teague was in the middle of the rapids, he was trapped by the raging currents and when the big wave broke over the bow he and the others in his boat were unable to move quickly enough to avoid it.

Our rescue helicopters were to take us to the confluence of the Middle Fork and Salmon rivers and Bill Guth would drive us from there to the town of Salmon.

As the helicopters lifted off the rockslide and started down the canyon we weren't just leaving the Middle Fork. We were escaping it.

The St. Croix—
Route of the Voyageurs

Roger Drayna

Roger Drayna grew up paddling the northwoods rivers. He absorbed their essence and learned their history. A former school teacher and principal, as well as National Park Service seasonal ranger and naturalist, Drayna is public relations director for the Wausau Insurance Companies and a free-lance writer in his spare time. We have run rivers together, from the San Juan to the Snoqualmie, from the Namekagon to the Nooksack.

There it was, the low, unmistakable rumble. We nosed the canoe around a point thickly cloaked in white cedar and straightened it to the quickening current. Ahead lay a corridor of river walled in by dense stands of evergreen, and at the end of it the white horses of Scout Chute, bucking and kicking. We had already run two small rapids, but this would be the first real white water test on this fifty mile run of the St. Croix National Scenic River in northwestern Wisconsin.

As the banks closed in and the river accelerated, I hastily rechecked the instructions for negotiating Scout. Committing details to memory, I returned my guide book to its plastic bag and shoved it under the flap of a Duluth pack. My sons, Mark in the prow and John amidships in a cockpit fashioned of camping gear, checked the straps on their flotation jackets and the tie-downs on packs and fishing tackle. I cinched shut the waterproof camera bag and lashed it tightly to a thwart. Now, we were as ready as we ever would be to take on Scout Chute!

In that instant before it becomes impossible to turn back, there is always a twisting in the stomach, a sense of forboding about thrusting the canoe and ourselves into all that churning water. But, that time for doubts is quickly swept away by the will of river. We could feel it now, under us and around us, strong and unrelenting, sweeping us inexorably into the notch of the first dark vee.

"Paddle!" I shouted above the din of crashing water and felt a sudden tug of pride as Mark leaned into a long, clean stroke. He'll be thirteen later in this summer of 1971; a squareness of young manhood had recently come to his shoulders and ropelike cords ebbed and flowed along his bare arms.

Then, we're into it, and long slide down the first dark-watered vee, the bow heaving upward to slam a standing wave and burst it into spray and droplets suspended in crystalline blue-whiteness. All of it, the pitching, the heaving, the whanging aluminum, lasts but an eternity of moments. Then we shoot into the flat water below.

Eleven-year-old John twists about in his pack sack enclosure, gives me a wide, even grin topped by tousled blonde hair. His blue eyes flash with excitement. "Hey, dad!" he shouts above the sounds of tumbling water, "Some ride!"

We slowed the boat just in time to play the role of spectators as Mike O'Malley and John McKenna took their seventeen-footer down the same route—saw them cleave the last standing wave and glide into the smooth water.

"Only thirty-two to go," McKenna shouted as they pulled alongside. And, that pretty much told the tale of this first day of our fifty mile float of the historic St. Croix.

In 1968, the 90th Congress, with the Wild and Scenic Rivers Act, had declared this famous river and seven others like it around the nation to be the nucleus of our country's Wild River System—rivers as yet unspoiled and destined to remain forever free-flowing and protected from the inroads of chrome and neon.

Far in the geologic past, two giant fault zones extended south from Lake Superior into this broad valley. They had guided huge continental glaciers of the Ice Age into this basin to carve a route to what one day, when men got around to naming things, would be called the Mississippi River. When, at last, the enormous masses of ice dwindled before the warm sun of a new age, Lake Superior brimmed and sent a part of its overflow cascading through this valley. Gradually, however, as the earth's crust was relieved of the crushing burden of ice, the land surface slowly rose to separate the St. Croix from the inland sea. In fact, the rising land mass, now called the Lake Superior Divide, created two famous rivers. The fabled Brule River rises within a half mile of the springs which are the source of the St. Croix. The one flows northward to ultimately add its clear-cold waters to those of the great lake; the other streams away to union with the Mississippi one hundred and sixty-five miles to the southwest.

There has been change, of course. First came the great forests which healed wounds wrought by glacial bulldozing. Much later, within the last hundred and twenty years, there came the men who would wrest untold fortunes in white pine lumber from those same forests. Many of them gave their lives in the log drives which slammed through this valley on the crests of spring floods.

The forests are pretty much gone now, yet the river remains, rather as it has always been, its waters filtered and cooled by dense stands of second growth crowding its banks. Considering that this strong-willed river lies only a long day's drive from Chicago and just a few hours from the metro area of Minneapolis and St. Paul, it does seem a wonder that it has held up so well.

So, on this flawless June day, lured by the sense of its history, by the promise of its reputation for small mouth bass, and by the wish to float one of the newly established wild rivers, we are on our way from the Gordon Dam to St. Croix State Park in Minnesota those many miles downstream. We had pushed off from the foot of the dam scarcely a half hour before our encounter with Scout Chute. The dam marks the upper end of the wild river portion of the St. Croix. It is not a power facility, only impounds the flow where a natural reservoir called Whitefish Lake had existed when fur traders followed the Brule-St. Croix route three hundred years ago. The original dam was a crude timber structure used during the log drives. In the 1930's, a public work project put in the present concrete structure which turned Whitefish Lake into the sprawling Gordon Flowage.

Plans call for the wild river portion, that part of the St. Croix which is to be managed as a free-flowing and undeveloped stream, to extend nearly one hundred miles to Taylor's Falls, Minnesota, where a power dam breaks the wilderness spell. It also includes 98 miles of a tributary called the Namekagon which matches the St. Croix's flow and was actually known as the South Fork of the St. Croix during the fur trading days.

This first day is all rapids, and we soon have the feel of pushing the heavily loaded boats through each new challenge. Mark and John both had shot rapids with me many times with a lightly loaded canoe; they quickly catch the feel of making the boat respond as they take turns in the bow.

John McKenna, a family physician who finds sport and escape from the telephone by occasionally getting away to white water rivers, was an old hand at this business. Mike O'Malley, manning the bow seat in John's canoe, is a transplanted Pennsylvanian and New Yorker new to this. But, he's a quick study and picks up the rudiments of white watering in a hurry.

We all relish the bright prospect of three days of fishing and just tuning in to life in the presence of this river. There is, after all, a

magical quality to a river float. With the flat water constantly punctuated by stretches of fast water, it combines the idyll of Huck Finn
rafting with the precarious existence of a river boat gambler.

The St. Croix is well known for small mouth bass fishing, walleyes,
northerns, even muskies. And, they are here although, as it turned
out, we came through with something less than a virtuoso performance
with the fishing rods.

In the first mile below the Gordon Dam, the river threads a maze
of ledge rock. As we worked the canoes through a slow zig-zag, picking
out leads to get the boats safely over the shallows where each
succeeding ledge slanted upward toward the surface, we saw dozens
of sturdy bass darting for cover. This is where we should have spent
a whole day, probing shadows and crannies of the tumbled rock,
casting under the cedars which arched over the clear water. But
optimism springs eternal within the human heart, and this was the
first hour of the first day. The sun stood high and bright, the river
promised miles of good water ahead, and we were anxious to put
some of it behind us. We pressed on, gradually building a feeling for
this splendid river which flows pure and untamed out of the north.

There were the rapids, of course, lots and lots of them, none too
exacting but all of them exciting and requiring concentration. There
was the look of it, the white water and the long sweeps of river
enclosed by cedar and tamarack, the pine and oak ridges standing
back from the river and walling the valley with varying tones of green,
and only our boats and ourselves on the whole reach ot if.

Once in a while we would startle a duck, usually a wood duck or
a merganser. Shorebirds, like killdeer and sandpipers, played along
shoals on the longer, slower bends. Once, a small doe, up to her
brisket in cool water, regarded our canoes as they slid quietly past,
twirling her ears and shifting her head from side to side like a Balinese
dancer.

Suddenly, as the sun arched for the zenith, we were at Coppermine
Sluice Dam halfway mark of our planned first day's float. Coppermine
is no dam at all, just the remnants of a logging era holding pond. But,
the water bursts through four boulder lined spillways, and our guide
book rated it as a number four—extreme hazard. We hauled the boats
ashore and decided this was as good a time as any to take our lunch
break. In short order, we shook up a batch of packaged lemonade,
sliced generous hunks of sausage using a paddle blade as a cutting
board, and quickly rid ourselves of the hunger pangs sprung from a
good morning's work.

After lunch, out of a sense of prudence, we unloaded the boats and hauled the gear to a landing at the lower end of the rapid, then prepared to portage the canoes. McKenna sidled up to me and pointed toward the frothing water. "Drayna, we've run worse than that!" I felt the same way; we dug out the map book:

> "Coppermine Sluice Dam: Turbulent flow through and over the old timbers creates a formidable obstacle. Protruding spikes in the old timbers add to the danger ... During periods of high water, the third sluiceway from the right usually has enough water to carry a canoe safely over the old dam."

Well, it looked like there was enough water. John and I shoved off and paddled back upstream, lined up with the suggested route, and, with a heart-pumping flurry of action, dashed through to the wide and quiet pool below without so much as a clang of aluminum against rock.

It had gone so well that O'Malley and I took the other boat and ran it through. After all, why make pack horses of ourselves if the river was willing to do the work for us?

This was getting to be fun. We hauled a boat back up and let Mark run through as bow man. Back again, this time to give my younger son a share of the action.

I don't know how wise it would be to run Coppermine on other days in other conditions. For us, it was a memorable episode on a memorable journey.

Here too, we broke out the fishing gear. Even at high noon, the deep pool below the rapid had the look of small mouth bass about it.

I paddled Mark over to a sand bar on the far side where he waded out almost to his armpits and began to loft hardware into the deep eddies. I moved the canoe into the shelter of one of the boulder sluices and arched a Mepps into the frothing tailrace.

Aside from the sense of expectation, it didn't work out very well. We had some bumps in the deep and roiling water, but only Mark succeeded in bringing anything ashore. That was a small northern pike which he promptly released.

Suddenly, we realized that it was past one o'clock and the day was getting away from us. Reluctantly, we loaded the boats and parted company with the deep pool which held such promise for the lengthening shadows of evening. Coppermine Sluice, with the high gravel wings of the old dam, would make an excellent camping place. If we come this way again, spending a whole afternoon by the dark and purling water will be part of our plan.

The afternoon fled away in a succession of rapids as we moved down the swift river as if on a descending staircase. There was the long Shelldrake where we had only to steer while the canoes glided silently through midafternoon shadows to the sounds of dappling water and warblers calling surreptitiously among the streamside foliage. Then came Steel Bridge Rapid and Bear Trap and Eagle Drop and all the smaller steps between them.

Perhaps it was the growing fatigue born of a long day of paddling that made us careless. Or, it might have been the sun slanting into our eyes and turning the river into dancing stabs of yellow and gold that caused us to misread the water. Whatever it was, calamity struck with a swiftness that caught us completely off guard. In what appeared to be a simple run of mildly white water—no more than a hazard of one on the four scale, we took a barely submerged boulder head-on, and it stopped us dead in the water. John, working the bow seat, was slammed into the narrow prow. Mark pitched forward and whacked his forehead on a thwart. I got off easy, going to my knees and bouncing my face off a pack. We were all okay although the boys were smarting a bit. But, before we could untangle ourselves, the little boat swung about in the current and got hung on rocks fore and aft. With the current swirling beneath us, the canoe rocked precariously, lurched suddenly and took a load of water over the upstream gunwhale. Just when we thought we had gotten it stabilized again, it dipped and more of the St. Croix came on board. With that, we simply sank without much ceremony right out in mid-river. The gear was water-proofed and the St. Croix is mostly a shallow river. We just got out, stood with the cool water washing about our legs, and waited for the other canoe to catch up.

Mike and John slid past, pulled ashore, and waded out to give us a hand. Slipping and stumbling, we hauled the packs ashore, then got to the task of freeing the canoe which seemed to have most of the river pouring into it. Somehow, despite the awesome hydraulic pressure, we got it up far enough to get the gunwhales out of the water. That gave us the chance to lighten it by vigorous bailing. Finally, it floated free, and we led it down the river to a sandspit.

All of this took place within sight of our intended camping place. Enough is always enough, we called it a day and pitched camp.

A big supper of freeze-dried beef stroganoff restored our spirits. In the fading light of a golden evening, we sat by our little tents, sipped hot chocolate and brandy, and watched a flock of cedar waxwings launch themselves from the snag-top of a dead white pine into an invisible swarm of insects.

Later, under an arch of star-filled night, we replayed the adventures of this first day and wondered about Big Fish Trap Rapids just two or three bends down the river.

We also talked, talked of this river and of its past—how in the late 1600s Daniel Duluth ascended the frigid and trout-rich waters of the Brule from Lake Superior—how, with the help of a Chippewa guide, he had found the two mile portage which lead from the cedar-shaded waters of that river to Lake St. Croix. Duluth—that's his name Anglicized, in French it was Daniel Greysolon Sieur Du Lhut and the Minnesota city is his namesake—thought he had found the fabled Northwest Passage, that elusive portal to the riches of the East which always seemed to be at the head of another river or at the end of another bay. In the seventeenth century, Northwest Passage led men into wilds and dangers which even the glossy pelts of fur-bearing animals would not take them. The Brule-St. Croix Portage did not take Duluth through the continent. What he had found, and it was important enough, was a water route from the greatest of the Great Lakes to the Mississippi drainage basin.

Whole generations of traders, trappers and adventurers followed him. In the mid-1800s, it was pine timber that brought men to the valley of the St. Croix. Axes rang in what seemed an endless forest and great river drives carried out the logs, lumber for farmsteads all across the midland prairies. By 1920, though, it was done. The river, still unfettered for the most part, was quiet. New forests sprang from the fecund earth to clothe the valley walls. That is how we found it in June of 1971, not virgin wilderness but rather presenting us with a sense of wilderness that fills the mind and talks quietly to the spirit about all the wilderness that has ever been.

In all our study of this route, Big Fish Trap Rapid took top billing as the most ominous. Rated as high hazard, it lived up to its reviews. With a combination of artful dodging and wading, the boys and I brought our boat through unscathed. The two Irishmen took it straight out and at full throttle. They got theirs. Less than an hour into the second day, we were back into the swamped canoe routine.

That was the last of our difficulties. At noon, we picked up the Namekagon and the increased flow was as if a huge hand was thrusting us down what had truly become a wide and strong river. Gone now was that sense of intimacy which comes from gliding through a shadowy cleft in the forest in slim boats.

Bluffs clad in pine and oak rose up from the river. At a place known as Riverside, we crossed under the first major highway in twenty-five miles and took an early afternoon break. Riverside had once been a bustling logging town, now it is nothing more than a combination store and saloon with a clutch of 1930s tourist cabins. Even that will change. Plans call for acquiring the property and moving them out completely.

Although this was far short of the goal for the day, it was fortunate we did stop. Water had somehow gotten into the gear when the boat swamped at Big Fish Trap. Had we continued, McKenna and O'Malley would have been faced with the uncomfortable prospect of a night in wet sleeping bags. We decided the better part of valor was to get everything dried out. Nylon ropes strung between pole-sized jack pines made a perfect drier and a warm June afternoon did the rest.

The early stop put us way behind schedule which was critical for John McKenna who had a clinic to get back to. We planned to make it up with an early start on our third and final day.

We were on the water as quickly after dawn as we could manage and were pleasantly reminded of the strong flow which seemed to propel us at a better clip than before. In no time at all we were dashing through State Line Rapid three miles from the launch. Now, the St. Croix was a border river with Minnesota on the right bank and Wisconsin to our left.

We sailed right on past Danbury, a small Wisconsin community where it is possible to resupply. That was eight miles.

On we swept, paddling leisurely under a cloudless sky.

For lunch, we pulled up on a sand bar and used a canoe prow for a table. The boys swam while we broke out sardines, kippers and rye bread.

Just a short paddle, and we sped over the Rock Ledge, the last rapid on our route. By four o'clock, we were unloading at St. Croix State Park on the Minnesota side. It's one of the governmental ownerships which will be joined with land donated to the National Park Service by Northern States Power Company to protect the hundred mile length of the river preserve. Twenty-five miles had slipped beneath the little boats; we had easily made the fifty miles in three days despite our mishaps.

That evening was celebration time—soda pop for the boys and Cold Duck for their elders. We reflected on what the river had given to us in these three days—talked about the barred owls conversing in the soft maple bottomlands downstream from Danbury, one calling out and the other coming back with an exact mimic just seconds later. We talked about deer wading out to drink or to submerge their backs in the shallows to gain some respite from the deer flies just beginning to visit pestilence on man and beast. We chuckled about the little buck which had quietly hunkered down on its belly in the rushes where the Clam River adds its flow to the main river. We talked of all those events, large and small, which bring us to these rivers again and again—the eagle sailing majestically overhead on six-foot wings, the miles of unblemished river, the prospect of coming back another time to run the next fifty miles and the much heralded Kettle River Rapids.

The St. Croix is not absolutely wild. There are occasional bridges, occasional cabins, occasional hamlets. For a total wilderness experience, the canoeist will still have to seek the outback of Canada or some of the remote Western rivers. For most of us, that is not always possible—sometimes not even in a whole lifetime.

I will remember the St. Croix not for the fish we might have caught had we stayed longer or tried harder. I will remember it as I saw it from the stern of my canoe looking past a boy with the squareness of new manhood coming to his shoulders and another boy grinning with excitement and shouting above the clamor of tumbling water. And, I'm pleased that this river, where I had fished with my own father twenty-five years ago, was still much as I remembered it. I'm hopeful that these sons of mine will be able to come here with their children twenty-five years from now and find it much as they have known it in these days.

Wild rivers are memorials to the land as it was—to us as we were in a simpler past. We hold on to a part of that when we live with such a river—even for a few days. In that, I think, is the enormous importance of our national commitment to keep at least a few of our rivers untamed. In that is the fundamental significance and real meaning of the Wild and Scenic Rivers Act.

The Survival of the Bark Canoe

John McPhee

John McPhee's writing is so varied and versatile that many people who have never heard of the New Yorker, *in which most of his material first appears, are familiar with his writing. He has produced more than a dozen books from his* New Yorker *pieces, at least three of which might very well be represented here:* Coming Into the Country, Encounters with the Archdruid, *and the source of this excerpt,* Survival of the Bark Canoe.

Whether he is writing about rafting the Colorado in Grand Canyon (Druid), folboating an Alaskan river (Country) or canoeing a Maine river with a maker of bark canoes, he knows his rivers and the people who float them. He captures the mood and the scene, painting a splendid picture with words. He can come along on any of my river trips and be most welcome.

The days are hot, and we often dip our cups in the river. Henri prefers Tang. He has the powder in his pack and a plastic jug by his feet as he paddles. He also has a supply of white bread—several loaves of it—and when he is hungry he pours honey onto the bread. In five minutes, he can prepare and finish a meal. Then he is ready to move on. We are in no hurry, like the shooting stars.

The river has many riffles, too minor to be labelled rapids. Nonetheless, they are stuffed with rock. The angle of the light is not always favorable. The rocks are hidden, and—smack—full tilt we hit them. The rocks make indentations that move along the bottom of the canoe, pressing in several inches and tracing a path toward the stern. It is as if the canoe were a pliant film sliding over the boulders. Still, I feel sorry and guilty when we hit one. I have been in white water and Rick has not, so he has asked me to paddle in the stern—to steer, to pick the route, to read the river—and I reward his confidence by smashing into another rock. Nothing cracks. If this were an aluminum canoe, it would be dented now, and, I must confess, I would not really care. Of all the differences between this canoe and others I have travelled in, the first difference is a matter of care about them. The canoes can take a lot more abuse than we give them, but we all care. Landing, we are out of the canoes and in the water ourselves long before the bark can touch bottom. We load and launch in a foot of water. The Indians did just that, and the inclination to copy them is automatic—is not consciously remembered—with these Indian canoes.

Once, on the upper Delaware, in a fifteen-foot rented Grumman canoe, I ran through a pitch of white water called Skinner's Falls. On a big shelf of rock at the bottom of the rapid, a crowd of people watched. When the canoe came through dry, they gathered around and asked how that was done. They said they were novices—a ski club on a summer outing—and none of them had been able to run the rapid without taking in quantities of water. "Well," said my wife, getting out of our canoe, "if you think you've seen anything yet, just wait until you see what is going to happen now. My husband spent his whole childhood doing this sort of thing—and so did that man up there in the other canoe. The two of them are now going to run the rapid together."

I walked up the riverbank. When I joined my friend and got into his canoe (also a fifteen-foot aluminum), I saw that one of the skiers had set up a tripod on which was mounted a sixteen-millimeter movie camera. My wife later told me she had said to them that it was good that they had the camera, because they would be able to study the film and learn a great deal. Skinner's Falls is easiest on the right. It gets worse and worse the farther to the left you go. So, for the rash hell of it, we dug in hard, got up to high speed, and went to the extreme left side of the rapid. The canoe bucked twice before the bow caught a rock that swung us broadside to the current and into a protruding boulder with a crash that threw us into the white river and bent the canoe into the shape of the letter C.

I have chosen not to tell that story to Rick Blanchette, for no one has ever cared more for a fifteen-thousand-dollar sports car (or, for that matter, for a work of sculpture) than he cares for his birch canoe.

Henri hits a rock; slides right; hits another. "I'd venture to say it would be easier to rip a wood-and-canvas canoe than a birch-bark," he says. "Anyhow, I've never, you know, ripped one." Henri paddles like an Indian. His stroke is a short, light, rapid chop. White people tend to take longer, harder storkes, which use a great deal more energy, he says. He appears relaxed in the stern of his canoe—leaning back, looking for wildlife, his paddle in motion like a wire whisk. Warren, in the bow, digs a large hole in the river with every stroke, contributing to the over-all effort the higher part of the ratio of power. We kneel, of course, and lean against the thwarts. There are no seats in these canoes. Kneeling is the natural paddling position anyway. It lowers the center of gravity, adds to the canoe's stability, brings more of the body into the stroke. Arms don't ache. You don't get tired.

We are seeing only ducks and muskrats on the big river, so we go into small streams in search of moose. These tributaries, tortuous and boggy, have all the appearance of moose country—Pine Stream, Moosehorn Stream. Moose tracks are everywhere—great cloven depressions in the mudbanks. Paddling silently, we move upstream— half, three-quarters of a mile. No moose. Henri is good at the silent paddle—the blade feathered on the recovery from each stroke and never coming out of the water. However, he is having difficulty travelling in the channel. The stream is only a few yards wide and has many bends. The canoes keep hitting the banks and sticking in the mud. With some trepidation, I suggest that there are bow strokes— draw, cross-draw, draw-stroke, pry, cross-pry—intended to help the canoe avoid the banks of the river. Trepidation because it is astonishing how people sometimes resent being told how to paddle a canoe. I have paddled on narrow, twisting rivers in New Jersey with good friends—easygoing, even-tempered people—who got royally incensed when I suggested that if they would only learn to draw and cross-draw they would not continue to plow the riverbanks. The look in their eyes showed a sense of insult, resting on the implication that every human being is born knowing how to use a canoe. The canoe itself apparently inspires such attitudes, because in form it is the most beautifully simple of all vehicles. And the born paddlers keep hitting the banks of the rivers. Mike Blanchette, though, in the bow of our canoe, to my relief, is not offended. Nor is Warren. They quickly pick up the knack of the pry and the draw—ways of moving the bow suddenly to left or right. Henri shows interest, too, inadvertently revealing that he knows almost nothing about paddling in the bow. His interest is genuine but academic. The bow is the subordinate position in a canoe. The person in the stern sets the course, is the pilot, the captain. The Blanchettes and I regularly change positions in our canoe, but Henri never leaves the stern.

Eventually, we give up the mooselook and go back to the main stream. Henri says it is all but impossible to go down the West Branch of the Penobscot River from North East Carry to Chesuncook Lake without seeing a number of—not to mention one—moose. Deriding us, a screaming seagull flies high above the river. We are two hundred river miles from the sea. Some substitute. In lieu of a moose, a seagull.

The Abnakis lived here. And the first whites to come into this lake-and-river country were hunters. They went back with stories of white pines so big that four men, grasping hands, could not reach around them. The next whites who came were timber cruisers. They made trips not unlike the one we are making—wandering at will in bark canoes—noting, and marking on inexact maps, the stands of pine. The big trees were there for the taking. They tended to cluster on the shores of the lakes. Loggers and log drivers followed, of course. Indian, hunter, cruiser, lumberer—this progression, in such beautiful country, could not help but lead to the tourist, the canoe-tripping tourist, and among the first of these (in all likelihood, *the* first tourist in the Maine woods) was Henry David Thoreau. He made two bark-canoe trips here, in 1853 and 1857, each time with an Indian guide. He went down this river. He went to the lake where Henri Vaillancourt—a hundred and twenty years later—would hide the felled cedar. Looking for moose in the night, he went up Moosehorn Stream. No moose. He had in his pack some pencils and an oilskin pouch full of scratch paper—actually letters that customers had written to his family's business, ordering plumbago and other printing supplies. On the backs of these discarded letters he made condensed, fragmentary, scarcely legible notes, and weeks later, when he had returned home to Concord, he composed his journal of the trip, slyly using the diary form, and writing at times in the present tense, to gain immediacy, to create the illusion of paragraphs written—as it is generally supposed they were written—virtually in the moments described. With the advantage of retrospect, he reconstructed the story to reveal a kind of significance that the notes do not reveal. Something new in journalism. With the journal as his principal source, he later crafted still another manuscript, in which he further shaped and rearranged the story, all the while adhering to a structure built on calendar dates. The result, published posthumously in hardcover form, was the book he called *The Maine Woods*.

Henri Vaillancourt's familiarity with books appears to be narrow, but he has read Thoreau—from *Walden* to *Cape Cod*, and most notably *The Maine Woods*. Rick Blanchette is saturated in Thoreau. In every segment of the river, they remember things Thoreau did there—places where he camped, where he collected flora, where he searched for moose. "I'm into Thoreau, too," Mike has said. "He writes about pickerel fishing, turtle hunting—the things I know and do."

Vaillancourt is transfixed by the knowledge that Thoreau, at North East Carry, actually watched a group of Indians making bark canoes. "All of them sitting there whittling with crooked knives! What a life! I'd give anything to have been there."

Back and forth between our two canoes, bits of Thoreau fly all day.

"Thoreau said the nose of the moose was the greatest delicacy, and after that the tongue."

"Thoreau said it is a common accident for men camping in the woods to be killed by a falling tree."

"Do you remember during the Allagash and East Branch trip when he said that all heroes and discoverers were insane?"

"No, that was in *Cape Cod*."

"Some people think he was humorless, you know. I disagree."

"Thoreau said . . ."

"Thoreau believed . . ."

"Do you remember the passage where . . ."

When it is not my turn to paddle and I am riding in the center of the canoe, I read to catch up. Thoreau's trips were provisioned with smoked beef, coffee, sugar, tea, plum cake, salt, pepper, and lemons for flavoring the water. His tent was made from cut poles and cotton cloth. He had one blanket. He carried his gear in India-rubber bags, and it included an extra shirt, extra socks, two waistcoats, six dickies, a thick nightcap, a four-quart tin pail, a jackknife, a fishline, hooks, pins, needles, thread, matches, an umbrella, a towel, and soap. For foul weather, he had an India-rubber coat, in which he sweated uncomfortably and got wetter than he would have in the rain. He ate his meals from birch-bark plates, using forks whittled from alder. For relief from mosquitoes, he wore a veil; he also threw damp leaves onto the fire and sat in the smoke. He slept in smoke, too—burning wet rotting logs all night.

Thoreau's guide on the first canoe trip was Joe Aitteon, and, on the second, Joe Polis—both Penobscots from Indian Island in Old Town, Maine. Henri Vaillancourt is at least as interested in these Indians as he is in Thoreau—particularly in Polis, who made his own canoes. Polis and Aitteon travelled light—no changes of clothing. Aitteon was a log driver. Polis was the better woodsman. Polis had represented his tribe in Washington. He had visited New York. He said, "I suppose, I live in New York, I be poorest hunter, I expect." Thoreau hired him for eleven dollars a week, which included the use of his canoe. Some eighteen feet in length, thirty inches wide, and a foot deep in the center, it was a longer, narrower canoe than the Vaillancourt canoes we are using. Thoreau's first canoe—on the 1853 trip with Aitteon—was more than nineteen feet long, and the bark was painted green. Our paddles are made from birch. Thoreau's were made from sugar maple. Thoreau was discomforted by the confinement of the paddling position, and he used the word "torture" to describe it. Sometimes he stood up in the canoe to stretch his legs. He appreciated nonetheless the genius of canoe technology. "The canoe implies a long antiquity in which its manufacture has been gradually perfected," he wrote in his journal. "It will ere long, perhaps, be ranked among the lost arts."

When Thoreau, from Mt. Katahdin, saw neither clearings nor cabins across huge domains of forest, lake, and river, he said, "It did not look as if a solitary traveller had cut so much as a walking-stick there." On closer view, though, from water level, he saw the stumps of timber a great deal larger than walking sticks. He saw dry-ki too. The first dams (small dams, built to raise the lakes a few feet to serve, in various ways, the convenience of logging companies) had been built in 1841, and now, after a dozen years and more, "great trunks of trees stood dead and bare far out in the lake, making the impression of ruined piers of a city that had been—while behind, the timber lay criss-a-cross for half a dozen rods or more over the water." Dry-ki (the syllables rhyme) apparently derives from "dry kill": wood killed as a result of the dams and now, as dry as bone—gray, resins gone—crudely fencing the shores of open water. Thoreau always hoped to see some caribou but saw none. Of the caribou, Polis said, "No likum stump. When he sees that he scared."

The stumps that scared Thoreau were the stumps of the giant pines. To cut and take those trees was "as if individual speculators were to be allowed to export the clouds out of the sky, or the stars out of the firmament, one by one." If the attitudes behind such rapine were to go unchecked, he said (a century and a quarter before the great ecological uprising), "we shall be reduced to gnaw the very crust of the earth for nutriment." And what of the remaining "stately pines"? Twenty years before the first national park, and more than a century before the Wilderness Act, he asked, "Why should not we ... have our national preserves, where ... the bear and panther ... may still exist, and not be 'civilized off the face of the earth'?" The Maine of his bark-canoe trips was the deepest wilderness Thoreau would see in his lifetime. Today, astonishingly, it looks much the same as it did when he saw it. Lake and river, many thousands of miles of shoreline are unbroken by human structures and are horizoned only with the tips of spruce. The lakes are still necklaced with dry-ki, some of it more than a century old. Dry-ki has come to be regarded as charming. It certainly makes good firewood, a smokeless fire.

After forty-odd miles of Penobscot River, we are impatient for a change. For all its big bends and deadwaters—larger dimensions the farther we go—the river is now hemming us in, and we anticipate Chesuncook Lake, a burst of space. The skyline is opening up some. The lake must be around the next, or the next, bend. Thoreau said that in this same reach of the river he found himself approaching the big lake "with as much expectation as if it had been a university." The river debouches. The lake breaks open. We move out onto it and look to the right down miles of water and far beyond to the high Katahdin massif. Katahdin is a mile high. The lake's elevation is less than a thousand feet. Katahdin stands alone. The vast terrain around it is the next thing to a peneplain. Wherever you paddle through this country, when you move out onto the big lakes you can look to the southeast and see Katahdin.

A steady wind is blowing from the direction of the mountain, and since we are heading north we hold the canoes together and put up an improvised sail. Supported by two paddles as masts, the sail is the largest plastic bag I have ever seen—five by five feet. It is something called a Gaylord liner and comes from the small plastics factory in Greenville, where both Blanchettes work. The canoes move smartly before the wind. Indians used great sheets of bark as sails, and moose hide as well. According to *The Bark Canoes and Skin Boats of North America*, Indians of prehistory "may have set up a leafy bush in the bow of their canoes to act as a sail with favorable winds." At any rate, "the old Nova Scotia expression 'carrying too much bush,' meaning over-canvassing a boat, is thought by some to have originated from an Indian practice observed there by the first settlers." Thoreau sailed using a blanket. Our plastic sail sets Henri Vaillancourt off on a long, surprising tirade against the mills and factories of Greenville, which he says are sweatshops, exploiters of immigrant labor. "I'm glad I don't have to work in one of those places," he says. "Particularly that plastics shop. What a rip-off!" For Mike, the plastics shop is a summer job. He is a student at the University of New Hampshire. His brother, Rick, who is already a college graduate, wants to be a librarian in a New England college. He works full time in the plastics shop and also takes graduate courses in library science at Fitchburg State. Water rushes by and between the canoes. Holding the polyethylene sail, Rick quotes one of his favorite lines from Thoreau, which was occasioned by Thoreau's first night here on Chesuncook. He had moose meat for dinner and afterward went for a walk. "For my dessert," he said, and Rick is now quoting him, "I helped myself to a large slice of the Chesuncook woods, and took a hearty draught of its waters with all my senses."

Vaillancourt sneers. "Some dessert," he says. "Thoreau was a great guy, but a little far-flung there at times. What a crackpot—a real featherbrain, a very impractical person."

Blanchette is annoyed. Vaillancourt is amused. Blanchette says, "Yes? Well, the most influential man of this century will turn out to be Thoreau, who lived in the century before."

"He was extreme," Vaillancourt goes on. "He would not cut down a live tree. You can use nature without destroying it. I have an aunt in Concord. I asked her what people there thought of Thoreau, and she said, 'He was a real bum.'"

"Thoreau actually started a couple of forest fires in his time," Blanchette admits. "One in Concord. The other on Mt. Washington. When the fires went out of control, Thoreau just walked away."

"He said he thought he could make a bark canoe," Vaillancourt adds. "I doubt very much if he could have. That Aitteon, for an Indian, didn't know much, either. Thoreau asked him about the canoe, how the ribs were attached to the gunwales, and he said, 'I don't know. I never noticed.' Aitteon saw a porcupine once and thought it was a bear."

The Gaylord liner is pulling us up the west side of Gero, a big island. Near the island shore, Vaillancourt sees two, three, four tall specimen birches, paper birches—perfection trees. He decides in an instant to camp below them tonight.

The River

Joel Vance

Joel Vance is an information specialist for the Missouri Department of Conservation and a free-lance writer whose articles and stories have appeared in numerous outdoor magazines, including Field and Stream, American Rifleman, Outdoor Life, Sports Afield *and* American Hunter. *At recent meetings of the Outdoor Writers Association of America, he and I discussed this book. His insights and suggestions have been helpful to me, and this article, which won the 1976 Johnson Wax Deep Woods Contest, is one of my favorites. It portrays a Girl Scout outing on the Eleven Point River in Missouri.*

The candles flickered in a soft river breeze. Fog shrouded the valley of the Eleven Point, result of a meeting between warm air and the cold, clear waters of the river.

We were on a Girl Scout float and our daughter, Carrie, was one of seven senior Scouts involved in a ceremony of farewell to scouting. The younger girls grouped around a campfire, listening to the seven say goodbye to their Scouting days. It was touching and the setting, along the river, was especially appropriate, for this is a river bunch. They have taken many float trips and, I hope, are the better for it, just as I hope my family is the better for all the trips it has taken down the rocky meanders of the Ozark rivers.

We love the rivers and all they mean and have meant to us. To some, rivers are sources of hydroelectric energy for an energy-starved society, to others a drink of water for a herd of cows. Some see the rivers as a place to channelize, others as a convenient dump for beer and soft drink cans, old refrigerators, bed springs, automobile bodies and the detritus of civilization.

All these uses (and abuses) of the rivers are focussed and narrow and are symptomatic of the problems that slowly strangle these incredibly lovely manifestations of nature at her best. Where there is running water, there is someone who can make use of it for a crippling project. I read the headlines: An official of a regional growth association is asking for funds to develop three new dams on three different rivers. A citizens' group is fighting a dam on a fourth Missouri river. In North Dakota, construction goes ahead on the Garrison Diversion project which will rip the heart from several National Wildlife Refuges and wreak enormous damage on vast areas of wildlife habitat.

Back in the mid-1940s, Aldo Leopold, the father of conservation philosophy, sighed for the lack of a conservation conscience, an ethic to guide man in his dealings with nature. Despite continuation of all the problems that Leopold saw then, progress toward a land ethic has been slow and painful. "The art of land doctoring is being practiced with vigor," Leopold said, "But the science of land health is yet to be born."

And he said, "Wilderness is a resource which can shrink but not grow." And he said, "There is as yet no ethic dealing with man's relation to land and to the animals and plants which grow upon it . . . The land relation is still strictly economic, entailing privileges, but not obligations."

The rivers serve as examples of the problems that Leopold saw. There is so much pressure to bend an ethical obligation to the river's integrity. What will one little dam hurt? What will a diversion of part of the waters hurt? After all, people need (a) energy (b) jobs (c) water (d) all of the above.

And the arguments are valid from a given set of standards. But somewhere there must be a higher authority, one that says: This river ethically cannot be altered. It must remain as it is. Leopold said, "The key-log which must be moved to release the evolutionary process for an ethic is simply this: quit thinking about decent land-use as solely an economic problem. Examine each question in terms of what is ethically and esthetically right, as well as what is economically expedient. *A thing is right when it tends to preserve the integrity, stability, and beauty of the biotic community. It is wrong when it tends otherwise.*"

Read that over. It should be engraved in the mind. It is the concept that is overlooked when a development is promoted. While Leopold said it simply and concisely, economist E.F. Schumacher didn't do badly either: "In the past, when religion taught men to look upon nature as God's handiwork, the idea of conservation was too self-evident to require special emphasis. But now that the religion of economics lends respectability to man's inborn envy and greed, and nature is looked upon as man's hindrance, what could be more important than an explicit theory of conservation? We teach our children that science and technology are the instruments for man's battle with nature, but forget to warn them that, being himself a part of nature, man could easily be on the losing side."

I wonder how anyone who has spent much time on the river could then return to do it harm, but maybe they don't see the same things, feel the same things that I do. Maybe they are driven by devils that, fortunately, I have escaped. Maybe I should pity them and maybe I would if they would leave the rivers alone.

The river seems quiet, with an ambient peace that relaxes tensions. Yet there is much noise, too. A belted kingfisher swoops across the river ahead with excited monologue. The Woody Woodpecker hysteria of a pileated woodpecker caroms through the forest and presently the big bird crosses the river with distinctive, rhythmic dips.

Ahead of me a bluff guards a bend in the river, its seamed face stained with the tears of leaching minerals. The pool is calm, but occasional boiling pulses on the surface indicate the current, quiet but powerful, below in the darkness. A snag bobs and nods, batted playfully about by the river as it passes. Water tumbles in from an uphill spring, bouncing over ledgerocks in an exact miniature of some grand, awesome waterfall that would draw millions of tourists who wouldn't turn their heads to look at this exquisite scene.

I think that what I love most about the river is sharing it with youngsters, both my own and others. There are times that I want to float the river alone and listen only to the irritable scold of the kingfisher and discover for my quiet pleasure the secret beauty of columbine nestled in a moss-coated niche in the cliff. But mostly I like to share the river with young eyes, those that see beautiful things for the first time.

How pleasant to squeal at the touch of icy river water for the first time. How exciting to negotiate a tumbling rapid for the first time. How wonderful to discover for the first time that there is a rich natural world beyond the backyard fence.

And how nice for me to hear soft young voices singing "Shenandoah" in a star-sprinkled spring night. Even the whip-poor-wills hush to hear the music and the gurgle of the river is counterpoint to the quiet old song.

Perhaps if my belly were sore from hunger, perhaps if the river offered a promise of better days, more money, I would feel differently and want to develop it, change it, alter it to be more profitable. I would look at is as an economic boon. But those who destroy the rivers are not those who cry with hunger. They are those who are driven by the Great God Progress, the concept of development, no matter the cost, and if they didn't gut the river, they would turn loose their big machines on something else, for their life is Projects.

I cannot believe that any of the youngsters who go with me on the river, who engage in joyous water fights, who seine for crawfish, who sing soft songs around a spiralling campfire, will in their adult years shout for a dam or channelization or other corruption of the river.

That is my hope. That is my consolation.

Rivers of the Rockies
Boyd Norton

Boyd Norton is one of a handful of former nuclear engineers who helped establish the environmental movement in Idaho. That movement sent Cecil Andrus to the Governor's chair and to Washington as Secretary of the Interior under President Carter, whose administration more than doubled the extent of the National Wild and Scenic Rivers System.

Norton, an easterner by birth and education, left Idaho for Colorado to work for The Wilderness Society, an organization well served by both Olaus and Mardy Murie. It was Norton who first introduced me to Mardy, and to Jim Campbell, under whose guidance I became a whitewater rafter. Boyd has guided river trips in Idaho and elsewhere. His Snake Wilderness *offers excellent background on conservation battles for Idaho's rivers and wilderness (see Michael Frome's "Must This Be Lost from the Sight of Man?" in this anthology, and Norton's "Last Great Dam" in* Audubon, *January 1970).* Rivers of the Rockies, *a classic in its own right, and, unfortunately, out of print, is a very personal story. In it you will meet authors whose works appear in this anthology.*

I am surrounded by the Salmon River. Clad only in tennis shoes, swimsuit, and a puffy red life jacket, I drift along in the current. Not far away is my raft, my sanctuary should these waters get too rough. But for now I am content to lie back, allowing the buoyancy of the life jacket to suspend me in my watery medium, and to look up at a fish-eye view of the wilderness passing by: blue gash of sky between high, forested walls; beetling gray granite; ponderosa pine; glaring white beaches; flowers and greenery brushing the river; side streams scrubbing themselves white as they rush down to join my river. There are no sounds. No, I take that back. There are no *man-made* sounds, but there is the low hiss of the moving blue-green waters carrying me along. And as they move me, these waters also pull and suck at my body, twisting me in subtle eddies that belie the seemingly smooth, quiet surface. The phrase "living river" comes to mind and if, indeed, a river lives, then I am feeling its pulse. But it is a cold pulse, for even though a hot July sun blazes down on me, my body is numbed by the snowmelt of the Sawtooth, White Cloud, Boulder, Beaverhead, and Bitterroot mountains. Every side stream—and there are countless numbers of them—is teeth-aching, palate-numbing cold, and they add to the chill of these waters.

I have no idea how long I have been drifting in the river and I really don't care. Time? What is that? Obviously some utterly meaningless concept here in my watery womb. What I perceive is movement, sky, water, earth color, form. But not time.

Suddenly I'm jarred from my trance by the voices of my companions calling to me. I lift my head to look and listen. From eyeball level the water is smooth as far as I can see. But somewhere downstream I hear a dull, ominous drone; an insistent sibilance that warns of a change in the river's mood. A rapid. A wild thought crosses my mind: What would it be like to run a rapid in life jacket alone, experience it at river level, and feel the full violence of the river as it foams and churns its way over the rocky constraints? The idea is intriguing, but as we drift closer I begin to have second thoughts. Maybe I ought to start on a smaller rapid or some riffles before taking on a large one. Convinced by my own logic, I scramble, somewhat relieved, onto my raft and once again take over the oars.

The rapid turns out to be a minor one, typical of the hundreds of places where the river is pinched together by canyon walls, forcing it to increase velocity and to tear itself apart as it makes a noticeable drop in elevation. We pitch and toss over some nice waves, and soon the river spreads itself into a placid sheet. And again we drift quietly along.

This is the second (or is it the third?) day of the trip. My companions have come from widely scattered parts of the country: Los Angeles, New York, Chicago, Dallas. All meaningless abstractions here. Our raft is part of a flotilla of three rafts in a party run by my old friend Jim Campbell, who owns and operates Wild Rivers Idaho. Jim is at the oars of one raft, Cort Conley mans another. Mine is the third and smallest of the three, and I prefer it that way.

This is a totally new experience for me. I've been on the Salmon many times before and on other rivers as well, but this is my first time as a boatman or guide manning the oars, responsible for the safety of my passengers. And added to the weight of responsibility is the thought that my own two children, Jean Anne and Scott, accompany me on this trip.

But such thoughts are not really burdensome in this country. In the spell and grip of this river nothing really matters. It feels good to be home again, back on the Salmon, *my* Salmon River. What is there about this place? Why am I drawn back here again and again? I dislike being analytical about it, yet there is something about this Salmon River country. It's a gentle wilderness, soft and welcoming, with no sharp edges or harshness. I have a feeling that I could step off my boat at some convenient landing, bid the others farewell, and settle down here easily. An abundance of trees would provide me with wood for shelter. And game is plentiful. Thus far we've seen many deer and there are countless elk in the high country. A struggle for survival? Seems more like living in the lap of luxury. But maybe I deceive myself, maybe this land is not as gentle as it first appears. People have tried for a hundred years or more and they've been beaten back, held in abeyance. All along our 90-mile journey is evidence of attempts to tame the country: Crofoot Ranch, Allison Ranch, Campbell's Ferry Ranch (no relation to Jim, our head guide), the Moore place, James Ranch, Shepp Ranch, the Polly Bemis place, and that's just about it. There was ample incentive here: gold. And remnants of the diggings are still around: Nabob Mine, Painter Bar Mine, Golden Anchor Mine, War Eagle Mine. Farther up in the high country were Leesburg, Grantsburg, Warren, Dixie, the boom towns that are now turning to rust and dust, decaying along with the remnants of the mines. For the gold seekers, this country was a temporary home, never intended to be more. But others decided to stay and they built with love and care their homes of immense, handhewn ponderosa logs, painstakingly cut, squared, and fitted one by one. Charlie Shepp's place took two years to build. With care it'll last another two centuries or more. And even the Moore place, abandoned for several decades, still has a sturdiness and solidity that seem almost geological.

But I digress. To get back to my original thought, why hasn't this land been tamed like the rest of our country, or at least like the rest of the West? Why aren't there roads, highways, cars, suburbs, factories, condominiums, trailers, hotdog stands, tramways, amusement parks, people, pavement, and pollution? Was this land so overpowering, the early pioneers so weak, that it resisted being subdued? Is this place both Valhalla and Hell? The answers to these questions seem to lie in examination of the total scope of this place, for, being confined to the depths of this great canyon—the second deepest on the continent, I'm told—we are cut off from the size and character of all this wilderness. Aside from occasional glimpses of the high country some

4,000 to 5,000 feet above the river, we have no feeling for the vastness, the great extent of the country surrounding us.

I remember once flying over here on a commercial flight to Seattle. It was evening, and the last flickering colors of an incredible sunset still lingered on the horizon when our pilot announced that we were over the "great Salmon River wilderness." I detected a curious mixture of pride and awe in his voice. All of us strained, of course, to see into the blackness below, but nothing was visible. Then it struck me: The blackness, that great expanse devoid of any sign of civilization—not even any lights—was the most obvious mark of a vast wilderness. We flew on for a long time at 30,000 feet and 500 miles per hour, and still no lights, no sign of roads or cars or towns, and I wondered how many places are left in this nation so free of man's presence.

As I learned later, this region through which our rafts now float is the largest expanse of wild country this side of Alaska, roughly 6,000 square miles and still roadless and wild. So far. And three of the continent's last wild rivers flow here: the Selway, the Middle Fork of the Salmon, and these waters of the main Salmon that bear us swiftly along. So perhaps it wasn't the harshness as much as the vastness that insulated it all from man, and still does to some extent. This incredible up-and-down, creased and wrinkled country of deep gorges, turbulent waters, and thick forests still has the ability to overwhelm man. It resisted Lewis and Clark and a good many others who came afterward. But one wonders how long it can continue to hold out.

Drifting along and discussing these thoughts with my passengers nearly causes me to miss Jim and Cort, who are pulled into a sandy beach around a bend on the right bank. I pull hard on the oars to slip out of the main current and into a back eddy where I can nose the boat onto the sandy shore.

Lunch break, we discover as we step ashore. The heat is fierce, and we seek shelter under the cool, graceful limbs of a ponderosa pine. I try one of Jim's Salmon River Specials, a sandwich comprised of salami, cheese, tuna fish, mustard, pickles, baloney, mayonnaise, and topped with a generous layer of peanut butter, guaranteed by my chief guide to give exercise to even the most indolent digestive tract. This gastronomical nightmare is washed down with delicious icy cold water dipped from a nearby side stream.

To work off my lunch I decide to have a look around. The little stream is edged by moss-covered rocks, and ferns grow in profusion. An Eden that needs to be explored. As I push my way upstream I discover that it's no easy task, however. It is a jungle of thickets and undergrowth, dense and lush. More reminiscent of a rain forest than the Rocky Mountains. It's a curious fact that there are many such micro-ecosystems along here. They exist along stream courses in protected side canyons and gulleys where there is a moister environment. These places are totally unlike the typical forests of the Rockies, which are characterized by a general sparseness of vegetation: slim, spare lodgepole pines, open ponderosa forests interspersed with parklike meadows, or alpine fir growing in clumps near timberline. A few years ago I discovered one of these Edens in an obscure, rarely visited side canyon here along the Salmon, a place so incredible, so beautiful, that each time I visit, it seems unreal. It lies some distance from the river, and getting there is a terrible bushwhack. I doubt that more than a few people have ever seen it. The walls of the canyon close in, and a little waterfall plunges over a lip of rock into a deep, secret pool. The overhanging walls of this grotto are covered with mosses and ferns, and the dense vegetation closes it all in, shutting out sky and sun. The carpet of mosses and ferns and flowers on the floor of this place seems so delicate that I walk very carefully, on tiptoe, to avoid disturbing anything. It is so lush, so tropical, that I half expect (and half hope) to find some lovely Tahitian girl sitting by the quiet waters of the pool.

With visions of discovering another such place, I stumble along this little stream. I recognize several plant species that are totally out of place here in the Rockies: maples, with their palmate, serrate leaves; and trillium, the delicate three-leafed, three-petaled flower. I would stake a case of my favorite beer that no trillium grows in all of Wyoming or Colorado.

As I'm about to step off a moss-covered, decaying log, I'm startled out of my thoughts by a high-pitched buzz. Having encountered many rattlesnakes in my travels, I recognize the sound instantly, and my response is learned: Freeze until you locate him. He's not difficult to find, lying coiled next to a broken extension of the log I'm on and about six feet away. Undoubtedly he heard me coming from a long way off, with my thrashing and crashing through this dense brush. But he chose to wait until an encounter was imminent before sounding off. As I stand watching him, he begins edging away, head and neck pointed toward me, but body slowly moving toward the protection of denser brush. Searching around, I find a broken branch nearby and I use it to halt his getaway, poking him gently back into a firm defensive pose. His buzzing rattle is loud and insistent. I hunker down on my log to study him. About six feet of space and a hundred million years in time separate us. He slowly flicks out a black, forked tongue and leaves it suspended in space a few moments. Tasting the air. Slowly his vibrating tail comes to a stop as I sit quietly, making no noise or movement. He eyes me cautiously through dusty, unblinking eyes, the elliptical pupils of which are dilated somewhat by the subdued lighting here. About two feet in length, his muscular body is sandy brown in color with dark brown blotches, or saddles, that are spaced regularly along his length and extend down his sides. Pacific coast rattler, I decide, or possibly a prairie rattler. No expert, I find it difficult to distinguish the two. No matter. He, possibly, is trying to classify me as well. This particular area is remote enough that I may be the first human he's ever encountered. "My God," he's probably thinking, "the gang back at the rocks is never going to believe this."

As a test I raise my arm quickly, and just as quickly he sounds his rattle again and tenses his body. When I make no further movements, he silences his tail in a few moments. It occurs to me that this would make a beautiful photograph, but here am I, dedicated photographer, without a Nikon or Rolleiflex shooting iron anywhere in reach. Finally I stand up, ready to head back to my companions, and he once more sounds his alarm. "That's all right, old friend," I tell him silently, "I mean you no harm. Thanks for letting me visit." I back away, then turn and retrace my thrashing path, cautious now that maybe a brother or a cousin of my friend back there might be lurking where I might step on him inadvertently.

Back at the raft, everyone is anxious to push off, move on, see what lies around the bend. I mention my encounter with the rattlesnake, and several people are horrified that I didn't kill him. "But why?" I ask. "He did me no harm. And besides, I was the intruder in his domain."

It gives them something to think about as we push off. Or perhaps they wonder what kind of a nut they have for a guide.

The river once more pulls us along. In a few more bends, we approach one of the major obstacles of the river, Salmon Falls, which is not really a falls at all, but an abrupt rapid. Those first few moments before slipping down into the watery fury are always a bit tense. Ahead, the smooth surface of the water ends abruptly at a thin, white line. Beyond, the dancing tips of white waves can be seen, and the sound is that of several freight trains rumbling through the gorge. I hang back, letting Cort then Jim run through. Finally I maneuver to start down the slick tongue into the rapid. Everything happens quickly, and there is little time to think, let alone react. After the first chute we plunge into some huge stationary waves that curl back on themselves and toss the raft around like a cork. As we pass swiftly through the middle of this madness, one curler reaches into the back of the raft and floats my friend Jimmy Collier clean out of the boat, then washes him back in, all in the same instant. In a moment we bounce madly through the tail waves and out into the placid water below, where Jim and Cort and the others all wait. Everyone is soaked and excited, still high from that hot, coursing jolt of adrenaline, and the raft spins slowly in the quiet water as everyone recounts his experience "Did you see that wave that . . ?" "I almost went over when . . ." "Hey, Jimmy, you're supposed to stay in the boat." Then we quietly settle into the peaceful mood of the river again. A hot sun blazes in the late afternoon sky, and the river becomes a slick glare, painful to look at. In a few miles we pull into Bruin Creek to make camp for the night, and the shade of the forest is welcome respite from the inferno. It is not long before the sun slips behind the high, verdant hills hemming us in, and the canyon is then steeped in cool shadow. There is no real sunset. Darkness simply sneaks in and steals away the remaining light. We sit around the campfire sipping coffee and digesting an immense meal, reading the mystic messages of our fiery oracle. Someone tells a story. Another relates a bit of adventure from today. Jimmy Collier, an up-and-coming folk singer from New York, plays some quiet songs on his guitar. The world outside and beyond these canyon walls could well be engaged in nuclear holocaust or a stock market crash or any number of calamities political or economic. But here the most troubling thought is choosing a comfortable spot on the sandy beach for your sleeping bag. As I lie there before dropping off, I hear Jean Anne and Scott not far away talking excitedly from their sleeping bags about the day's happenings. I resist a fatherly impulse to suggest that they should get to sleep. To hell with it. Let 'em stay up and count stars all night long. The world needs a lot more star counters.

A River Runs Through It
Norman Maclean

> *Norman Maclean's trio of short stories, published in*
> *1976, has struck a vital cord, especially the title story, which*
> *is one of my favorite pieces of river writing. It is a fishing*
> *story and a personal experience that is as moving as the*
> *river that runs through it. Maclean grew up in Montana*
> *and taught for years in a big city. He returns to his home*
> *country to write, as Hemingway says one should, about*
> *what he knows.*

I sat there and forgot and forgot, until what remained was the river that went by and I who watched. On the river the heat mirages danced with each other and then they danced through each other and then they joined hands and danced around each other. Eventually the watcher joined the river, and there was only one of us. I believe it was the river.

Even the anatomy of a river was laid bare. Not far downstream was a dry channel where the river had run once, and part of the way to come to know a thing is through its death. But years ago I had known the river when it flowed through this now dry channel, so I could enliven its stony remains with the waters of memory.

In death it had its pattern, and we can only hope for as much. Its overall pattern was the favorite serpentine curve of the artist sketched on the valley from my hill to the last hill I could see on the other side. But internally it was made of sharp angles. It ran seemingly straight for a while, turned abruptly, then ran smoothly again, then met another obstacle, again was turned sharply and again ran smoothly. Straight lines that couldn't be exactly straight and angles that couldn't have been exactly right angles became the artist's most beautiful curve and swept from here across the valley to where it could be no longer seen.

I also became the river by knowing how it was made. The Big Blackfoot is a new glacial river that runs and drops fast. The river is a straight rapids until it strikes big rocks or big trees with big roots. This is the turn that is not exactly at right angles. Then it swirls and deepens among big rocks and circles back through them where big fish live under the foam. As it slows, the sand and small rocks it picked up in the fast rapids above begin to settle out and are deposited, and the water becomes shallow and quiet. After the deposit is completed, it starts running again.

On a hot afternoon the mind can also create fish and arrange them according to the way it has just made the river. It will have the fish spend most of their time in the "big blue" at the turn, where they can lie protected by big rocks and take it easy and have food washed to them by big waters. From there, they can move into the fast rapids above when they are really hungry or it is September and cool, but it is hard work living in such fast water all the time. The mind that arranges can also direct the fish into the quiet water in the evening when gnats and small moths come out. Here the fisherman should be told to use his small dry flies and to wax them so they will float. He should also be informed that in quiet evening water everything must be perfect because, with the glare from the sun gone, the fish can see everything, so even a few hairs too many in the tail of the fly can make all the difference. The mind can make all these arrangements, but of course the fish do not always observe them.

Fishermen also think of the river as having been made with them partly in mind, and they talk of it as if it had been. They speak of the three parts as a unity and call it "a hole," and the fast rapids they call "the head of the hole" and the big turn they call "the deep blue" or "pool" and the quiet, shallow water below they call "the tail of the hole," which they think is shallow and quiet so that they can have a place to wade across and "try the other side."

As the heat mirages on the river in front of me danced with and through each other, I could feel patterns from my own life joining with them. It was here, while waiting for my brother, that I started this story, although, of course, at the time I did not know that stories of life are often more like rivers than books. But I knew a story had begun, perhaps long ago near the sound of water. And I sensed that ahead I would meet something that would never erode so there would be a sharp turn, deep circles, a deposit, and quietness.

The fisherman even has a phrase to describe what he does when he studies the patterns of a river. He says he is "reading the water," and perhaps to tell his stories he has to do much the same thing. Then one of his biggest problems is to guess where and at what time of day life lies ready to be taken as a joke. And to guess whether it is going to be a little or a big joke.

For all of us, though, it is much easier to read the waters of tragedy.

Exploring a Desert Legend— the Dolores River

David Sumner

David Sumner (1937–1983), to whose memory this book is dedicated, was a New Englander by birth and education. He spent only the last third of his too-short life—he died of leukemia at 45—in the west where he made his reputation as editor (Colorado), writer and photographer. He was a well-known free-lance writer and photographer whose articles have appeared in the Sierra Club Bulletin, National Wildlife *and* Backpacker. *He worked as a citizen employee on the Dolores River Study. We ran a number of rivers together—the Snake in Hells Canyon, the Green through Dinosaur National Monument, the Main Salmon and its Middle Fork—and frequently talked about this book as we shared campfires. His presence gave an added dimension to every trip we made together. The Dolores was his favorite river.*

Long before I caught a glimpse of its vertical, slickrock canyon walls and the seething maw of whitewater and rock known as Snaggletooth Rapids, the Dolores River had taken on a legendary quality in my mind.

From the tight-lipped cadre of Colorado river rats who'd been sneaking off to run it since the late 1940s, only an occasional word leaked out. Usually, it was a superlative of some kind, or a vivid, descriptive fragment. And then a hush. The Dolores was one of those secret rivers precious few knew about, and those who did wanted to savor their treasure alone as long as time would allow.

I tucked the rumors away in the back of my mind, tantalized by the incompleteness of what I could find out, and waited. Finally, in June 1973, I met the Dolores—El Rio de Nuestra Senora de los Dolores, as she is formally known, The River of Our Lady of Sorrows. The name was bestowed by Spanish traders wandering north from Santa Fe in the mid-1700s. No one knows why.

The veil of mystery around the Dolores was disappearing by 1973. The river was threatened by a dam (and still is) and also a desalting project; it also was being looked upon as a candidate for the National

Wild and Scenic Rivers System, albeit only in a preliminary way.

Stirred by this interest, a group of us decided to have a look, and what we found made indelible impressions. In four days we covered 108 miles, flipped two rafts, wrapped a third around a bridge pier, lost four members of our party overnight, had an airplane searching for them the next morning, and, thankfully, found them safe. But in the end, these were not the strongest memories; they were overwhelmed by the simple discovery of the Dolores herself.

Our put-in was at the standard spot for launching trips on this river, Bradfield's Ranch, about midway between the southwestern Colorado communities of Dolores and Cahone, which bills itself as "The Pinto Bean Capital of the World." Almost from the beginning, the river took hold.

For the first 20 or so miles, the canyon gradually deepens. This is Dolores Canyon, the first of six deep gorges the river has carved. The rock grows redder as the river flows into the geologic province known as the Colorado Plateau—the same red sandstone realm as Canyonlands and Arches National Parks in Utah, and the tragically inundated Glen Canyon on the Colorado River.

The walls on this first leg of the Dolores are stair-step rather than sheer, the red contrasting vividly with the dusty greens of juniper and pinon pines that grow and twist at oblique angles. Save for a few farm and ranch fences just below Bradfield, and a pumping plant down a ways, signs of civilization are nil. This is a dry, tough canyon, and it has not encouraged settlement.

At Snaggletooth Rapids, 400 yards long and dropping about 20 feet, we portaged the gear, running rafts, rubber ducks and kayaks through empty—careening off rocks, shipping waves of water, spinning, veering, but somehow making it, despite the standard advice on Snaggletooth: "Portage at all stages."

Our run went at about 2,500 cubic feet per second, which is optimum. Above that suckholes begin to grow monstrous; below it, rocks clog the channel. Some have run Snaggletooth at 4,000 cfs, others at 1,000 cfs; their challenge was more extreme than ours.

Below Snaggletooth, Dolores Canyon reaches a maximum depth of over 2,000 feet, but we hardly had time to take notice. For 25 miles, there is an intermittent staccato of rapids, none of these much more than Grade IV, but they kept on coming at a galling, erratic pace—unpredictable, like guerrilla warfare. Gnarled yet stately cottonwoods appeared along the stream terrace, also several hawks, a prairie falcon, repeated flights of ducks, and on shore, three groups of mule deer, all does and fawns. We drifted past an abandoned homestead, a relic of broken dreams.

Toward the one-cafe, two-gas-pump settlement of Slick Rock, the canyon opens out and the rock fades from rust to tan. We were through the rapids now, drifting lazily in the high desert.

Below Slick Rock, the Dolores drops suddenly into its second canyon, this one recently named Little Glen (in memoriam). The walls grow sheer, mostly red again, and streaked with blue-black desert varnish. The rims are topped with goblin-like buttresses and domes. The song of a canyon wren trilled and tumbled down the musical scale, over and over.

More variation. The canyon falls away to rolling cow country (white-faced, behind barbed wire) and the Dolores flows into Gypsum Valley. We pulled ashore to investigate two petroglyph sites, and discovered grinning stick-men pecked in sandstone faces. The river meanders past sandbars and beneath more cottonwoods.

Beyond Gypsum Valley, the land heaves upward and the Dolores dives into Slick Rock Canyon—33 miles long, sinuous, red-walled and deep. Ever since Bradfield Ranch, we had been waiting for this, but it still came as a shock. No rapids here, only an occasional whitewater riffle and one delicious chute. Ever since Slick Rock, it had been canoe water.

If the fury of the Dolores fails to show in the present, it is amply evident from the past, from the work done in slow, geologic time. Here, running water has cut through layer upon layer of ancient seabed, beach, sediment and dune. This is a classic desert canyon, steep and twisting to the point of disorientation. Sandstone walls seem to crash down everywhere; sometimes the faces are smooth, sometimes chipped, fractured, cracked and spalled.

At one point, the river swings beneath the roof of a long, arching cave. At another, we pulled ashore to behold more signs of "the ancient ones": maroon pictographs on a slanting wall. Oftentimes there is no shoreline, only the clean, hard contact between flowing water and sheer rocks. High on the canyon rims (1,800 feet overhead) are towers, domes, turrets, spires and the beginnings of a natural arch.

Below Slick Rock Canyon the Dolores flows into Paradox Valley, past the tiny settlement of Bedrock and the end of that first trip. From here, it is still another 70 miles before the river spills into the grand Colorado near Cisco, Utah. All can be run by canoe—all except a violent rapids known as "The Narrows" straddling the state line—though some of it is tricky and tight. There are three more canyons, Red, Mesa and Utah. And many long, lazy stretches where the world dreams along beneath the high desert sun.

Few places in the West offer such an opportunity—a chance to float and shoot a wild river in the desert for a solid week. Signs of civilization are still precious few. Only the communities of Slick Rock, Bedrock and Gateway, plus a paralleling state highway for about 20 miles, significantly change the impression the river must have given Spanish explorers more than two centuries ago.

From the Bradfield Ranch to Slick Rock, the Dolores cannot be run in canoe, only in inflatable raft and kayak. Below, however, it is different save for a single portage—maybe two, for the cautious.

On subsequent trips, I've seen even more wildlife both on shore and from the river. There are many deer here, the mountain lions that prey on them, brilliantly colored collared lizards, duller whiptail lizards, myriad songbirds. On one trip, as we drifted lazily below Gateway beneath ranks of cottonwoods, a pair of bald eagles attacked a great blue heron almost directly above our raft.

The river-running season on the Dolores is comparatively brief, however. Only during the spring snowmelt season, from April into June, does the Dolores carry enough water—and this doesn't happen every year. After July, invariably, the river is drained to a trickle by upstream irrigation diversions near the town of Dolores. If dams are built, as is likely, the season will be even shorter.

In January 1975, legislation cleared Congress and the President authorizing a Wild and Scenic Rivers study of the Dolores, a necessary first step before the river is formally included in the National System. Throughout 1975, that study moved rapidly, though not to the satisfaction of river-runners and conservationists. When recommendations were formalized by the U.S. Forest Service and the Bureau of Outdoor Recreation, only the Bradfield Ranch-to-Bedrock segment, plus the last 30 miles above the Colorado River, were tabbed for Wild and Scenic Rivers status.

While this will preserve the most outstanding reaches of the Dolores (about 140 miles in all), it denies the fact that any river is a living, continuous whole, and this omits protection for the Dolores' headwaters high in Colordao's San Juan Range, and also for a 40-mile desert segment between Bedrock and Gateway.

In addition, an alliance of landowners and ranchers along the river (their holdings are comparatively small) are waging a pitched campaign against any Wild and Scenic Rivers designation for the Dolores. Their voice has already been heard in Congress, where the ultimate fate of this, the last truly classic desert river in the West, will be decided.

The battle promises to be both rough and drawn-out. A national treasure is at stake.

Alive But Not Well

Verne Huser

Poling and paddling northward down the Allagash Waterway, a canoe party knifes through quiet water past ghost conifers half-hidden in the morning mist. Before nightfall they will run rapids, portaging the bigger drops; see moose, deer, and bear. They will hear loons call; camp; and watch the stars wheel overhead. Depending on the season, they will battle blackflies or headwind or shallow-water ledges and rock gardens. More than a century ago, Thoreau cruised the headwaters of this 92-mile corridor through rivers and lakes in northern Maine that today bisects the largest semi-wilderness in the eastern United States. A century before that, the Native Americans whose ancestors created the canoe called this area home, and they still claim much of it . . .

Another party quietly drifts the Eleven Point River in southern Missouri in a johnboat, lazing along the cool, clear, spring-fed stream, enjoying autumn in the ancient Ozark hardwoods. They fish for bass or bluegills, or perhaps hunt or trap along the route. Their craft reflects the skill and design of a hundred-year-old family secret . . .

A wooden dory anchors near a shallow riffle of the Skagit River in Washington's North Cascades, its slicker-coated occupants fishing for steelhead in the soft rain. An inflatable raft full of colorfully garbed, raincoated nature-lovers floats by. Its passengers look for bald eagles that congregate to feed on the spawned-out salmon, even as more of the huge fish struggle upstream to spawn.

Three different rivers in three different parts of the country—each being enjoyed by people in different ways at different levels. All three are part of the National Wild and Scenic Rivers System. Each has been added to the System through a different mechanism, and each is administered by a different agency in a different manner. Diversity is one of the characteristic qualities of any natural system. In many ways, the National Wild and Scenic Rivers System preserves the diversity of rivers, their often-competing uses, and opportunities for the general public to enjoy them in a variety of ways.

A river can be a means of transportation, as it was for early explorers and settlers, who found rivers both a ready means of access to new country and a barrier to their passage. It can also be a means of commerce with foreign markets and of transport for raw materials and finished products.

A river can supply water for industrial and municipal consumption, for irrigating crops and hayfields, for watering livestock and slurrying minerals. It can provide hydroelectric power and cooling water for thermoelectric plants. It can be a sewer for carrying municipal, industrial, and agricultural wastes out of sight and out of mind, or it can be a source of aesthetic pleasure—a ribbon of blue through a concrete city or a pool reflecting wilderness moonlight. Its beauty—in settings both bucolic and industrial—is inspiration to painter and photographer, composer and writer.

A river can serve as habitat for fish and wildlife. And it can serve as a source of food and recreation: fishing, hunting, trapping, swimming, and boating. It can provide sand and gravel—the most abundant mineral mined by man—or reveal the gold stored in its mountain vaults.

A river may be dammed, dewatered, or diverted for any number of uses for the benefit of the human race—or it can be allowed to flow freely to its ultimate goal for other, competing uses. What is the best use of a river? Obviously, that depends on several factors and value systems. And since different people embrace different values at different times, it is often a complex problem to determine the best use of a river.

In 1968, the people of this country decided, through their elected representatives in Washington, DC, that a balance needed to be struck between competing uses. Congress declared that "the established national policy of dam and other construction at appropriate sections of the rivers of the United States needs to be complemented by a policy that would preserve other selected rivers or sections thereof in their free-flowing condition to protect the water quality of such rivers and to fulfill other vital national conservation purposes." The Wild and Scenic Rivers Act was an attempt to legislate a balance among competing uses of American rivers. Obviously, not every river belongs in a protective system, but Congress decided—in 1968—that some rivers do.

The Act declared it to be "the policy of the United States that certain rivers, which, with their immediate environments, possess *outstandingly remarkable* (emphasis mine) scenic, recreational, geologic, fish and wildlife, historic, cultural, or other similar values, shall be preserved in a free-flowing condition, and that they and their immediate environments shall be protected for the benefit and enjoyment of present and future generations."

How are such rivers to be selected? Protected? Initially, eight rivers were designated by Congress as part of the System, with 27 additional rivers listed in a study category (that list has since grown to 88). Two mechanisms were established for adding rivers or river segments to the System: federal legislation and state legislation with the approval of the Secretary of the Interior. Selected rivers were to be studied, then administering agencies were to make recommendations for their inclusion in or exclusion from the System. Inclusion could be in any of three categories in a progressively more protective designation: recreational, scenic, or wild. But the intention of the act was to provide protection for rivers and their immediate environments—a narrow corridor not more than half-a-mile wide—that in effect would allow existing uses to continue but preclude uses which would impair the character of the rivers involved.

The act creating the System selected several cream-of-the-crop rivers but ignored dozens of qualified rivers. During the Nixon-Ford Administration (shortly after the passage of the Act) a more comprehensive mechanism was developed: the Nationwide Rivers Inventory, which examined 1,524 river segments covering nearly 62,000 miles of free-flowing streams (about two percent of all streams in the United States; the 6,943 miles in the System today constitute only about one-fifth of one percent of the river miles in the nation).

The first rivers to be designated under the Act were nicknamed the "Instant Eight:" Middle Fork, Clearwater (ID); Eleven Point (MO); Feather (CA); Rio Grande (NM); Rogue (OR); St. Croix (MN/WI); Middle Fork, Salmon (ID); Wolf (WI). From those initial eight in 1968, the System has grown to include 61 in 23 states at present. Thus 53 rivers have been added: 26 through the Alaska National Interest Lands Conservation Act of 1980, 11 each through the study system and the state mechanism, four through direct Congressional action (the Snake on the Oregon-Idaho border and the Rapid in Idaho as part of the Hells Canyon National Recreation Area Act; the Middle Delaware in New York, New Jersey, and Pennsylvania; and the Missouri in Nebraska and South Dakota), and one as a joint federal-state river (the lower St. Croix).

Of the 88 rivers in the study category, 42 studies have been completed (46 have not). Of the 42 completed studies, 10 resulted in federal designation, two in state designation, and one in joint federal-state designation. Four were found unqualified (the Allegheny and Clarion in Pennsylvania, the Maumee in Indiana, and the Cahaba in Alabama). Two others were found to qualify but were not recommended: the Big Thompson in Colorado (because it is already protected as part of Rocky Mountain National Park) and the Sweetwater in Wyoming (because it is too short at less than 10 miles—even though it was an important part of the historic Oregon Trail).

Thirteen reports recommended state or local designation, and 10 reports recommended federal action that has not yet been taken by Congress. For all of its base in law, the National Wild and Scenic Rivers System is obviously a political system subject to political changes. Eight rivers were added during the Johnson Administration (the original eight); 12 were added during the Nixon-Ford Administration (four under Nixon, eight under Ford); 41 during the Carter Administration; and none to date under Reagan. (In mid-September, the Administration recommended inclusion of eight more rivers into the system. The eight, however, are still in the proposal stage.)

This thumbnail analysis is misleading, however, because it takes some time for a new mechanism to begin to function properly. The act allowed 10 years for the original studies to be completed, one reason the Carter Administration could claim such an impressive record—the System simply reached fruition then, and the Alaskan rivers were added to nearly double the System. Conversely, one reason so few rivers were added during the Nixon and Ford years is that the mechanism for adding rivers was not yet in place and few of the studies had been completed.

Now, however, the mechanisms are in place and the studies have either been made or are under way. But the expansion of the System has slowed down—just as the economy has slowed. Studies have gone begging for funds; land acquisitions have been dropped; management plans for existing rivers in the System have not been developed or implemented; and the mechanisms for adding rivers to the System have been largely ignored. The National Wild and Scenic Rivers System is in place, but it is not well.

Many would place the blame on Secretary of the Interior James Watt, who knows the System well. In its early days when the Bureau of Outdoor Recreation was responsible for the system, Watt headed that agency. When he became Secretary, he abolished the Heritage Conservation and Recreation Service, which at the time had policy review for the System. That responsibility subsequently shifted to the National Park Service (also within Interior)—though several rivers are administered by the Forest Service (Agriculture) and at least one by the Army Corps of Engineers (Defense).

And though the budgets for the National Park Service, Fish and Wildlife Service, and Bureau of Land Management—all involved in administering the System—have all been reduced, the Bureau of Reclamation, Interior's dam-building agency, has had its budget increased by Congress above and beyond Watt's requests (from $742.3 million to $771.2 million for FY 1982, with $950.3 million requested for FY 1983).

The National Wild and Scenic Rivers System is not a high priority with Congress or the Reagan Administration—or, for that matter, with the American people. Given the Reagan budget and the current economic climate, that may be understandable. Several politicians who have tested the water find little enthusiasm for expanding the System at present. In some quarters at least, there seem to be higher priorities.

Has the general public changed its priorities since 1968? Can the nation no longer afford to protect selected rivers? Are we too poor to seek the balance that the National Wild and Scenic Rivers System was directed to seek 14 years ago? Is the present economic atmosphere so unfavorable to protecting rivers in a free-flowing condition that the System will not survive?

The answers to all these questions lie with the people of the United States. If they are willing to sacrifice the System to temporary circumstances, then the System is in deep trouble. Only the people who use rivers can make that determination—through their elected representatives in Washington and in their respective state capitals, for roughly half the states have their own protective systems for rivers.

As a nation, we have been building a balance for more than two centuries: through a civil war, two world wars, and numerous economic disasters. Even as a river constantly seeks a dynamic equilibrium, so the nation may respond to the current circumstances and continue to protect selected rivers and continue to select rivers to protect. The present problems may be merely another rapid to negotiate, an eddy in the gravity-induced flow toward completion of the System, a rock garden that high-water flows will obviate as the System returns to health.

The National Wild and Scenic Rivers System gives us pride in our history and cultural heritage, offers us recreational pleasure, and provides us with the diversity that helps us find balance in our own lives.

The Big Drops
Robert O. Collins and Roderick Nash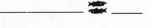

Robert O. Collins and Roderick Nash were both profes-
sors of history at the University of California, Santa
Barbara, in 1970 when I ran the Salmon River with them.
Both men continue their tenure at the University, Collins
in administration and Nash in the classroom. Both are
experienced river runners.

It is Nash, whom I have known since the summer of
1957, when we worked at Jackson Lake Lodge in Grand
Teton National Park, who wrote the chapter on Clavey
Falls and with whom I had my first taste of the Tuolumne
in the spring of 1980. Author of Wilderness and the American Mind *and several other books on conservation history,*
Nash is an authority on wilderness management, a term
which he sees as contradictory.

He and I have shared trips on the Selway and the Snake,
have rowed the Colorado through Grand Canyon and sat
around many a campfire talking about this book and
embattled rivers like the Tuolumne, which is even now
threatened by new hydro-development projects.

We said there warn't no home like a raft, after
all. Other places do seem so cramped up and
smothery, but a raft don't. You feel mighty free
and easy and comfortable on a raft.

MARK TWAIN

Along with large rocks, gravel bars, and resistant bedrock
formations, a river's rate of descent creates Big Drops. The
slope of a stream is usually measured in feet per mile, and some
comparisons are useful in putting the Tuolumne (pronounced to-OL-
uh-mee) River and Clavey Falls into perspective.

A mature river like the Mississippi lumbers from St. Louis to New
Orleans at a rate of descent of about two feet per mile—just enough

to keep Old Man River rolling along. The Colorado is a much younger, hence steeper, watercourse. Through the Grand Canyon of Arizona it drops 2,167 feet in 279 miles, an average of just under eight feet per mile. Water flowing down this kind of slope produces an alternating pattern of major rapids follwed by mile-long calm stretches. Oregon's Rogue River averages 12.4 feet per mile, and its rapids are steeper and more frequent than those of the Grand Canyon. A still sharper rate of descent is found on the Middle Fork of the Salmon River in Idaho, which races downstream at an average of 27 feet per mile. In high water conditions, a river like this, or the Selway, just to the north, seems like one continuous rapid.

Then there is the Tuolumne. Pounding down a deep canyon through the golden foothills of California's Sierra Nevada, this river's runnable section drops 54 feet per miles, or seven times the rate of the Colorado in the Grand Canyon and twice the rate of the Middle Fork. Particularly during high water, many boatmen regard the Tuolumne as the most challenging raftable river in the West. It is a relentless force, with rapids blending one into the other; only occasionally can a boatman escape the grip of the current to catch his breath and ease strained muscles. Then, as he looks back upstream, the Tuolumne appears to be a white staircase descending the Sierra.

The unusual name of this unusual river has its origins in the local Indian dialect. *Talmalamne* meant a cluster of stone wigwams. But given the multipurpose functions of most aboriginal words, *talmalamne* may well have referred to the circle of tepee-shaped granite peaks that form the main crest of the Sierra at the Tuolumne's source. Mount Lyell, 13,114 feet, is one such pointed landmark. The meltwater of two small glaciers clinging to its northwestern face starts the river.

In the next phase of its 158-mile length, the Tuolumne lives in high country, flowing through forested valleys that spread out at 8,600 feet into the largest upland meadow in the Sierra. A paved road brings thousands of visitors to Tuolumne Meadows every summer. Below this point, however, the river is seldom seen as it enters Muir Gorge and rages along the bed of a deep, precipitous canyon. A century ago John Muir scrambled through here, the din of falling water pounding in his ears. No one boats the Tuolumne at this elevation.

At 3,800 feet—still in Yosemite National Park—the river dies for a time. In 1913, after a protracted controversy, Congress authorized a dam at the lower end of Hetch Hetchy Valley. Completed ten years later, it created a granite-walled reservoir in a place once considered the aesthetic equal of Yosemite Valley, a few miles to the south. Many people today believe the Tuolumne ends in the Hetch Hetchy impoundment, its water diverted into aqueducts and destined for power plants, irrigation ditches, and the pipes and faucets of San Francisco. Some of the Tuolumne does, of course, go this route, but enough water remains in the river below Hetch Hetchy to make possible one of the West's most exciting whitewater rides. Indeed, to give the dam builders their due, the released water from hydroelectric operations has the beneficial effect of making the Tuolumne runnable in California's dry summer months.

Thirteen river [miles] below the Hetch Hetchy spillways, the Tuolumne can be run by experts in kayaks, decked whitewater canoes, and modified rafts. Eight miles farther, at Lumsden Camp, the increasing amount of water and decreasing rate of descent usually permit the use of standard inflatable rafts. Barring mishaps, it takes only two hours to run the five miles to Clavey Falls, but the Tuolumne can spoil the best laid plans. Regardless of their skill, first-time boatmen on the Tuolumne pay their initiation dues to the river in the form of broken oars, upsets, and torn boats. The United States Forest Service, which manages the river once it leaves Yosemite National Park, used to place its registration box not at the put-in, but after the first two rapids, on the theory that any boatman who reached the registration point in one piece was either good enough or lucky enough to have a reasonable chance of completing the run.

The Tuolumne moves so quickly and drops so precipitously around so many blind corners that boatmen require several runs to decipher its obstacle course. The rapids present several possible channels and the need for an instant decision in very fast water. The wrong choice is quicky rewarded, and the unfortunate boatman is left draped around a rock, pinned on a log, or overturned at the base of an eight-foot waterfall. It is, of course, possible to walk down and scout the whitewater ahead, but how much river can one memorize? The Tuolumne's rapids are so long and complex that keeping a planned route in mind is extremely difficult. Once on the racing water, chosen landmarks or "keys" blur into a pastiche of waves, rocks, and shoreline vegetation. Moreover, the Tuolumne is what boatmen call a "technical" river. It consistently demands a degree of precision in rowing and finesse in reading and running fast water, seldom required on the larger western rivers. Broken boats and bodies are commonplace on the Tuolumne. Those theoretical two hours to Clavey Falls can easily become two days, and Clavey can put a permanent end to a river journey.

Just above Clavey Falls the Tuolumne relents a bit, as if to anticipate its biggest drop. After threading slots only inches wider than the raft and setting up to ride down a succession of sudden, sharp ledges, it is a blessing to sit at the oars and look at the scenery. Then ahead on the right appears a flash of whitewater that first-timers mistake for Clavey Falls. It is, rather, the last few yards of the Clavey River, blasting through boulders to make a grand entrance into the Tuolumne.

The Clavey is a major tributary with branches reaching sixty river miles to the top of 9,000-foot ridges north of the Tuolumne's canyon. The name comes from an English immigrant, William Clavey, whose widow and son tried to run cattle from the 1890s to the 1940s in the chaparral-choked foothills between the Tuolumne and the river that bears their name. The Clavey funnels water and, during storms, large rocks, down a very steep gradient along the north side of Jawbone Ridge. Tumbling into the Tuolumne, these boulders make Clavey Falls. The Tuolumne powers through them and smashes into a sheer, two-hundred-foot cliff opposite the mouth of the Clavey River. The cliff restrains the river, forcing it into the boulders. The result is a long, spectacular clash of an irresistable force against an immovable object that leaves even the most hardened boatmen stunned when they see it for the first time.

Clavey Falls is divided into two main channels by a large island of boulders that clogs the middle of the Tuolumne. The flow on the right side is larger, but leaps fifteen feet down a rock-studded chute into a maelstrom of green and white. The vertical drop of the left channel is only half that of the main falls on the right, but a left-side run brings boats dangerously close to the base of the cliff and its churning whirlpools. Below the boulder island, the right and left channels converge just in time to plunge through a formidable hole, and twenty feet farther on, the current splits savagely around a large rock. Below this obstacle come two sharp drops in low water or a series of large standing waves in high, and finally a tight, rocky bend to the left. From the top of the main falls to the bend is almost a third of a mile.

The challenge of running Clavey Falls begins with the landing to scout the rapid. Because of the cliff, scouting must be done from the right shoreline, which also features the Clavey River confluence. Usually the Clavey is too fast and too deep to ford safely, so the only alternative is to remain in the boats until its mouth is passed and then pull to the right bank. The maneuver sounds easier than it is since only thirty feet separate the Clavey confluence and the start of the fast water at the top of Clavey Falls; moreover, the Clavey enters the Tuolumne with a force sufficient to kick a boat into the main current and propel it straight for the falls. With everyone intensely aware of the Big Drop just ahead, there can be momentary panic as the boatman powerstrokes onto the little gravel beach just a few yards from the brink.

With bow lines tied and double-tied to brush or a boulder, it is time to go and look at Clavey Falls. Styles vary. Some boatmen dash down the shoreline, leaping rocks and splashing through small pools. They hurry to wait, unmoving, on the ledge below which the main falls thunder. Others try to play it cooler, perhaps lighting a smoke or joking with passengers; but soon they too stand silently on the ledge over the falls. By unspoken agreement boatmen at first say little in such situations. Their eyes move constantly, searching for routes. After a time someone will venture an opinion. It will be discussed, modified, and discussed again with much pointing and even stone-tossing in an effort to pinpoint a location in the rapid.

On a right-side run the first difficulty is the small rocks above the main falls. The boatman must pick his way through them carefully in order to reach the lip of the falls with his bow pointed straight down the only clear chute. Too far right and he will plunge into a churning white vortex that could hold an overturned boat and its former passengers indefinitely. If he misses the chute in the other direction, the boat will hurtle over the lip of the falls to smash on the jumble of sharp, black rocks in the center of the river. The least serious mistake is to slip into the main chute sideways; the boat will simply capsize and its occupants swim the rest of Clavey Falls. Entered correctly, boats in the chute tilt sharply downward at angles approaching sixty degrees. Standing almost vertically on his foot brace, the boatman anticipates the jolt at the bottom on the fall. Two water-covered ledges flash by underneath, then dagger-sharp rocks appear to the left and right. Oars are useless at this point. Even if a boat impelled by such force could be controlled, the amount of air beaten into the water by the fall makes it futile to dig and pull a blade; you cannot pull against bubbles and foam. Accurate prior positioning is the only key to a successful passage through the top of Clavey.

The alternate way to run the first part of these falls is down the left-hand channel, to the left of the boulder island and close to the cliff. In low water this run is mandatory. It begins with a row across the Tuolumne; there is a little room on the left bank before the cliff to land and read the water. At first glance it appears impossible to get a boat through the jumble of table-size rocks with which this route through the rapid begins. The lesser of many evils seems to be a narrow, twisting passage about fifteen feet out from the shore. The current is fast here, and the boatman must pivot repeatedly to keep from jamming his raft against a rock. There is little room to maneuver. Broken oars are a distinct possibility, and to lose control in this way would be disastrous since the twisting slot drops boats into a foaming pool just above the falls. There is only time for one, perhaps two, strokes, and they must accomplish two things: keep the boat off the cliff face and straighten it for the plunge over the fall. The frightening price of not making effective use of the moment in the pool is to have a boat pinned into a crevice in the cliff. Held as in a vise by the raging current, the boat fills with water and either capsizes or moves sluggishly sideways over the fall to a probable flip.

Once below this fall, the worst may seem to be over, but Clavey holds more surprises. One moment a boat is ten feet out from the cliff in five-foot waves and more or less in control, the next it is up against the rock wall. The explanation is the powerful current pouring down the right side of the rapid and intersecting the left-hand route at this point. Anything floating, such as a riverboat, goes along for an unwelcome ride headlong into the cliff. Only by anticipating the sideways blast, angling the boat, and rowing hard can boatmen avoid eating rock. It is no different for boats using the right channel. So great is their speed coming off the chute over the main falls that they are propelled straight across the Tuolumne and into the cliff.

Some boatmen try to fight the hydraulics and keep off the cliff. It is also possible to go with the flow and play the cliff as one would the side of a pool table, deliberately allowing the boat to ricochet and, according to the angle of rebound, making the necessary adjustments to ride through what is known as "the big hole in Clavey." A large rock, eight feet off the cliff, is the problem. In low water it is exposed, inviting boats to wrap around its upstream side; quick thinking and rowing are essential to dodge it on either side. Higher flows cover the rock, but creates a monster hole. Most boatmen simply straighten out and slam into its center. They know their rubber boats will fold into a "V," but they count on the speed of the current to spit them out on the downstream side.

All that now remains of Clavey Falls is a long, dragon-shaped rock with a sharp upstream edge that can slice rubber like a razor, and another hundred yards of waves and ledges. Invariably a boat is so heavy with water at this point that control is difficult. With a final effort the boatman pulls to the right and attempts to land in the fast water along the steep right bank. Many fail in this endeavor and are obliged to run several hundred more yards through another, very rocky rapid before they can relax.

Within a half day's drive of fifteen million people, it is remarkable that the Tuolumne was not run until the 1960s. The first known attempt was that of a group of fishermen from Sacramento who thought it would be easier to float the river than walk along its banks. They were in for a big surprise. By the time they reached Clavey Falls both boats and morale were in tatters, and they wisely portaged the Big Drop. Their report, and that of the few hikers who reached the bottom of the Tuolumne's canyon, discouraged river runners until 1965, when Knoel Debord, a Sierra Club member from Oakland, took a kayak down the river. Debord portaged Clavey, as did Gerald Meral and Richard Sunderland on November 4, 1968, when they took kayaks down the Tuolumne. Meral and Sunderland did, however, exercise the privilege of pioneers and name several pools and rapids. Excited by what they had seen in the canyon, the men returned the following May and, with Jim Morehouse, kayaked the river. Its flow was 4,800 cubic feet per second—ideal for an attempt at the right channel in Clavey Falls—but inexperience bred conservatism, and again they carried their boats around the rapid. The first known run of Clavey occurred on July 20, 1969, at a flow of 4,000 cubic feet per second. Sierra Club kayakers, including a fourteen-year-old girl named India Fleming, made the run without incident.

The summer of 1969 also marked the beginning of rafting on the Tuolumne. Bryce Whitmore, a veteran California river outfitter, had been searching for an alternative to the Stanislaus River for his commercial trips. He wanted a longer, more challenging journey on a less crowded river. Whitmore and a team of his best boatmen tested the Tuolumne for a week in late July and found the flat "Huck Finn" rafts they used quite capable of handling the river. At Clavey, however, they lined the rafts down the right shoreline. The next season Whitmore scheduled several trips on the Tuolumne, but his brochure carried the warning that the river "requires the best equipment, most skilled oarsmen, and lightly loaded rafts." The run, he added, was "not recommended for your first whitewater trip, or for the faint hearted." But, he concluded, the Tuolumne offered more thrills and more challenge than any eighteen river miles in the American West. Few who made the run with Whitmore disagreed, even though they continued to line their boats around Clavey Falls.

In May 1970 the authors became the first rafters to run Clavey Falls. Bryce Whitmore told us the Tuolumne run would take lots of time, and that was an understatement. We spent hours crashing through thickets of manzanita and poison oak along the river to study its rapids, but we still had trouble. One of our boats ripped open on a rock, lost air, and wallowed helplessly down a quarter mile of rock-strewn waves. Another wrapped around a rock, filled with several tons of water, and had to be extricated with fixed ropes from shore. Running scared by the time we reached Clavey Falls, we landed well above on the right and barely managed to stumble across the torrent coming down the Clavey River. The sight of the rapid left us limp; there seemed no way it could be run. We paced the right shoreline again and again, memorizing the rocks, waves, and currents.

Today's perspective is different, but since no one had yet put a raft down this Big Drop, we would not be sure if a boat would make it down the falls, between the rocks, and through the big hole. At length we decided to portage and walked back to where the boats were tied. But our minds continued to churn, and as we reached the boats we turned to look back downstream to where the Tuolumne vanished into the space above Clavey Falls. "Why not?" we thought simultaneously. After all, we had come to run, not walk, the Tuolumne, and it was precisely challenges like this that had brought us to wild rivers in the first place.

Once we were committed, the run went smoothly enough. It was unnerving above the falls, slaloming through random rocks, aiming for a chute we saw only in our memories. At what seemed like the last possible second, the chute opened ahead of us. For a moment we hung poised on the brink. Then, unbelievable speed. The rocks we had studied from shore for so long went past in a blur. Ahead was the cliff: we leaned on the ten-foot oars, not really rowing but straining, in a kind of isometric exercise, against a constant force. Even so, one boat glanced off the rock wall. The beauty of inflatables is that they bounce rather than shatter or dent, and this time we won the billiard game between rubber and rock. Rebounding off the cliff, the raft spun into perfect position for the big hole. It seemed much larger on the river than it had from the shore, but there was a thread of water moving through the reversing wave. We adjusted to hit it square on; then, with Grand Canyon instincts, we pushed with the oars to increase the raft's momentum going into the hole, thus giving it a better chance of popping through. It did, but knee-deep with water, and there was no time and no one to bail. We struggled to keep the unwieldy craft facing downstream as we plowed over and through the lower waves and ledges. In one sense the weight was a blessing—a boat carrying an extra ton of water has a low center of gravity and is very hard to flip. In landing such a heavy boat, however, you pay the price. Only after several abortive attempts could we make the raft stick into a semblance of an eddy along the right shore, leap out, take a turn with the bow line around a rock, and notice our hands shake as we tied up.

In time others came to try their hands at Clavey Falls. Some got through and some did not, but everyone learned this was a "boatman's" as opposed to an "equipment" rapid. The distinction is clear and important. On big water, such as the Grand Canyon's Lava Falls, the equipment brings you through. A big boat compensates for the boatman's mistakes; it may get pounded, but it will float out the downstream end right side up. It is almost (but not quite) impossible to flip one of the giant thirty-three-foot pontoons, or multiple pontoons. These big rigs are usually run straight down the middle of a rapid. They eat every hole, yet they flush out. Try the same technique on the Tuolumne, and your trip, if not your life, will end in the first mile. The Tuolumne is a "boatman's" river because expertise in reading whitewater and rowing it precisely is mandatory for a successful run. A mile on the Tuolumne calls for more maneuvering than a hundred miles on the Colorado. But with Sierra snowfields melting down the Tuolumne in May and June, it is sometimes the case that neither big boats nor skilled boatmen ensure a safe passage.

One June a few years ago a group of campers near the Tuolumne put-in were startled by the sudden appearance at their evening fire of a boatman who worked for a leading western river outfitter. He seemed shaken, but after several cups of coffee began the story of his day at Clavey Falls. Because of the high water his company had canceled its scheduled trip and bused the would-be passengers out of the canyon. The boatmen, however, decided to run for their own fun. There were two boats: a rowed raft carrying two men and a stripped-down boat which five persons attempted to steer with canoe paddles. With many of the Tuolumne's rocks covered by the high water, they shot down to Clavey Falls in an hour. No one had ever attempted the Big Drop with so much water in the river, but the crew was in a "go for it" mood. The raft with oars ran first, careening down the main falls and somehow negotiating the quarter mile of ten-foot waves beyond. The paddled raft ran second, with the boatman at the campfire among its crew. He was washed over the side below the main falls and recalled nothing but an occasional gasp for air until he was pulled from the river by the rowers at the end of the rapid. The three men waited and waited, peering upstream for a sight of the paddled raft and the four remaining members of the group. Nothing appeared, and, fearing the worst, they ran up the right shoreline. Still no raft. Then they saw it, pinned into an eddy against the cliff and trapped so securely that the four remaining paddlers were helpless in their efforts to work back into the downstream flow. The possibility of their swamping and drowning in that whirlpool was desperately evident. The cliff prevented any rescue from river level, so the three on the right shoreline ran back to their boat, crossed the Tuolumne in calmer water below Clavey, and climbed the back side of the cliff with a long rope and some rock-climbing hardware known as Jumar ascenders. Locating a big ponderosa pine on the top of the cliff directly over the beleaguered boat, the rescuers tied on and lowered their rope. One by one the people on the river climbed the line a hundred vertical feet to safety. The last task was to pull the empty raft up the cliff and carry it below Clavey Falls.

Whitewater boating had barely begun on the Tuolumne when it seemed destined to end. On December 4, 1968, the San Francisco Public Utilities Commission released a report proposing more intensive use of the river's "remaining power drop" for hydroelectric generation. A new dam below the one already restraining the river at Hetch Hetchy Valley was proposed, along with a series of tunnels and a generating plant right at Clavey Falls. Actually this was repetition, not innovation. In 1907 the Tuolumne Electric Company erected a hand-fitted stone powerhouse a mile below Clavey. It supplied electricity to rim communities until 1938, when a giant storm put 38,000 cubic feet per second in the Tuolumne and cleaned out all but the foundations of the bridge and building.

Initially San Francisco's 1968 proposal did not elicit much opposition. Few knew what was at stake, but the Sierra Club, remembering Hetch Hetchy like the Alamo, was instinctively suspicious of the city's plans for the river. Rather than build new dams, the Club argued that the existing ones on the Tuolumne should be removed. As Michael McCloskey explained, "We've already had the experience of reclaiming logged-over land for parks. We think it's time the same concept be applied to dams." By the early 1970s McCloskey, along with many environmentally conscious Americans, was asking quite seriously if dams added to or detracted from the quality of a society's life. In a state that had intensively utilized its flowing water and, in the case of the Stanislaus River, was about to eliminate its most popular whitewater run, a wild Tuolumne was an especially precious resource. The United States Congress, at least, held this view. On January 3, 1975, it designated the Tuolumne a "study" river for the National Wild and Scenic Rivers System. This action placed a moratorium on further development and mandated public hearings. Congress will ultimately decide the issue (probably not before 1980), and Clavey Falls has a fighting chance at a future of turning boats rather than turbines.

Meanwhile the rapid continues to generate improbable stories. One evening Bryce Whitmore camped several miles below Clavey on the big beach opposite Indian Creek. As the rafts were being unloaded, it became painfully clear that the box of cooking pots was missing. To his chagrin Whitmore remembered leaving it in his garage at home. Lacking the means even to boil water for coffee, the party scoured the bushes for rusted pots prospectors might have abandoned, or any container that would hold water. As dusk fell, Whitmore saw a box floating down the middle of the Tuolumne. Someone rowed out and brought it into camp. To the astonishment of the hungry campers, it contained a complete set of pots and pans. There was no explanation, except prayers, for its presence until several other packs and bags appeared in the river. Then an overturned raft floated past. Whitmore towed it to shore, but found no sign of its former occupants. By this time it was dark and dinner was simmering in the newly acquired pots; then out of the darkness came a shout from upstream, and into the circle of firelight staggered four disheveled river runners. They told how they had flipped in the big hole in Clavey that afternoon. Their boat had continued on downstream too fast to follow on foot through the Tuolumne's dense riparian vegetation, so there was no alternative but to walk on down the river in the hope of finding the boat caught in an eddy. Just as they were about to give up the search and climb out of the canyon, they saw the light of Whitmore's fire through the trees. Dinner, served from their own pots, never tasted better.

Run, River, Run

Ann Zwinger

Ann Zwinger, whose sketches grace the pages of this book, happens to be one of my favorite writers. Her books make me miss my bus stop as I ride to work in Seattle.

When I read Run, River, Run *shortly after it was published, I was so thrilled by the book—its fabric of history and geology, fauna and flora intermixed with the flow of the Green River—that I wrote to the author and we've been corresponding ever since.*

Her other books include Beyond the Aspen Grove, Wind in the Rock, *and* A Conscious Stillness *(with Edwin Way Teale), a book about a couple of Thoreau's rivers. Her book about Baja, California,* A Desert Country Near the Sea, *has just been released, and she is working on a book of letters written by Xantus, "a crazy Hungarian who lived at San Lucas 1859–61 and wrote letters to Spencer Baird, for whom he collected scientific samples." She's remarkable in her energy, always working on a writing project or illustrations for a book or for her own pleasure.*

The afternoon river is golden and olive and clear, the surface netted with debris from rising water. Ripples pattern the sandy bottom, sinking into shadowed pools. Three feet beneath, crisp dark fronds weave in all the various filamentous, intertwining subsurface currents. Often a single plant grows, forming a mound on the bottom, where it catches sand that builds up around its roots. As the current flows over, it tends to form a vortex that eats away sand on the downstream side, eventually loosening the plant and tumbling it away. Since underwater plants spread largely by vegetative means, the tufts and handfuls floating in the currents beneath help to colonize downstream.

On the left bank, the stone building beneath the cottonwoods was the old Jarvie store, modernized with an irrigation pump and a new trailer. John Jarvie, who established the first post office in the park and ran the store here, was murdered by a half-breed and his partner in 1909, the body set adrift in a skiff, a grisly flotsam found months later in Lodore Canyon. One of the few ferry crossings in Browns Park lay between Jesse Ewing Creek and the Jarvie Ranch, where the river banks are open and low. A mile below is the site of abandoned Bridgeport Post Office, Browns Park's connection with the outside world between 1881 and 1887. After it was closed the lack of mail delivery isolated the park's inhabitants; mail could be brought in monthly from Vernal, at $50 a run, but the road was so hazardous in winter that the postman refused to deliver. Another short-lived post office was established in 1889 on the Bassett ranch, and after that the mail came only weekly from Maybell, Colorado, until modern rural free delivery.

Whiskey Creek slips in through a terrace that it has notched deeply. In recent years many of the streams of Browns Park have renewed downcutting. The result is a lowering of the water table and a change from the grasslands, so characteristic of the park in trapper days, to the greasewood deserts we find when we get off river.

Thinking that the rapids are over, I am pleasantly surprised to hear the river's burbling float upstream and to enter a narrow rock-studded reach. Although the current switches through the rocks, the river steers us and we bob and swivel through. The rock-garden rapids precede the windless respite of Swallow Canyon. Now that the birds are gone for the year, it seems ghostly quiet. It is a small, charming canyon cut through a spur of the Uinta Mountains that projects northward. This whole area was once covered by the softer layers of the Browns Park Formation, on which an ancient river system initially established its course. When the river cut completely through, it reached the harder quartzites of the Uinta Mountain Group beneath. Confined in a channel determined originally in the softer strata, it continued cutting in the same channel, into this spur, a geologic process defined by Powell as superposition.

On a low ledge toward the mouth of the canyon, a beaver works on his lodge, stuffing sticks under a triangular overhang, the only one we see in Browns Park. Crouse Creek enters the river just below the mouth of Swallow Canyon, a lovely shaded slot of a canyon with green thickets. Butch Cassidy allegedly had a cabin high on a sandstone ledge up the canyon where Mrs. Crouse delivered jam and goodies. Perhaps, in a time of more open hospitality, Cassidy was a personable addition to a lonely, isolated household. Or perhaps the fact that he often left his hostess a five- or ten-dollar gold piece under his plate assured him of a devoted welcome wherever he hitched his horse.

Gunnison Butte rises on the right skyline, a reminder that Green

River, Utah, was once called Gunnison's Crossing, after Captain John
W. Gunnison. The original crossing was one of the few places for
miles in either direction where there was a stable bottom and easy
access to the river. Used as a ford by the Utes from times unknown,
it became one of the major fords on the Old Spanish Trail, that began
in Santa Fe and ran northwest to this crossing. At best never more
than a trail, the Old Spanish Trail was practical and usable during the
spring, summer, and fall. So much stolen livestock traversed it in the
1820s and 1830s that it earned the sobriquet of "Horsethief Trail." It
was not until the winter of 1830–31, when William Wolfskill led
twenty-one trappers west, that it was opened all the way from New
Mexico to California.

The acquisition of Oregon in 1846, the termination of the war with
Mexico in 1848, and the rush of gold seekers in 1849 pressured for
better communication and transportation between the Mississippi
River and the West Coast. At the close of the 31st Congress in 1852,
an appropriation was made for a railroad survey, and in March of the
following year exploration was authorized to follow a central route
suggested by Senator Thomas Hart Benton. Although Benton would
have preferred his son-in-law, Frémont, to be appointed, Captain
Gunnison was made head of the small survey group that included a
botanist, a geologist, a cartographer, and a military escort.

The expedition was directed to the Old Spanish Trail crossing of
the Green River by an Indian guide. Here Gunnison was to split the
expedition into two parties, one under his command, the other under
Lieutenant Edwin Beckwith, who described the crossing:

> We crossed the river by an excellent ford, which we had
> observed the Indians crossing, from a few yards below our
> camp (on the Spanish Trail) to an island opposite, and from
> its upper end to the shore. The river is 300 yards wide, with
> a pebbly bottom, as we forded it, but with quicksands on
> either side of our path. The water, rising just above the
> axletrees of our common wagons, flows with a strong
> current, and is colored by the red sandstone of the country
> through which it passes, having here the same red muddy
> character which the Colorado has far below, where it enters
> the Gulf of California.

Gunnison and his small party proceeeded to the Sevier River. There
all were ambushed by a group of revengeful Indians, Gunnison shot
while he knelt and washed his face in the river. None survived.
Beckwith took the remainder of the expedition to Salt Lake City,

where they wintered. They returned east the next spring, going north to cross the Green River above the Uinta Mountains. They followed it nearly to its source, preceding the Hayden Survey by twenty-six years.

A pump transfers water from the river to a broad farm on the right bank. In the West, water rights must be applied for, and can change hands quite apart from the land on which the water is used, in sharp distinction to an eastern water owner's more permanent and absolute, or riparian, rights. In the East, rainfall normally exceeds evaporation, and the riparian doctrine gives the owner of the streamside property exclusive rights to its "natural use." Where water is plentiful, this system is practical. But west of the ninety-seventh meridian water is scarce, and the doctrine of prior appropriation holds: the state ordinarily possesses title to all water within its borders, and individuals appropriate it on a basis of "first in time, first in rights," and these rights may be forfeited by non-use. Irrigation rights carry a limitation of cubic feet, adjusted so that users up and down the river may remove specified amounts, which are both sufficient to needs and will not overtax the amount available.

In the Gunnison Valley agriculture can be successful only with irrigation since rainfall ranges between five and ten inches yearly. Although there are some excellent bottomlands, their extent is limited, and individual tracts are often small and irregular; in addition, those up canyon are isolated. Much of the remainder of the land is poorly drained and patched with alkali, the Mancos Shale flooring forming a variable soil that has a tendency when wet to imbibe roads, air strips, and miscellaneous farm machinery. Rustlers ingeniously took only small groups of cattle through at a time during the wet season, or made a circuitous trip to avoid leaving track molds that hardened into cemented evidence until the next gully washer. In fact, the landscape looks today just as it looked to Dr. James Schiel, geologist with the Gunnison expedition, in 1853:

> There could be no thought of any subsistence by the hunt, for one can travel for weeks without finding any game besides a pair of lonely jackdaws, or a few contented lizards, which seem to represent the animal life here. . . . The soil is so dry and bad that even the fields of artemisia and cacti, which in the Grand River territory are a nuisance for the traveler, disappear soon and only single specimens remind us of their existence.

A familiar sound comes upriver, that of a rapid, yet somehow steadier. Ahead a straight line of dancing water marks the top of a diversion dam. The raft slips down the spillway into the continuous smack of a three-foot backwave. On the left bank a big waterwheel stands silent. When the Kolbs came through in 1911, Ellsworth noted several waterwheels along the river here, some

> twenty feet or more in height,—with slender metal buckets each holding several gallons of water, fastened at intervals on either side,—were placed in a swift current, anchored on the shore to stout piles, or erected over mill-races cut in the banks. There they revolved, the buckets filling and emptying automatically, the water running off in troughs above the level of the river back to the fertile soil.

Around the farmhouse, iris and peonies are blooming. Years ago a housewife put her mark on the river and it blooms every spring.

As we approach town, gutted, wheelless cars lie like grotesque carnage on the river bank, piled there to keep the new shorter channel, cut when the highway bridge was built, from shifting. The roofs of Green River appear through the trees. Founded officially in 1878 as a mail relay station between Salina, Utah, and Ouray, Colorado, it is one of the few Utah towns without a Mormon background.

An apocryphal story avers that Gunnison Butte once bore a profile closely resembling that of Brigham Young. Since the town was a railroad community rather than a congregation of the faithful, the profile received less than proper respect. One dark night, after a lengthy session of hundred-proof debate, it is said that some of the more energetic of the town's notables made their unsteady way to the appropriate promontory, and with a little dynamite surgery irrevocably altered the Butte's configuration.

I walk away from the lookout and face upriver. Even with a group, it is possible to have a great deal of time alone with the river. I sit on the edge of the Chinle parapet and dangle my feet over the side. It occurs to me, somewhat vaguely, that I who am normally afraid of heights am sitting comfortably above a large segment of empty space. The cottonwoods below follow the river's curve in an esker of green. The river is brown and the clanking hot shale beneath my hand is gray-green. I should be writing or drawing, recording, but I can only ponder, feeling immobilized by the weight of the sunlight on my back. Rock, tree, sky, a hand shadow on the page, a morning breeze, a sunlight-webbed river: I suppose it is the proportions that count, how much is stone, strong, how much is green, yielding, and how much is river, going on and never coming back.

The Green River, at this time of moderately heavy runoff, is probably carrying more than half its silt load for the year. The average load held in suspension by the river is estimated at 19 tons a year, plus 2.5 million tons dissolved. The silt content near the mouth of the Green, by volume, was once estimated at 0.5 percent; it seems a minute amount, but evenly distributed by the current it forms an effective screen, creating the year-round turbidity in the river from the Gates of Lodore south.

The sandpaper surface of the rock, unslicked by algae, provides a sense of stability in a flowing, swirling, moving world. How to explain the pure delight of being here—some of it no doubt stems from the fact that, after a day of unrelenting sunshine, almost any kind of ablution feels welcome. But there is an ineffable sybaritic pleasure beyond the necessity. The cool slide of water slips down the back of my neck, down my arm, drips off my elbow, picks patterns on the river's surface. The water that tugs around my ankles is pure hedonistic enticement, issuing a reminder of downriver delights in a branch that bobs by, on its way to other appointments.

After seeing ruins all day, I am extremely conscious of those who came here before me. So too, on a warm spring evening, a thousand years ago, someone must have stood like this, soothing calloused feet, cactus-scratched legs. I feel no time interval, no difference in flesh between who stood here then and who stands here now. The same need exists for the essentials of food and shelter, the same need to communicate and to put down symbols for someone else to see, and, so I cannot help but believe, the same response to cool water and warm sun and heated rock and sandstone on bare feet.

The last rays of the sun keep it warm enough to air dry. The sun hangs for a moment above the cliff. As it disappears behind the rim, the air cools. And yet it is not cold; maybe time to robe and leave, but not yet, not cold yet. As long as I can stand, ankle deep, without civilization, without defense, going back to self, as long as there is yet enough warmth in the air to respect needful body temperature, so long as possible I stand here, submerged physically only to the ankles, psychologically to the base of being.

Paddy

R. D. *Lawrence*

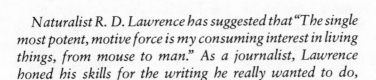

Naturalist R. D. Lawrence has suggested that "The single most potent, motive force is my consuming interest in living things, from mouse to man." As a journalist, Lawrence honed his skills for the writing he really wanted to do, about the natural world that he has explored widely and come to understand deeply.

The passage I have selected is from the second chapter. It tells of the author's struggle to reach a lake where he plans to spend several months. His route leads through a maze of channels in a cattail marsh and offers some interesting route-finding problems.

Similarly, on that morning in marsh country, the breaking day with its kaleidoscopic colors gave me a new perspective on the tangled, obstacle-ridden country that had hitherto seemed intent upon foiling my purpose. Yesterday the marsh was a troublesome barrier between me and Old Alec's Lake; today it acquired personality and character and it made me aware that though it was unruly it was also the guardian of the lake, slowing the escape of water and by its very unruliness preventing the invasion of the lakeland by unscrupulous members of my own species.

A short while later I was ready to leave, but first I took time to cut a ten-foot push pole to help me fight the marsh. I chose a straight, two-inch poplar, axed it down and trimmed off its main branches; then I cut off the tender top and threw it into the water for the beaver to enjoy, and after stowing the long pole into the sixteen-foot canoe, I boarded and pushed away from the shore.

Ten minutes later the warmth of the sun encouraged me to take off my shirt, not because I was hot, but because I find pleasure in the touch of the wind and the sunlight on my bare skin and I seem better able to feel nature like that, to absorb the events of the wildwoods and to attune to their sounds, as though naked contact with the elements has the power to bridge the gap between modern civilization with its attendant strictures and the abandoned freedoms inherent in the world of nature.

For an hour I followed the twisting course of the beaver canal and at the end of that time I was pleased to note that the water was still deep enough for easy paddling and the channel wide enough to allow me to move along without brushing into the walls of cattails.

Then the main channel ended. Three secondary openings faced me. Which one to take? Each canal was just a little wider than the canoe and none of them appeared to go in the desired direction; yet any one of the openings, or even all three, could suddenly turn and lead me to the lake. To help me decide which one to take, I tested the outflow of water from the lake.

Paddling to turn the bows into the wall of cattails so as to anchor the canoe in one place, I broke off three pieces of dry stem, each about two inches long, and threw one into the mouth of each watercourse and timed their progress toward the canoe, reasoning that the outgoing lake water might flow faster along the canal that led more directly to the source of the current. The reeds moved very slowly, but the piece from the left-hand channel was just a little faster than the others. Into its course I turned the canoe.

The canoe became more difficult and I had to hold the paddle almost perpendicular to the gunwale in order to keep the blade clear of the reeds. And I had to put my shirt back on because the cattails were closing in over my head and scraping against my body and showering me with bits of dried leaf, pollen dust, various tiny insects, and spider webs. I was glad that some whim had prompted me to wear my broad-brimmed canvas hat instead of my favorite orange cap, though the physical irritations were minor compared to the directional confusion created by the twists and turns I was forced to make.

In a large marsh such as the one through which I traveled, the channels form a series of waterways that can vary considerably in width and length; some are short and narrow, muskrat-built openings; others are wide and long and winding, swaths cut through the reeds by the combined efforts of beaver and current. Unless a traveler knows the country, or has definite landmarks as guides, it is quite possible to wander through such mazes for a long time, and on more than one occasion I have slept in my canoe when darkness forbade further travel. Such experiences are not necessarily dreadful, but they are uncomfortable enough to avoid if possible.

Soon after entering the narrow channel, visibility was reduced to a few yards in any direction and only the dry rustling of my own progress broke the stillness. When I had been in the tunnel of cattails for an hour and half I began to get irritable. Pushing through the labyrinth was hot work, little itchy things were sticking to my sweaty body, and I was bothered by the knowledge that I would have considerable trouble should I decide to try and turn the canoe around if I was forced to go back and seek another channel; and the alternative to turning the craft was moving my load of gear from the bows to the stern, so that I could change places and paddle forward.

I kept moving as best I could. Soon I put away the paddle and used the pole. The going was easier in the straight places, but to negotiate some of the sharper bends I had to drop the pole and use the paddle, or pull the boat around by grabbing the cattails. In this way almost another hour went by and I was seriously thinking about turning back, even if I had to sit on top of my gear, when it seemed to me that the canal was getting wider. I pushed more heartily with the pole and after traveling about four more canoe lengths I saw uninterrupted blue sky and the boat no longer touched the sides of the channel. Five minutes later I was able to paddle again and in another ten minutes I came out of the tunnel into an area of open water. As I paused to look around, a small flock of black ducks winged sibilantly overhead, losing height rapidly as the birds headed in what I fervently hoped was the direction of the lake. The ducks, I thought, would confirm my hope: if I heard them land on open water, I could be certain that the lake was near. I listened. In about twenty seconds the clear sounds of their splashdown became audible, and in another moment the ducks began to gossip. Old Alec's Lake was not far away!

Ahead of me appeared the opening of a solitary channel and, guided by the voices of the ducks, I paddled into it. Ten minutes later I cleared the marsh and found the lake. The black ducks took wing when I appeared; a beaver swimming toward the cattails slapped his tail and dived. I gave a couple of hard strokes and then let the canoe drift while I rested and looked around and noted at one point that I was gliding over a flooded dam; it made me realize that there might be others in this area that were also underwater as a result of the heavy spring runoff.

Down the River

Edward Abbey

> *Ed Abbey has been running rivers for a quarter of a century. He ran the Colorado River through Glen Canyon before the dam that created Lake Powell, an experience he writes about in a wonderful chapter in* Desert Solitaire. *Many of his best friends are river runners, and his well-known novel,* The Monkey Wrench Gang, *begins with a river trip. One of its main characters is Seldom Seen Smith, a mutual friend of ours. I've met Abbey a few times but have never run a river with him. He is a philosopher, no matter what he or his detractors may say.*
>
> *In a sense, the very fact that he has detractors tells you something about the man: environmental iconoclast of the Southwest, desert rat, river rat, blasphemer, damn good writer. It was Boyd Norton who introduced me to Abbey's writing when he recommended* Desert Solitaire *(currently available in three different editions) to me back in 1968, and I've been reading Abbey ever since. For this collection I selected the more recently published* Down the River, *in part because I took my son down the San Juan on a sportyak trip this past spring, just as Abbey took his daughter a couple of years earlier with the same outfitter, Cort Conley's brother.*

Bluff, Utah

Not another river trip? Yes. This time it's the San Juan in southeast Utah. We have twenty plastic rowboats, the kind known as Sportyaks, lined up on the beach, plus two rubber support rafts. Since this is a commercial tour, outfitted by Wild & Scenic Expeditions, Flagstaff, Arizona, we have three paid professional river guides with us, plus two cook's helpers and swampers, and myself; I have been invited along in the capacity of "wilderness philosopher." The pay is not very good—nothing—but it's a good job. As near as I can figure out I am not expected to do anything but look wise, keep quiet, and stay out of the way. I accept.

My daughter Susie, age twelve and three-quarters now, is coming with us. Not her first river trip—she rode the Green through Desolation Canyon last year—but the first in which she will be in sole charge of a skiff, a Sportyak II, all her own. She is elated by this advancement and understandably excited. She packs her waterproof ammo can and her waterproof river bags with care, secures them inside her boat with line and the proper half hitches, and fastens on her Mae West life jacket.

Head boatman and trip leader Randy Tate assembles the customers and gives the customary prelaunch lecture: how to handle the Sportyak, the rudiments of rowing, the push, the pull, the ferry, the pivot-turn. He demonstrates the right way to don and adjust the life jacket. Very important; the San Juan is the fastest major stream in the United States, dropping an average of eight feet per mile over the eighty-four miles of our projected journey. He talks, at length, about the "Groover," the camp toilet, a device and subject of great interest to everybody or nearly everybody. He concludes his talk by stressing the importance of keeping baggage firmly lashed to one's boat; in case of a flip or upset, the loss of sleeping bag or food or other gear could be the source of much distress.

We customers and philosophers listen to it all; though some of us have heard the lecture already, we are engaged as before by Randy's wit and charm. He likes to talk and he does it well, with authority. He's an attractive man, about thirty, brown, muscular and athletic, with sandy hair and beard, intelligent eyes, and a small gem of turquoise set in the lobe of his right ear—the California touch, although he has lived in Utah now for several years, wintering at Snowbird near Salt Lake City, summering on the Utah rivers.

Randy's fiancee, Marilyn Rivas, stands nearby. She too is a professional river guide, a member of our crew. A slender woman, with long flowing brown hair and warm brown eyes, she moves with the grace of a dancer.

The third guide is Gary "Silvertip" George, a native Utahn and "wild Mormon," as he calls himself, who stays mostly in the background, smoking his hand-rolled Bugler cigarettes and puttering about on the big raft with his dog Teddy. Gary is both a boatman and a cowboy, equally at home on the rivers or on the range, as familiar with oars and rapids as with horses and cattle. His dog is a good mutt, well behaved and alert, but with a wary, haunted look in the eyes; Teddy once spent four days and nights in a #5 coyote trap and has the stump of one hind foot to show for it. Knowing his story, you are not tempted to call him Hopalong. Teddy sleeps at his master's feet every night and rides the raft through the rapids by day—with ease, with nonchalance.

We put in, push off, row into the current. The San Juan is a muddy brown, cool but not cold on this day in June, fast but not high: it's been a dry winter in the San Juan Mountains in Colorado, the river's source. The water hisses past the mud banks, swirls toward the main channel, and rolls under the blue sky toward the Sea of Cortez and the Pacific, the "cold mad faery father," which it will never reach. Like many rivers these days the San Juan is bound for practical ends, condemned by industrial agriculture to expire in a thousand irrigation ditches, transmogrified from living river into iceberg lettuce, square tomatoes, celery, onions, Swiss chard, and radishes. Not an entirely unworthy end, I suppose, since we Americans do like to eat and God only knows there are so *many* of us, but—it makes me sad. If I think about it. Like fish, chickens, cows, pigs, and lambs, the rivers too are penned and domesticated and diverted through manifold ingenious ways—some which will not bear witnessing or thinking about—into the bottomless gut of the ever-expanding economy. There must be, somewhere, good reasons for our collective gluttony, but if there is a Judgment Day and a God of justice we humans are going to have much to answer for. If I were a good Christian I would dread that day.

Don't think about it. Nobody else does. Except animal liberationists. And vegetarians—those murderers of zucchini! those bean sprout killers!

Randy takes the lead in the smaller, fifteen-foot rubber raft, looking back anxiously at the twenty bright orange rowboats bobbing behind in a long, wavering, straggly line stretched over a quarter-mile of river. The Tupperware navy. I'm in the middle—plastic man in a plastic boat—trying to keep my daughter in view. She seems so small in her seven-foot Sportyak; only her straw bonnet shows, and her bare arms rotating the oars with a regular and expert beat. Like a pro, like a true-born river rat. Only her second float trip and she's addicted already, hooked like a trout on the lure of flowing water. May she never run out of rivers.

Far in the rear, as planned, Gary George, with Teddy for company, rows the eighteen-foot raft. He is the sweep man, meant to pick up the pieces and gather in the strays if anything goes wrong.

I'm rowing a Sportyak III, eight feet long. Like the others, it's made of a tough and durable orange plastic, a double-hull construction partially filled with foam, "virtually" unsinkable. I can see by the dents in the gunwales that it's been bounced off a few rocks. One oar is wrapped with duct tape but seems sturdy enough; I have a spare oar slung to the side. Weighing about fifty pounds, this ridiculous-looking little toy boat can carry up to four hundred pounds. It is highly buoyant, riding the top of the waves, and easy to handle; with one cross stroke of the oars I can turn it 180 degrees. The Sportyak does not have the elegance and beauty of a dory, or the utility of a rubber raft, but—it's workable. A river trip in Sportyaks is the only kind of commercial tour that offers the passengers an opportunity to fully participate in the delights and hazards of wild-river boating.

An old-time river runner named Dock Marston, I recall, went down through the Grand Canyon in a Sportyak. At low water levels, to be sure. And only once. But he did it. One of these days . . .

Floating backward, looking upstream (the deja view), I see the green cottonwoods of Sand Island wheeling slowly out of sight around the river's bend. No return. The temperature on shore was in the nineties, but here on the river the heat seems tolerable, even pleasant, and if it were not I could easily make it so by pouring a little water over my head and shirt.

At any minute now, among the veteran boaters, the water battles will begin. My Susie is one of the worst of the troublemakers. But I also have to keep an eye on Scott Frezza, a young fellow from Philadelphia, and on Berna Hahn, the glamour girl from San Diego, and on Jim Ferrigan, the gentleman from San Francisco, and on Honest Bob Reeve, a car salesman from Michigan. Nor do I like the sly smile on the face of Marilyn Rivas. In fact you can't trust any of these Sportyak types, they're all inclined to mischief. I pull my big hat down low over my eyes, hoping they won't see me. Like any honest riverman, I detest getting wet. But I've got my bailing bucket close at hand and full of water, ready for action if an aggressor strikes.

Scott comes gliding near, rowing a bit faster than necessary. He pretends to be looking at the scenery but has something—probably his bailer—clutched between his knees. As he comes alongside, starting to pass, I empty my gallon of muddy water down the neck of his shirt.

The battle immediately becomes general. Through waves of flying water I hear shouts and screams, see my daughter jumping out of her boat—bailer in hand—and into the river. Ferrigan shouts, "Stand by to repel boarders!" amid the splash and crash of bodies falling overboard. I am besieged by Scott on the portside and his girl friend Lynne on the other, both of them hurling water by the bucketful into my face. Randy stands on his raft fighting off two or three Sportyakkers circling round him like Indians. Within minutes everybody but Silvertip and his dog Teddy, far in the rear, is soaked to the socks. The battle fades, the swimmers struggle back into their boats. The sun blazes down and we begin at once to dry out; the evaporative cooling effect, in this intense heat, is doubly refreshing.

Thus we while away the time while drifting at the rate of seven or eight miles per hour toward the Raplee Anticline and the first gorge through the world of rock. Rock the color of rusted iron, rock the color of sand, rock that resembles the formal patterns of a Navajo rug. Old stuff to my unjaded eyes and always new. But in quirky ways. After thirty-five years of contemplating this bizarre landscape I can still find no human significance in it and remain emotionally un-moved—though intellectually persuaded—by the geologists' involved theories. What do I care whether these cliffs and buttes and clines, these synclines, anticlines, and monoclines have been here a billion years or only for a geological moment? Deep time is too shallow for me, about as interesting as charts in a textbook. What matters is the strange, mysterious, overwhelming truth that *we* are *here now*, in this magnificent place, and never will know why. Or why not.

The cool water flows between my fingers. My kid-daughter plies her oars three boat lengths ahead, serenely delighted by everything. My friends lie sprawled on the boats beyond, floating and sunning and dreaming. The fiery sun beams down. A great blue heron sails ahead. A beaver noses upstream close to the willow banks. Three black ravens yawp at us from the crags above and Jim Ferrigan yawps back at them, setting off a lengthy and repetitive dialogue. The crystalline blue dome of the sky turns with us, turning, still turning. And the fiery sun beams through it.

We go ashore to inspect some petroglyphs and the cliff-bound ruins of an Anasazi masonry village. The Ancient Ones were here, of course, until eight hundred years ago, tilling their fields of maize, squash, beans, and melons on the river bottoms, and whiling away the ample leisure of *their* hot afternoons in the making of pottery—the fragments are everywhere—and the chipping of arrowheads, the painting and carving of pictures on the panels of the canyon wall. They too had their scientific explanations for everything, no more and no less mythical than ours will appear to our descendants a thousand years from now. The ladies ground corn with mortar and pestle, the naked gentlemen convened in sacred committee meetings down in the kivas, smoking their sacred joints, and the swarms of children romped in the river, climbed the stony walls, chased lizards, and tormented the village dogs. I can hear the children shouting even now.

And then one day they all left. Departed. *Vanished*.

The world dissolves around us, hour by hour. Whole ranges of mountains come and go, mumbling of tectonic vertigo. Nothing endures, everything changes, and all remains the same.

I could be wrong about this.

We stop again, farther downriver, to climb the old Mormon wagon trail that leads around the base and over the hump of a giant monocline known as Comb Ridge. In 1879 a party of pioneers—men, women, children, babies—left the town of Escalante in south-central Utah to establish, under orders from Brigham Young, a new settlement at the site of Bluff in extreme southeastern Utah. After six months of toil and travel, almost within sight of their goal, they came up against this five-hundred-foot-high sandstone barrier that reaches unbroken for fifty miles from the Abajo Mountains to the river. There is no pass, no gap, no natural passageway through it that is accessible to livestock and wagons. Therefore they forced a way through the rock with hammer and drill steel and blasting powder, and constructed a crude track up which their wagons could be hauled. The track is still here, modified by weather and erosion, impassable now even to a Jeep with four-wheel drive. Near the summit we find an inscription in the rock:

Oh God
We Thank Thee

Four years after their arrival the Mormons abandoned their mission at Bluff. No one could make a living there. The climate was too dry for farming, the Indians were troublesome, and the San Juan River, always flooding and then receding, filled their irrigation ditches with sand. Bluff was revived later by the cattle business and survives today on tourism, mining, and the sale of alcoholic beverages to the Navajo Nation.

We make Camp One by midafternoon. Jim Ferrigan, master flagman, designer and retailer of flags, plants a twelve-foot pole in the beach and hoists a black banner with a strange device: one red monkey wrench. The lords of misrule are here. Later than evening, joining the circle around the campfire, he tells a long shaggy story which begins, "Is it true that in a clearing somewhere deep in Africa, Tarzan paints white stripes on black zebras, blacks stripes on white zebras, and black and white stripes on plain zebras? And if so, why?" The answer comes half an hour later: "Yes. Tarzan stripes forever."

Birds sing in the gray dawn. Off in the brush the pheasants—chukar—are cackling. A lean and hungry coyote stalks through camp, weaving among the sleeping humans on the beach. Teddy growls a warning; the coyote trots away, stopping now and then to look back over one gaunt hip. Teddy goes back to sleep.

Rising early, I step to the river's edge. A small beaver swims toward me, within a foot of the bank, only its nose showing, followed by a slender wake. The beaver seems unaware of me. I freeze, watching. The beaver swims by, goes under the first raft floating on the water, under the second, and right past the nose of Teddy, who is sleeping with his head twelve inches from the bank. The dog fails to notice. The beaver swims steadily on, direct and purposeful.

The penitents from last night's party sag around the fire, red-eyed, hungover, sipping hot coffee. Kevin Briggs, a black-bearded young literary scholar, also from San Francisco, chants his morning pledge, paraphrasing Chief Joseph:

"From where the sun rises and the river now runs, I will drink no more forever. . . ."

This pledge like most pledges is guaranteed good for at least six hours.

Ferrigan arrives, demanding coffee, and immediately begins a new story: "Three hippies are discussing the meaning of Easter . . ."

We clamber into Sportyaks and hit the river. We float through the ancient cut in the anticline, through the great upwarping of the earth's crust. Here we see not sandstone but cliffs of pink and gray limestone rising in tiers, benches, and ledges toward the crest. The walls of this canyon resemble the interior of a grotesquely oversized Roman Colosseum, the seating arrangements designed for patrons fifty feet tall. Along shore and in the river are chunks and slabs from the walls, boulders of blue-gray limestone inset with fossil crinoids and brachiopods.

We approach the fine white noise of troubled waters. The first rapids. We ride through in style. Nobody flips a boat. Even the rankest beginners make it look easy. The old-timers watch with mixed amusement and chagrin; what's the pleasure in feeling superior if you're not?

That was Four Foot Rapids, where the river drops four feet over a length of fifty yards. Next we come to Eight Foot Rapids. We beach our boats on shore above the rapids and walk close to plot a course through the waves, suckholes, and rocks. Nothing difficult, really. Back to the boats. We launch. I follow Susie through the big waves, we ship a little water, but have no trouble. She maneuvers her Sportyak like an expert, gliding into the center of the tongue, facing the waves, pushing over them, pulling away from the rocks, straightening into the glittering riffles in the tail of the rapids.

When in doubt, straighten out, that's the boatman's motto. Never broach on a rock. Always face the danger. Keep a three-boat interval between your own boat and the boat ahead. Would never do to tangle oars in the middle of a rapid. And watch that downstream oar—don't crab it on a hidden rock. Avoid the big holes if possible or, what the hell, go for the gusto and run right through them. But maintain momentum—if you get caught in a keeper you're in trouble. Watch the bubbles and the drift, follow the current, look for sandbars and gravel shallows, read the river. Read the river like a book. And if still in doubt—?

Jump out. Stay at home. Read a book.

We pause on a beach for lunch. The air quivers with heat, with albedo reflectivity from the radiant canyon walls. Must be close to a hundred degrees in the shade and the sand is much hotter than that. Gary unlaods the cooler, the crowd goes for the drinking water and the Tang. The hardcases among us snap the tabs from cans of beer, kept cool like catfish in gunny sacks trailed in the river. *Fssst!* The others stare. Impossible to muffle that sudden release of CO_2 under pressure, the conspicuous *pop!* Sounds like a grenade attack. *Incoming!* Nobody here flinches but everyone knows who is drinking the beer. And who's been hoarding it. Would be helpful if some clever lad invented a more discreet, a more genteel mode of opening beer cans. A soft, susurrant, suspiring sort of ... *s i g h* ... might serve nicely. A sound that could pass, let us say, for the relaxed, simple, artless fart of a duchess. Ingenuous. But our technology continues to lag behind genuine human needs.

Onward. On through the gorge. On down the river. How come it's always *down* the river, never up? A good question, and I am willing to offer an answer. The answer is that some do go up the river. In July 1960 a New Zealander named Jon Hamilton drove a high-powered jet boat from Lake Mead upriver through and over Lava Falls and the other great cataracts of Grand Canyon all the way to Lee's Ferry, the usual put-in point for a Grand Canyon voyage. His was the only successful uprun of the Canyon; other attempts had been made, and one jet boat was lost at Grapevine Rapid. The Park Service forbade upriver runs thereafter. Too much downriver traffic.

Hamilton's stunt was impressive but I am more impressed by Bert Loper, one of the pioneer river runners, who *rowed* a boat, alone, not once but several times, 150 miles upriver from Lee's Ferry through Glen Canyon to his river home near Hall's Crossing on the Colorado. Now that was not a stunt but a feat, an achievement, a labor of oarpower, finesse, and love.

And no man, or woman either, ever loved the river more than Bert Loper. In 1949 he took his final voyage—the last of hundreds—down the river and died while running 24½ Mile Rapid in Marble Gorge.

His wrecked boat was not found. Bert Loper was seventy-nine years old at the time of his death.

We emerge from the anticline. Mexican Hat appears, a mighty slab of sandstone resting like a sombrero on a dark, head-like pedestal. A few miles farther and we come to the original hamlet of Mexican Hat itself: the highway bridge across the river, a gas station, cafe, motel, and picnic supply store. Nothing more here, although there is a post office and other establishments a quarter-mile up the highway. We stop to replenish the beer supply. Last Chance Oasis. Salvation Station. There will be nothing more in the grim and thirsty wilderness ahead. The boys come stumbling and sweating down the dusty road through transparent waves of heat, shouldering their cases of Budweiser, Millers, Olympia, Michelob, and the sweet green Coors. Six cases of angel piss. Everybody knows there's hardly a decent beer, aside from homebrew, made in the United States anymore. The last good American beer I ever tasted was Iron City Pilsener, brewed in Pittsburgh. The death of local breweries was the death of good beer. Although, by general agreement, some American beers are worse than the mediocre norm. At a ballgame in Tucson—Toros leading Dukes 3–1 in the fourth—I called down to the vendor for more beer. The boy looked in his bucket, shouted back, "Sorry, sir, all I got left is Schlitz."

As I always say, capitalism sounds good in theory but it just doesn't work.

We plunge at once into a new canyon, the beginning of the Gooseneck meanders, leaving Mexican Hat out of sight out of mind in an instant. The river rushes down into the limestone bowels of the Monument Upwarp, heedless of the ignominious fate that awaits sixty miles ahead, the gentle commergence of this mad stream with the bland, soft, clear, stagnant reservoir of Lake Powell. Better known as Lake Foul, or Government Sump, or the Gangrene Lagoon, or Glen Canyon National Recreation Slum, property of the Del Webb Corporation, Inc. We never give it thought.

I think instead of my previous journey down this river, two years before, in a cold rainy week in March. The river was high then, surging with power, and the banks were strewn with giant cakes of ice coated with frozen mud. We read the river with great interest then, you can bet your life on it. We wore rain suits or wet suits—hypothermia was only minutes away without such protection. And one poor devil did flip his boat, submerged himself in the icy river. We rushed him onshore, stripped him, wrapped him in an unzipped sleeping bag, built a big fire. The man came out of it well, although, as he admitted, his bones stayed cold for the next three days.

But now in June it's quite different. Making camp Number Two in late afternoon, just below another rapid, some of us leave our boats and walk upshore—wearing life jackets—to a point above the rapid, wade into the river, and go bobbing like corks down over the big waves. This is the way to truly feel and know the power of a fast river. Facing downstream, feet and legs lifted to act as shock absorbers in case you hit a rock, guarding your tailbone, you flounder into the current and are suddenly, helplessly swept away. The waves soar above your head, blotting out the sun. You gasp for air just before the water wallops you in the face, rise into the light at the crest of the wave, and descend like a duck into the next trough. Cheap thrills.

We ride to the bottom of the rapid, backstroke hard out of the current and into the peaceful eddy at the beach.

A few go trotting up the beach and over the boulders for a second body-run, my daughter Susie among them. I still get nightmares when I recall that day last year, on the Green River in Desolation Canyon, when we discovered that Susie's life jacket had a pinhole in it. Swimming the rapids nearly every day, she came out of the tail of one choking and gurgling and blue in the face. She complained that her life jacket seemed too heavy, that it was taking her through rather than over the waves. Checking it, we found that one of the four kapok flotation pads in front had somehow been punctured, probably by cactus, had soaked up water and turned hard as a stone. Susie was wearing what river folk call a sinker.

Ferrigan the Flagman sets two driftwood poles in the beach this evening. Up the first he runs the expedition flag, the one we've seen before. Kevin Briggs makes a bugle of his fist, playing "Salute to the Colors." On the second pole Ferrigan raises another exotic totem, a dark sun edged in gold on a field of royal blue. The meaning? He shrugs: "A literary allusion." Beer cans pop like pineapples; we salute the flag-maker. The two flags whip smartly in the evening breeze.

Stanislaus:
Struggle to Save a River
Tim Palmer

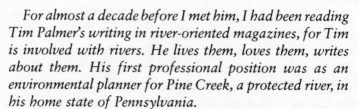

For almost a decade before I met him, I had been reading Tim Palmer's writing in river-oriented magazines, for Tim is involved with rivers. He lives them, loves them, writes about them. His first professional position was as an environmental planner for Pine Creek, a protected river, in his home state of Pennsylvania.

It is not strange that Palmer, an easterner, should be writing about a western river, for he travels all over the country running rivers and writing about them, trying to save them from destructive practices and patterns, trying to keep them free-flowing and natural. His books include Rivers of Pennsylvania *and a book about the Youghiogheny River in his native state. He is currently writing a history of river preservation, perhaps a companion piece to Rod Nash's wilderness history.*

Tim's input to this book goes beyond the short excerpt below, for we have spent hours comparing notes on river writing and river writers. I appreciate his counsel. This passage constitutes the final pages of his book on the battle to save the Stanislaus, a lost cause—or is it?

July, 1981

Back up at Parrotts Ferry, where we have returned again and again since we first arrived in Catherine Fox's raft, there is no river in the spring of 1981. The only sounds are from small waves lapping in the chaparral and in the pines at a bend in the flooded road, not a bend in the Stanislaus. The campers are gone. The kayakers and their bright boats are gone. All those barefoot people in shorts are gone. The field where the June 2 rally was held is murky deep, and the clump of willows where Gaguine, Grimm, Pickup, Lynch, and the others chained themselves is a watery tomb. The trees that Don Edwards, Pete Stark, and Huey Johnson planted in July 1980 are gone. No boatloads of laughing passengers wash up on that sandy shore, and no suntanned river guides gather around to drink a can of beer apiece as they pack up their rafts. The Stanislaus River at Parrotts Ferry is no longer changing anybody's life. Everybody is gone. Who has come? Motorboaters, and their exhaust stinks. The place seems full of ghosts, haunted. But I don't believe in haunted things.

I am looking, thinking about what I don't see, at what is underwater. At what is dead and gone—for what? California author James Houston writes, "Economically, ecologically, the history of the far west has continued to be a saga of exploitation, land abuse, bloody struggle, and enormous thefts." Maybe the loss of this river is like the turn-of-century land grabs from Central Valley wheat farmers by the railroads; like the empires of timber amassed by lumber companies under the Homestead Act; like the water rights bought up from Owens Valley farmers; like the diversion of the Trinity River and the death of the Indians' salmon; like Hetch Hetchy.

Above the sick brown shore, I begin walking upriver through the tangled chaparral. I am retreating higher, as people have done for centuries to get away. Go higher and higher to get away from what is happening. Try to get away, then hope that it doesn't catch up with you.

I crawl through oak, manzanita, pines, toyon. Climbing over rocks I watch for rattlesnakes chased from their dens by rising water. I think of Jennifer Jennings, who knew how hopeless this struggle seemed. Looking out to the river, she was stone-still and silent. "What is it?" I asked, and she said, "Oh, I was just thinking how nice it would be if there was an earthquake." As I scramble, I think of the weight of this reservoir. It is heavy. Ever pick up a five-gallon jug of water? I think of the weight of this reservoir pushing down on the restless California earth. I think of the hanging planters in the Department of Water Resources in Sacramento office trembling and swaying during the Oroville quake, seventy miles away, after DWR's Oroville Reservoir was filled.

I come to the place where I used to camp. It was a sandy beach with a big ponderosa pine at its upstream end, a flat rock where I'd pile my gear, a shady oak with a fire circle where I'd cook. It is gone and I keep walking. I hear the drone of a motorboat. I pass the house-sized rocks that rose above Chicken Falls, but the falls is deep under, and I see only the summits of rocks where people used to sunbathe and lie and laugh at rafters as they were clutched, then released by the big hydraulic. At Chinese Dogleg, at what used to be the graceful, dancing bend that Catherine Fox loved so well, I cannot see the river, but the surface of the reservoir is agitated. Now and then it quivers and swirls as a remnant of current boils underneath. I am getting closer to the river again, near the upper edge of the rising reservoir. I walk through a flat that is covered with berry bushes, over ground that is lumpy from the work of old miners. I walk closer and closer to the water. The limestone-cobbled shore is dry and untouched by the silent backwater, and up ahead, very faintly, I can hear a sound.

Rapids. The river again. The Stanislaus not yet touched by the dam. The going is rough, and I scramble over, around, and between boulders. Then I see the wild sight of whitewater. Cliffs climb to pointed tops and the Stanislaus curves smoothly around a bar of colored stones. I've made it back to the river.

What I see—this place—has been the main thing for several hundred pages now. The main thing can be babies and children, a warm lover, a friend who reached out and saved you, your soft-eared dog, a job and a paycheck in the bank, your future, the twisted past, war, evil, crops, or God. But here it is this place. Just a river and a canyon and its life. So what that it's the only one of its kind, so what about that irreplaceable stuff. It's just shapes and forms, a low space for water to run, craggy rocks up high, blue sky, sand, stones, sounds, trees, and animals. Big deal. How can a place do this to people? How can a simple place do what the Stanislaus Canyon has done? I sure don't know. All I know is I feel good sitting here in the sun near the South Fork and listening to the river run by. Why do I feel good? Maybe I was bored and this is different. Maybe I was the opposite of bored, and this is just enough of nothing.

There are powerful places on this earth. Places that uplift people's spirits, as Alexander Gaguine says. He says the Stanislaus Canyon is one of those places. I don't know how this works. There is something here that I cannot hold, but cannot let go of either. Now that this book is almost over, there is something more that needs to be said . . .

Harold Gilliam, a California journalist, writes "To walk by a river or flow with it down rapids and through quiet stretches, to swim in it, to feel on your skin the power of its currents, is to have a direct experience of the flow of time and history and the cycles of the earth that bring the rain and snow, the winds and the waters that flow down the mountains to the valleys and to the ocean again. This is the mystique of the Stanislaus."

Mary Regan, beautiful, crippled Mary, spoke for the disabled who have been to the Stanislaus, "The river and its canyon was our greatest teacher . . . it became for us a wilderness cathedral."

Then there is the other side. When Mark Dubois talked to the Ripon Young Farmers Association and said his spirit belonged to the canyon, they laughed at him.

John Hertle said, "All the talk about a canyon and other things is superfluous. The issue is rafting." Hertle went to China, returned, and said, "They would look at this issue differently. People there don't care about Russia, Taiwan, atomic bombs. The only issue is where their vegetables are coming from. Rafting compared to food to them is utter stupidity."

It was Chief Sealth, from the Pacific Northwest, who in 1854 called the coming of white men, "The end of living and the beginning of survival."

Milton Kramer says this about the canyon: "It provides pleasure. We're so much in pursuit of pleasure that we're losing values that have built the country. It's the sign of a decadent society."

I wonder, is the pursuit of pleasure the same as the pursuit of happiness? You know—life, liberty, and the pursuit of happiness?

This is decadent? I'm looking upriver as the Stanislaus rips around a sunlit bend and picks up the South Fork. A raft drifts into the bend, and the people in the raft paddle and have the gall to laugh while others are working.

I have nothing against a good time, but an important question has been posed: what, if anything, does this canyon provide besides fun?

"It's really hard to find words," Mark Dubois says. "It's not kilowatt hours or recreation days. It cannot be counted, but it is still a value that is important and real to many people. On trips I usually ask people to try to go and sit alone. They return with a glow on their face. They've touched something that they haven't touched anywhere else. This canyon feeds people's spirits."

This is so vague. No matter how you say it, it sounds like thin air. I'd rather just sit on my boulder and not bother, but nobody is going to call me a rafter for wanting to save this canyon. Rafting gets you to some nice places, I'll say that for it, but I'm not a rafter. I'm a canoeist.

Some people believe in nature. That is part of what's going on here. Water cycles, the chain of life, all that. The fact that we're made from earthy elements and when we die, these things go back to the warm ground and feed some other life. It is a belief in life, a reverence for it.

A wild river shows life like no other place. Simple truths of the earth—as Gilliam said—are seen more easily here. That helps to make this place powerful.

Then there is this thing about flowing water. People love it. Maybe some of it stems from being 75 percent water ourselves. Maybe it stems from a heritage of gills and webbed feet. Loren Eiseley said,

"If there is magic on this planet, it is contained in water." Whatever magic is.

Alexander Gaguine says, "There is so much beauty and perfection. To realize that it exists adds a huge new dimension to what I thought the world was." Gaguine is coming close. Keep talking, Alexander . . .

"Trying to keep up with the demand for more water or more power does not uplift people, but spending a day in the Stanislaus River Canyon often does. The experience can raise people's spirits or bring out feelings of wonder and joy. The Stanislaus becomes a very real part of their home, whether people are there for three days or three months.

"I feel that two of the most important things are home and community, and we have both in the Stanislaus River Canyon. It has been the home of people for thousands of years. We can see that heritage more clearly than in any museum, and now the canyon is our home.

"On the river, people work as a community and even strangers find themselves helping each other, getting to know each other because of the special demands, the special opportunities that are faced in the canyon. You don't find that in other places today.

"Europe has its great cathedrals, but in America it is our own great natural landscape which uplifts our spirits and souls as individuals and as a whole nation."

Deep in our past is the ideal of a perfect place. A paradise, an island, Shangri-la. The original garden. It is what many people work toward, whether we think it can be right here or someplace else. To get there is the reason that a lot of people do good. People devote their lives to getting there. Though I have never done that much good, I look at this river and I think I have made it.

The story goes that way back, an apple was eaten. Poor Eve has taken all the blame. What can be so wrong with eating one shiny apple? Even an apple a day. She may have turned around and tenderly planted the seeds, for all we know. It is easy to blame Eve, since she is long gone, but it seems to me we are missing the point. What we are doing now is not eating an apple, but smashing barrels of them into cider that will sour in no time. Eden is being lost today. "What will inspire us when the holy places are gone?" Gaguine asks.

I feel a spirit of the earth. These river people dream that others will feel it too; but here, in this canyon, it is a dream that has not yet come true.

February 1981, Parrots Ferry covered by New Melones.

March 1981, Chicken Falls covered.

April 1981, Chinese Dogleg covered.

Because of low runoff, the level of the reservoir receded through the summer of 1981, uncovering Parrotts Ferry once again. For now, the Stanislaus remains. The other rivers remain, and a very special friend says that you can make a difference.

Kayak Adventuring
in a Desert Gorge

J. Calvin Giddings

> Dr. J. Calvin Giddings is a professor of chemistry at the
> University of Utah, but in river circles he is better known
> as a kayaker. A former president of the American
> Whitewater Affiliation, Giddings has been active for dec-
> ades in kayaking and kayak exploring in North and South
> America, including trips on the mountainous headwaters
> of the Amazon in Peru. He has pioneered many of the
> desert canyons of the southwest, including Cross Mountain
> Gorge on the Yampa River in Colorado, a segment immedi-
> ately upstream from Dinosaur National Monument,
> which is presently threatened by a proposed dam.
>   Giddings was one of the founders of the American Rivers
> Conservation Council, and he continues to fight river-
> destroying water-development projects.

My feet slipped on wet rock and the rope from above pulled
me into the waterfall. A tumbling brown torrent hit me in
the chest and began to wash over my face, nearly smothering me with
dense spray.

"Slack!" I cried, "let me down!" The rope uncoiled and I plunged
deep into the pool, into the churn and boil of the river. A big cushion
of water pushed me right toward the main stream and I fought to
escape along its edge, fought for the opposite left wall, fought for the
streamer of current aimed like an arrow at the thin slot between the
wall and the rock. The water focused on this lonely exit and at that
spot concentrated all its momentum to escape the madness of the
pool. I felt myself whipped into the aperture, felt sandstone faces
closing on both sides, funneling the writhing snake of water that had
swallowed my body. Suddenly I burst out the other side like a
champagne cork, and felt solid rock at my foot. I groped for a place
to stand, reached up to the edge of the formation, and pulled my
dripping frame out on a gently sloping platform of pink rock.

"Yah-hoo!" I shouted in ecstacy, and my voice echoed and reechoed
700 feet up the shadowed walls of a desert gorge. It was the kind of

feeling that floods over you like an ocean wave when you face a big uncertainty then pull it off in an instant. I was infinitely happy, at life, at success, at the sweet desert air lapping brown desert water from my city-white body. I pulled up my rope, strode to the top of the rock and called back over the tumult of water, "Let's have a boat!"

ADVENTURE, *noun.* A remarkable or hazardous experience; an unexpected or exciting occurrence . . . (Funk and Wagnall).

Kayak adventuring is a term I use to describe unorthodox, adventuresome passages down a river. Kayak adventuring is facing a tough canyon or a terrain problem or an unusual obstacle which requires more strategy and wit than getting down a series of separate rapids. It may require special tools and skills outside of kayaking, such as you need to rope down a waterfall or a canyon wall, to fight off icebergs, or to get past crocodiles. I won't try to define its whole limits. I will just say it is something more than kayaking, something less than exploration, something with a special challenge that can scare your wits out, or float your soul to heaven.

Some of the best kayak adventuring is found in narrow gorges. Here plummeting walls fall straight into the water, leaving no place to pass on foot. You may not have the portage option if the rapid is too rough. It can be dangerous business unless you know something of the rapids and the escape routes and the paths of retreat. And something about hanging on to life no matter what.

I love the incredible redrock gorges of the west, fallen like giant knife cuts across a sage and pinyon land, blazing with egg yolk sun and ripped by winds on the rim, shadowed and cool and wet and rumbling far, far down the darkened walls, down where the knife still cuts at the heart of the world. Nowhere is there a more magnificent place to shed civilization's cocoon and become a man again, to see through an ancestor's eye, to mobilize brain and muscle against challenge, for a survival deserving the name.

Utah has a number of them. Zion Narrows on the Virgin River. The Chute cut by the Muddy River below Hondoo Arch. Some of the canyons of the Escalante. And the queen, the San Rafael.

Since these rivers course through desert land, they must be nurtured by mountain snows. Their moment of glory is brief, usually in late May or June, when the snowpack liquifies beneath the sun. You take what is left over from irrigators and cooling towers, and it may not be much. You have to have patience to find them full of water, full of bucking waves, loud with noise, ripping away toward adventure.

For pure gorge spectacle, Zion Narrows is the place to go. This long slit canyon entombed beneath incandescent rims becomes a target for backpackers in late summer when the stream is a trickle. But in May and June it can flood and clog with wayward logs that stick sideways from wall to wall, forming deadly traps. Zion National Park forbids boats on its waters. We ran it in May 1975 by special permit—to study it the paper said—and gloried and shivered a little committed to the deepness of its vaults.

The Muddy River has a problem and that is what men call it. Who would go to a place whose name suggests such drabness? You can see in your mind's eye a turbid stream, tamarisk banks, alkali flats beyond. But only if you have never seen the splendor of the gorge below Hondoo.

I idolize the Muddy. I have since May 1975 when we dragged boats down its shallow waters and got caught at night in its recesses. We ignited driftwood but the increasing cold penetrated to our bones. I snuggled with my 8-year old son Mike for warmth, finding him worth all the furnaces in the world.

Go see it! Its watercourse is gentle. Its cliffs are spellbinding 12-feet apart parallel wonders of our world.

The Escalante, unlike the Muddy, is a name of honor. It is titled after one of the earliest explorers of the west, Father Escalante. It has color, cliffs, and arches along the way, Glen Canyon to pour into, and Ed Abbey to write it into fame. And, what most people don't see, it has some fair rapids when the water booms.

We ran it in June 1975. J. Dewell, his son John and my son Steve, Les Jones and I. We cooked in the fiery heat of the desert one day and froze in cold rain the next. To get out of the canyon we roped our boats over the low cliffs of Coyote Gulch and shouldered them up an inclined expanse of Sahara known as the Sand Bank beneath the reborn desert sun.

Escalante walls are steep but they are not drawn tight over the river like those of the other canyons. It is an adventure, but it will never be a San Rafael.

The San Rafael. Born in snowfields in the eleven thousand foot Wasatch Plateau. Tumbling down Cottonwood Creek and Ferron Creek and Huntington Creek. Soaked up by Electric Lake to feed a new, ugly power generating station. Soaked up by the fields of lovely Castle Valley. Then, what's left, flowing into the San Rafael Swell.

The San Rafael Swell is a 30 by 70 mile upthrust of colored rock lying west of Green River, Utah. Sixty-five million years of erosion have carved it into buttes and pinnacles and layercakes of strata. And deep in its heart runs the slotted cut of the San Rafael River.

Lanky Pete Hovingh—biochemist and desert rat—first told me

about the canyon of the San Rafael. It had dinosaur bones and big red cliffs and fast water, he said. Pete got really caught up in it and rafted down to its main crossing at the San Rafael campground in 1969. My first trip there was in 1970. It was as spectacular as he said.

Then, around a campfire one night, Jim Byrne added an element of madness to the San Rafael.

"I'd like to try the Black Box," he said with a twinkle in his eye.

"The black what?" I asked.

"The Black Box. A deep gorge. Below the campground. I hiked up from the bottom a ways when it was dry. No problems."

Jim poked at the fire, added wood, sat down, and we listened to crickets.

At length he added rather flatly, "Of course, I couldn't see the upper part. Too narrow to look around the bends. Not sure what's up there. Shouldn't be too bad though."

Sure, I thought.

Jim Byrne, a wiry nuclear engineer plastered with red hair and beard, is infectious with dry humor. But put to the test in a canyon, Jim is much more: he is an analytical thinker, a fixer of broken paddles or what have you, a solver of tough strategic problems. In short, if you had your choice of one thing to take adventuring with you, you would be wise to take Jim.

June 13, 1971. Jim and J. Dewell and Roger Turnes and I unloaded boats in the shade of a cottonwood grove beneath shimmering buttes. We launched in low water, headed for Mexican Mountain. It was a late start—2 p.m.—but since Jim thought it was so easy, we felt we could push through by dark. Instead we spent the night on a sandbar in the middle of the canyon—in the middle of an adventure. Jim, it seems, had missed more than a few bends in his reconnaissance of the course of the San Rafael.

We paddled out late the next morning, hungry, thirsty, but thrilled like kids at what we had found. Then, at the head of a great, flat meander around Mexican Mountain—poised at the edge of an even greater wilderness of redrock—we carried our boats out to the terminus of a jeep road.

All next winter I wondered what it was like in the canyons in that expanse of red, raw land below Mexican Mountain. I asked Pete Hovingh who had hiked down the riverbed in the dry season, and he said that there was another black box down there, narrower than before. I couldn't believe it. Suddenly, I couldn't wait.

The same group, back down the same jeep road. We launched in low water in June 1972. We drifted and scraped all the way around Mexican Mountain, and down there came face to face with the narrowest black box of all. It was an unforgettable experience.

The 1970s slipped by and I got enmeshed in other gorges and in the exploration of Peru's Apurimac River, source of the Amazon (see *Mariah*, Vol. 1, No. 3, Fall 1976). But always in the back of my mind the San Rafael flowed, and I dreamed more and more of going back and running the entire 50 mile stretch below the campground in a single run, a single grand adventure in those singular black boxes.

In these years my son Steve grew from four foot four to six feet tall, to be a young man of 16 who loved adventure. But at the same time Electric Lake grew up behind a new dam on the main tributary, sacrificing the flow of water for the flow of electricity to help power can openers and keep civilization intact. J. Dewell predicted glumly we would never run the San Rafael again.

The winter of 1977-78 was heavy with snow and a spark of hopefulness gripped up. But by late May there was still no water and I thought, dammit, J. was right.

On Friday, June 9, facing a free weekend, I called the BLM office in Price on a long shot and could hardly believe it when I heard that a stream of water was flowing down the river bed.

"It's still coming up," the ranger said.

"How much water is there?" I asked.

"Oh, bank to bank."

"How deep?"

"Too muddy to tell. I wasn't really paying much attention."

I would have to drive 200 miles to see for myself, maybe for nothing. But after all, there is only one San Rafael.

The next thing I did was call Les Jones.

Les Jones is one of a kind, a living legend in his time. Explorer, inventor, thinker, an original man. Independent, creative, determined, devoutly Mormon, tough as a rock, Les Jones would rather die than let you down. His square face beneath a shock of black hair, his analytical mind, his strength laid out on a 6-foot frame, were all designed in heaven for adventuring, I am sure of that.

Les said yes instantly. After all, isn't life made for moments like these?

Saturday morning, June 10. Steve, Les and I carried gear across the dusty campground to the river. Deer flies attacked in swarms along the grassy banks. We hurried to escape them and got off at ten. The water was amazingly high, perfect we thought. We coursed through eight miles of riffles, stunned by the view.

The river meandered through an open valley beneath incredible landforms, stacked one on another, tens of millions of years a'building, all for us it seemed.

Layers on layers of rock. Yellow rock, purple rock, pink rock and red rock. Orange and buff orange, powdered with cream. White stripes, black nodules. Big red feet holding up tabled yellow strata. Color, color, color, that is the sacred ingredient of this land.

Late that morning the strata cut by the river began to change. We dropped back in time millions of years from Moenkopi shale to Kaibab limestone, then into the most ancient and spectacular and deepest rock of the Swell, Coconino sandstone. With this transition the canyon narrowed and soon became a crevice, little more than a boat length across. The yellow sandstone slabs spun skyward out of the water, out of the shadows. Black velvet capes of desert varnish smothered the walls, ancient and awesome and dark. This was the first of the gorges whose somber aspect has led to the name: Black Box of the San Rafael. It should be called a cathedral.

The river rolled in silence through its sanctuary, maybe a mile from end to end, then emerged into a deep canyon of rugged, fractured sandstone. The pink and yellow walls were dabbed black with spots of desert varnish, graced by pinyons on the rim, bushes clinging in cracks. It was a fine view, but we couldn't look now: the rapids had begun.

It was 12:30 p.m. We battled rapids an hour then stopped for lunch beneath a cottonwood tree. We napped a while in its leafy shade, throwing back the fatigue of a long night of driving.

We departed at 2:30 p.m. The rapids came thick and fast now, broken only by pools where we could get a breath and plan the subsequent drop. Sometimes we climbed up on shore to scout but usually we could plot a course from our position in the river.

The rapids grew in fury as the water twisted tighter around the giant rocks, and pulsed and fell through narrowing gaps between stone faces. We nosedived down the throbbing ramps of water, so close to rock we could touch it, and buried in the froth of pools below, only to be forced tightly left or quickly right past subsequent obstacles.

Our difficulties were compounded by the shallowness of the water, and by its appearance, which I have only hinted at. The water was more than just silty, it was flecked with foam; it felt slipppery like sudsy dishwater but it looked worse, thick as bean soup. The patches of foam and the opaqueness hid the shallow brown rocks, forcing us through mazes of small rocks even as we twisted among the big ones. It was tough going, but we did okay until about 5 o'clock.

At five, Steve was forced off-route by a patch of the small brown devils. He dug in hard to get past the face of an elephant-size rock and back in the channel, but too late. The water slammed him against the face full force, and tipped him upstream before he could posture himself for recovery. He began to bury in the water, and it looked like his boat might collapse around him and pin him beneath the surface.

I leapt out of my boat and thrust it to shore. I stumbled through the buried, bruising rocks toward the surprised boater, for he was my flesh and blood, my son.

I must explain that Steve, although barely 16 years old, was a strapping young man, a good boater, an accomplished rock and ice climber, a budding mountaineer. He was rightfully a teenager, erratic in mood, sometimes in another world. But more often he was thoughtful and helpful, and he was intensely serious: he had already pushed through two years of calculus toward a clearly bright science career. If we got him off the rock.

As I battered and cut my shins on the race through the hidden riverbed, Steve found a corner of rock to hold onto, and he pulled with all his strength toward the edge. The boat inched forward, then suddenly broke free and spun around the edge of the monolith and washed into the current on its side. Steve casually righted himself by bracing on his paddle.

I came to a stop in the middle of the swirling water, my shins bleeding, my mind relieved at his recovery, suddenly cognizant of my son's transition to a man.

The sun had disappeared behind the high walls, but it still blazed on the rim. We pushed on through relentless rapids, getting tired, each finally capsizing upon collision with a rock or cliff. Each time we recovered with no harm done.

At 8 o'clock the walls began to close ahead, getting ready for a more serious section of black box. An exaggerated darkness fell into the depth of the canyon, gloomy against the ribbon of azure sky that arched above our heads, a distant roof to our world. We camped.

Dinner. Reminiscences. Cricket and water sounds. The ribbon of sky turned to a ribbon of stars then melted into dreams.

We arose early the next morning, in anticipation of adventure. By 7:30 we were on the river, surging into a closing canyon. The trees disappeared from the banks, the banks became occasional sand spits, and the spits melted into black varnished cliffs. We were in the heart of the glory of the San Rafael, so deep in the earth that 250 million year old Coconino sandstone welled up around us to sun streaked canyon tops.

Suddenly house-size blocks loomed ahead, filling the blackened gorge from wall to wall. The river burrowed left and we clambored up the broken fragments on the right to find out how to get around. We tunneled beneath some of the great pieces, climbed over others, then dropped down to a patch of shore where we saw we could launch. We returned and formed a human chain to pass our boats from one to another up over the high angled rock, ultimately down to the beach. We launched again, aimed for the crux of the canyon.

Uncountable years ago a mounstrous block was pried off the gorge wall by the forces of erosion and it thundered down between the cliffs in what must have been a grand, grand show of whizzing stone and dust and echoes of rock splintering on rock, and finally at the bottom the explosion of water into a trillion rainbow drops. The San Rafael was dammed by the rubble and it backed up behind, cascading eventually over the far right side and through a break near the center. It plunged fifteen feet into a caged pool and frothed from wall to wall until it broke over rocks below. It left no beach, no ledge, no stepping-stone rocks. Nothing but wild, pulsing water and the endless blank walls.

We landed left on the blocks of rubble, climbed the pinnacle rock of the dam, and stared down over 25 feet of stone face into the swirling water. We stared and stared at the diabolical barrier, the cut in our time line that partitioned our future off into something mysterious and questionable and totally uncivilized.

We couldn't climb down the falls anywhere, couldn't find a landing in the sheerness of the rock, couldn't launch our boats. We couldn't find a ledge or even a crack leading us around the pool to the side.

But we could swim.

We began to set up an approach like the one that got us by here in 1971, but we wondered if it would work in the face of the stronger flow and the heightened turbulence down in the pool. I edged toward the lip of the falls with a loop of climbing rope in my hand, something I could let go of instantly so I wouldn't be pinned down there and drown like a rat in a flooded hole. Steve belayed me from above.

I dropped down slowly, awash in brown water, then slid into the heaving pool. I reached down with my feet to check its depth but couldn't touch bottom anywhere. We needed to know for the last man would plunge in unsupported, alone.

Then came the wild swim which I described at the beginning, and soon we had 80 feet of rope arching from the top of the waterfall down across the brown water to my island rock. With one end of the strand Steve and Les lowered each of the boats into the pool with its cockpit cover tied closed to keep it dry inside. With my end I guided it into the narrow channel alongside my rock. As each bobbed by I grabbed it and pulled it up beside me.

Steve dropped into the pool and swam down. Then Les. We coiled our ropes, organized our gear, and soon the roar and then the echo of the waterfall receded behind us.

Eighty-five Strokes Per Minute

Eric Evans

> *Eric Evans, a competitive kayak paddler (he won the National Slalom Championship nine times during the 1970s) teaches high school English at Putney, Vermont. An occasional announcer for NCB Sports special events and a contributing editor to* Canoe, *he writes about many outdoor recreational activities. He is coauthor of* Whitewater Racing.

Corbin could be had. From the moment Ron Williams and Al Rudquist beat Serge Corbin and Richard Tetrault by 63 seconds after 86 miles of racing last May at the Hyack Marathon in British Columbia, the word had spread.

The next week it raced across marathon canoeing's heartland, the Midwest, to waft uneasily like the threatening clouds over hundreds of milliing canoe racers on Otego Lake in Cooperstown, New York, early in the morning, May 31. The word was not spoken aloud, but drifted amongst them, dreamlike, as if by mentioning it the bubble would burst, and an opportunity vanish.

The word was especially poignant for Bruce Barton of Homer, Michigan and Tim Triebold of Porterfield, Wisconsin, as they checked the registration desk behind the Lake Front Motel prior to the start of the 21st General Clinton Regatta. Last year at this race they had lost to the *Quebecois*, Corbin and Tetrault, by half a boat-length: they'd been told by race officials to stay on the outside of the buoys at the finish (on the outside of the turn) and then watched Corbin, coming up behind them *on the inside of the buoys*, nip them at the end of the 70-mile endurance event. Cooperstown '82 had left a one-second bad taste in the Midwesterners' mouths. The word from the Hyack race was the start of exorcising a year of injustice, of confirming what they'd been telling themselves all winter. *Corbin could be had.*

The word reached Quebec as well. *Le Nouvelliste*, Quebec's third largest newspaper, serving the cities of Trois-Rivieres, Shawinigan, Victoriaville, and Corbin's hometown, Cap-de-la-Madeleine, had chorused word of Corbin's demise the next day on the front page: "Corbin Loses To Williams" was all the bold headline said. For the canoe-wise folks of the area, more was unnecessary. Newspapers in other parts of North America would be forced to amplify the headline, explaining that this was *canoeing*, but Corbin's name needs no explanation along the St. Lawrance. Sports? They began on page 12.

A rare loss at the Hyack, added to that funny business of losing at the ICF Worlds last year in a slow boat as an "unofficial entrant." Cracks were appearing. And Barton-Triebold, the Stockton brothers and Rudquist (with "go-fast" partner Mike Bohannon) were readying their Pro Boats.

Corbin could be had.

The reason so few people openly brandished the notion of Corbin losing was that Corbin is the most prolific winner in the history of canoeing. In basketball there can be hot-stove-league *repartée* over who was the better player: Chamberlain with his statistics or Russell with his championships? In football was it Jim Brown or O.J. Simpson? In track, is Sebastion Coe faster than Steve Ovett? But in marathon canoeing there is no discussion, simply indisputable fact: Serge Corbin is the finest paddler, ever.

Corbin, mostly with older brother Claude, but also with Ron Williams, Michele Beauchesne and, lately, Tetrault, has won more than 130 races during his career. Cooperstown six times . . . Au Sable . . . Minnesota . . . Mont Laurier . . . and save for the ICF Worlds last year in Luxembourg where he and Tetrault competed with an unfamiliar boat (slowest design on the river), he's gone undefeated over 96 races and seven years.

Ask any distance paddler which race he or she'd most like to win and the answer would be Shawinigan: the Classique Internationale des Canots de la Mauricie, or Classique for short. Three days and 125 miles of racing in front of 300,000 spectators for $25,000 prize money. It's marathon canoeing's Olympics, World Championships, and Golden Fleece combined. Corbin has won it *nine times in a row*.

Bruce Barton, 26, is America's preeminent marathon paddler and, when trained, one of our best Olympic-style kayakers. He's the scourge of the USCA circuit in C-1 and C-2. He's won 12 titles at the USCA nationals over the years. A well-coordinated athlete of unbelievable drive, Barton has the motor to excel in any endurance sport.

Bruce Barton has never beaten Serge Corbin.

The only discussion might be over Corbin's qualifications as North America's best canoeist, period. But how does one compare canoe sailors to polers to whitewater slalom racers to Olympic-style paddlers? Mathematics is one way. There are dozens of canoe sailors and polers, hundreds of open- and decked-boat whitewater racers and Olympic-style paddlers. But there are thousands of marathoners. Champions rising from a gene pool of dozens or hundreds are, statistically, less significant than a runaway champion culled from a pool of thousands.

For nine years, Serge Corbin clearly has been the champion of canoeing's most thoroughly competitive arm.

And he's only 26.

By 7:30 a.m., the crowd of General Clinton-watchers on the grassy park of the boat-launching area behind the Lake Front Motel began to thin. Most of the racers who had been tinkering with their boats (readying fluid-replacement bottles if they were serious, coolers if they weren't) had already started their 70-mile odyssey down the Susquehanna in earlier classes.

At 7:40 a.m., a hush drew over the crowd and activity slackened; around the corner of the restaurant came boat X10, carried on the shoulders of Serge Corbin and Richard Tetrault. Behind them swirled a band of red-coated elves, with "Assoc. Coureurs en Canot de la Mauricie" emblazoned on their backs, walking briskly to keep pace with their Pied Piper. Corbin and Tetrault went immediately to the first narrow ramp jutting into Lake Otego and promptly stepped into their boat as the crowd drew closer, whispering, with cameras starting to whirr.

As their manager, Richard Toupin, fluttered above them on the dock, offering last-minute imprecations in French, Corbin and Tetrault nodded repeatedly, like one would nod half-listening to a mother's "be careful" warnings, and then pushed off.

As if on cue, Barton and Triebold materialized from the crowd and headed for the second dock, but most attention remained glued to Corbin and his entourage.

Toupin eyed Barton and Triebold, and whispered to one of the elves, "Today Barton is going to pay for Ron Williams' aggressiveness last week."

Pro Boats are narrow, low-sided, delicate, dicey creatures. They're tippy, like sitting astride a Coke bottle. Incredibly, Barton and Triebold stepped into their boat (jumped is more like it) as if they were stepping off a curb: total defiance to the word "instability."

Obviously, elite paddlers spend lots of working hours in their canoes, and there develops an ineradicable harmony between craft and crafts-men. Long-distance racing demands long-distance training; there's no escaping the irrefutable. Bulging muscles don't win marathon races. It's highly tuned cardiovascular systems, livers which can still kick the glycogen into a depleted bloodstream after many hours of hard work, and muscles accustomed to repeating the same movement mile after mile after mile. Like good wine, honing a marathoner's body takes time.

Bruce and Tim had put in 200 hours of 1983 water time before Cooperstown. Both ski cross-country competitively, but the '82–'83 winter's poor snowfall and warm temperatures allowed them extra practice in the boat. Triebold, 30, said it was the best spring of preparations he'd ever had.

Corbin and Tetrault had 150 hours. During the winter, they lift weights three times a week, swim, ski cross-country, run, and work on flexibility. When the ice breaks on the St. Lawrence, Serge and Richard are on the water, often in frigid, wetsuit conditions. Races are easy after long afternoons in a Pro Boat on a swollen, ice-choked ocean of a river with chilling 30-mph sidewinds. The dues of spring are repaid on victory podiums in the summer. Leading up to May, they paddle daily, including one long (four-to five-hour) stint a week. In racing season, they decrease practice time to allow for the demands of racing and travel. From May 7 to September 5 they race every weekend without a break; seven times during this period, they have two races on a weekend.

Such is the regimen of a serious marathon paddler. In the summer, don't call one until nine at night. They're working 'til five; after that they're on the water until dark, grinding out the miles, adding up the hours, payin' the cost to be the boss like no other competitive paddlers.

Training of this magnitude produces efficient metabolic pathways. On the maximum oxygen-uptake test,* using solely his arms on bicycle-like pedals, Corbin has recorded a 66. Given the smaller muscle mass of the arms, this figure is truly extraordinary when compared to runner Bill Rodgers' 67 using his legs.

The General Clinton Regatta, held each Memorial Day weekend, is now in its 21st year, and for the inhabitants of the southeast-central region of New York immortalized by James Fenimore Cooper, it's a rite of passage from spring into summer. As a result, this is a regatta with a 19th-century flavor and concomitant fanfare. It's a three-day, 12-town festival encompassing craft shows, fireworks, road races, a wrestling tournament, bicycle events, folk music, and balloon rides. The competitive events alone draw 3,000 participants. Adjacent to the finish of the 70-mile canoe race in Bainbridge is a grassy fairgrounds where a carnival midway rollicks day and night. Just obtaining entry to the fairgrounds (and the finish) demands a 15-minute wait for a parking space. At this regatta there is no loneliness for the long-distance paddler: 80,000 spectators will watch Monday's race.

But the heart of the affair is canoe racing. On Friday, Oneonta's *The Daily Star* publishes a 33-page guide for the weekend which includes schedules, start orders, and maps. On Saturday and Sunday the first canoe races take place: relay races, sprint races, and shorter distance events.

Monday morning brings the main event, a 70-mile endurance race from Otego Lake to Bainbridge, via the Susquehanna and three portages. It is billed as "the world's longest one-day canoe race," which is slightly hyperbolic considering the 86-mile Hyack a week earlier in British Columbia. But no matter, the test is genuine. For contestants, it is the first major event of the year in the East, a chance to establish an early pecking order for 1983.

At 6 a.m., the aluminum canoes depart. Most of the 200 boats in this class are hoping for mere survival—a day on the river with provisions, frosty and otherwise, inspired perhaps by a bet, a dream, or the desire just to be part of the rite. A few sleek tin-foil craft raise the pace across the lake to the river entrance, but most of the fleet is propelled with rental paddles and arms more accustomed to pushing Lawn-Boys than Grummies. Here is a spirit to belong, to participate, a spirit duplicated a month earlier by those who run without numbers at the rear of the Boston Marathon.

At 7 a.m., the 100 amateur cruisers begin. Although the odd Coleman or fake "birchbark" boat can be spotted, the overall mood is more serious, the tempo accelerated. The boats are light, sharp and fast, as are the racers—good, national-level-quality athletes. Athletes like Peter Heed of Keene, N.H., with an upper body from a Nautilus ad. Athletes like wiry, intense Dick Weber of Syracuse. Athletes like Rochester's Tanna Gaustad and Canandaigua's Shari Eaton, with motors that would make any track coach drool, two women who last year finished third *overall* in this division. But there's an inescapable feeling that the *crème de la crème* is yet to come, that although these amateurs will drive themselves to the bone in the next eight hours, there's a limit to how fast people with full-time jobs can push a canoe. Heed is a lawyer, Weber runs a chain of outdoor stores, while Gaustad is a nurse; inherent limits are imposed by job demands.

At 8 a.m., the best of the pros, the men who explore and then redefine limits, are ready. Granted, most of the 43 pro teams entered aren't competitive, but the top 15 teams are racing with dead-serious aspirations: first prize is $1,200. This is the heavyweight division, classified not only by faster boats and the lure of monetary gain, but also by the quality of the athletes drawn to it and the amount of commitment they must bring to be competitive. The winners, despite a one- or two-hour handicap, will pass almost every canoe on the Susquehanna before the day is over. The record is seven hours, two minutes and 20 seconds, set on high water in 1979 by Serge and Claude Corbin. Given this year's mediocre water level, that record will not be broken today.

For the first five miles of the race, Corbin's canoe will carry no fluids, nothing to drink. "Why shave the weight of the boat and then add five pounds when it's not necessary?" he noted. One crucial reason is that the fluid loss of high-speed canoeing must be replenished or dehydration will ensue in later miles. It must be replenished early on, because no amount of water or magic potions can bring an athlete back into the race once dehydration sets in. Corbin will get his water at the five-mile point, late enough to take advantage of five fewer pounds but barely early enough to start the replacement cycle. He'll start drinking regularly from then on. It's a risky move: manager Toupin must deliver the goods at the pre-arranged checkpoint. If he gets stuck in traffic, becomes lost, or the car breaks down, or . . . the 85 strokes a minutes that the Corbin boat produces while rifling across the lake will be for naught. A bold move. Would fortune favor it?

Toupin is lost. After watching their team come off the lake in first place, Toupin and Helen Francoeur, Corbin's girlfriend, drive along the eastern side of the Susquehanna which has less spectator traffic. Soon they are miles from any body of water. Panic rises, and the speedometer keeps pace. They check their maps, and in Keystone Cop fashion, roar off in the opposite direction.

They miss the lead pack at the Mile Five checkpoint.

But at Mile Seven they are waist-deep, water bottles in hand, eyes searching upriver. Soon the Corbin canoe whisks into view, veers toward the bank and the exchange takes place: water bottles and a few choice *gros mots* (big words). The Stocktons are 20 seconds back; Barton, 30.

A key to Corbin's success is Richard Toupin, 40, manager of the Discosalon Val Mauricie in Shawinigan Sud, Quebec, who is equal parts agent/accountant/ trainer/Svengali for the Corbin-Tetrault duo. Marcel La Joie usually pitches in with the same duties, but this weekend he was helping other Quebec teams at the General Clinton.

As agent, Toupin plots Serge's schedule, organizing when and where the team will race and under what financial conditions. As accountant he pays the bills for room, board, and travel, then collects the winnings at the awards ceremonies. With his boldly lettered Discosalon Val Mauricie "I" van, Toupin is better equipped than Nancy Reagan's appointments secretary. A spare boat rides on top, extra paddles in back. A topographical map of the Cooperstown area is taped to the dashboard, the race-day route highlighted and practiced the day before. Dry clothes, Top Ten and XL-51 sport drinks, and lunch provisions are stowed together with two briefcases of Corbin newspaper clippings, past results, and schedules.

The Toupin van is a well-known fixture at Shawinigan's Classique, recognized immediately by course marshals and police. Toupin always lands the choice parking spots while other support crews fight congestion miles away. At Cooperstown, Toupin is somewhat out of his element, but his tenacious improvisation yields results. His nearly faultless English is employed when requesting information from race officials; it quickly becomes non-existent when a policeman asks him to move his van from the No Parking zone next to a portage. "*Monsieur, je ne comprends pas*" amidst classic Gallic hand gestures and shrugs.

Other teams use friends and wives for catch-as-catch-can support crews. Corbin and Tetrault have an energetic, experienced ally working behind the scenes, smoothing the wrinkles that mean minutes and seconds in races. They worry about paddling, nothing else.

Toupin's metabolism is revved at a high pitch. He's skinny, nervous, and mouthy. This last quality often gets him into hot water when his unabashed cheerleading grates on the ears of Serge's competitors. At the end of the Classique last year, Toupin kiddingly said to Barton, "Here, Bruce, better get a drink now from the Cup; it's the closest you'll ever get to it." Said in jest, but enough to fuel one more chin-up from a spent Barton body during the winter. Indeed, Toupin loves to talk. Boatbuilder Ev Crozier has a photo of Toupin at last fall's Molokai Hai race in Hawaii. Toupin is sticking out his tongue. It is sunburned.

Why Toupin's fealty? Why the time and money invested? Part of the answer lies in altruism—Toupin, relatively unathletic himself, is a canoeing fan in the purest sense of the word. And part of the answer is advertising. The name of Toupin's discosalon written on the side of Serge's canoe, on his T-shirt both on and off the water, and on Toupin's van, has been seen on television and newspapers in Quebec for years during the summer. It's inexpensive exposure when compared to the cost of purchasing that same space.

On the narrow, serpentine, shallow Susquehanna it behooves the team that takes the lead to increase it. Out of sight—out of mind, so to speak. At 16½ miles Corbin and Tetrault are well out of sight: 1:22 up on the Stocktons and 1:57 up on Barton-Triebold. Toupin begins to relax. "Barton is going to *hate* Ron Williams for beating Serge last week," he chuckles.

Of the 43 pro teams, 15 are from Quebec and several of them are in the top 10 at this point.

Such quality and depth has not always been seen from our northern neighbors. Although canoeing as a sport courses through the veins of the Quebecois (remember *les voyageurs*), in the 1950s and 1960s Americans dominated the Classique, and one man in particular, Minnesotan Irwin "Buzz" Peterson, is still revered there. Peterson won the event nine times with a variety of partners. Buzz was a paddler from the school of old salts: work an eight-hour day, paddle some at night during the week and then hit the training hard on weekends. And he was not above having a good time or a good laugh. Many a mass start would see him sprint out to a sizable lead, whereupon he'd stop and have a cigarette, even offering same to his competitors as they grunted past. Once down to the butt, he'd resume paddling and catch up to the leaders within a few miles.

"The reason we did well for so many years," reflected Peterson, "was that we trained more than the locals. The Quebec boys would only train four or five times a summer before Shawinigan, when we were at it on a regular basis. Then, once one of them got the idea about training, the others followed."

Guy Beaumier got the idea and brought Quebec back into the winner's circle with a 1968 Shawinigan win. He built canoes, promoted canoeing, ran the paddlers' organization, even paddled across Canada to publicize the sport in 1967 as a part of the Canadian Centennial. In Beaumier's shadow was a 20-year-old electrician named Claude Corbin who became the champion Quebec had waited for so patiently. Starting in 1969, Claude went on to win both the Classique and Cooperstown eight times.

In 1973 Claude was short a training partner and shopped around. He settled on his younger brother, Serge, who had been messing about in canoes for four years, since the age of 13. The chemistry worked, and they began racing as well. That year they finished second in the Classique to the last Americans to win it, Dan Hassel and Gene Jensen. A Corbin has been in the winning canoe ever since, Claude's last victory with Serge coming in 1979.

Quebec's organization has matured with its champions. The Association des Coureurs en Canots de la Mauricie now schedules 15 races a year, raising enough revenue from licensing fees and the $25/year memberships to send teams in 1982 to Vancouver, Cooperstown, and nine paddlers to Hawaii for the October Molokai Hai.

The lead is stretched at the 21-mile mark: 1 minute, 46 seconds is what veteran canoe racer Al Camp of Otego reports on WDOS radio which is monitoring the race. After 16 years of successive Memorial Day bashes (including a win in 1969), Camp is sitting this one out: "I needed a break. The racing's fun, but the training can be boring."

At first glance marathon paddling does appear to be the essence of ennui. Similar "fun" could be had with simpler equipment: a cement wall and one's head comes to mind.

But the essence of marathon paddling lies just below this shallow surface. "There's magic in making a canoe go fast," says Corbin. "I like the feeling of raising a fast boat to its limit and keeping it there, slicing effortlessly through the water."

Downhill ski racers call this mesmerizing magic "glisse"—whereby an athlete with his equipment does not overpower natural obstacles and forces, but subtly joins them in a delicate partnership of rhythm and control. The feeling captivating Corbin and others of the marathon world in his wake, however, is not the raw burst of sensuality experienced by anaerobic participants, such as downhillers, but the more protracted affair of repeated motion by long-distance runners, cyclists, and cross-country skiers. Stride . . . pedal . . . glide . . . paddle . . . again and again and again, the heart pumping, the breathing hard but controlled, the muscles contracting, relaxing, contracting—at speed and in shape and feelin' good, one is flying through space, not grinding over it. It's all a heady intoxication which is a curious reversal of what sedentary America takes to be the norm. Glisse is a phenomenon of racing, and as Al Camp noted so bluntly, appears infrequently in training, which is why marathoners in canoeing race so often.

Unlike swimming, long-distance paddling has visual rewards. "Canoeing is a way for me to see a changing countryside from a different, slower perspective," said Corbin. There are other facets as well and they manifest themselves on the Susquehanna. Reading water to find the fastest six inches of current, riding another canoe's wake (like drafting on a bike), and portaging at top speed are all sciences. "Marathoning is far more interesting than Olympic flatwater racing," noted Bruce Barton.

Barton's reaction at the 31-mile point would also be interesting:

he's 2:30 down to Corbin, with the Stocktons and Bohanon/Rudquist on his wake.

On June 8 Corbin will assume a position working for the Canadian Government which will involve testing canoes: design, safety, and materials. Prior to Cooperstown he and Tetrault had been looking for work, collecting unemployment, and living off their winnings, approximately $6,000 from the previous summer.

The son of a journeyman paper worker at International Paper Co. in Trois-Rivieres, Serge was raised in a large family of five girls and three boys. But Corbin keeps his family and personal life away from the inquisitive eyes of the press and public. He rarely lets interviewers inside his home, which is fine with his father who to this day has not followed the canoeing trail his two sons have blazed.

Serge graduated from secondary school and attended technical school for a year and is currently a certified electrician.

At 5'11" and 147 pounds by the end of the summer, Corbin's build is lithe. Full but supple through the chest and shoulders, Corbin is blessed not with bulging muscles, but with a more subtle advantage for canoeing, long arms. These provide Nature-given mechanical advantage for paddling that no amount of training can produce. His body tapers through slim hips to downright skinny legs.

"The secret to Corbin's success, other than hard work, is his weight," said Al Camp. "He and Tetrault are a lightweight team, 40 to 45 pounds lighter than Barton and Triebold. On a shallow river where excess weight means more drag and friction on the hull surface of the canoe, this is a crucial factor."

Like most endurance athletes, Corbin is unhurried and soft-spoken off the water. And the quiet words he uses are always French, making him a bit enigmatic amongst his American competitors. Strikingly handsome, Corbin has eyes that women could spend a lifetime gazing into.

The eyes of Richard Tetrault, 23, however, glisten like those of a cat. These are the eyes seen beneath a hockey helmet in the face-off circle; eyes that silently warn before the puck is dropped that all hell is about to bust loose. If Corbin is the sleek panther moving quickly only when forced to, Tetrault is the chunky banty rooster.

At a pre-race dinner, Corbin and Tetrault were discussing strategy with Toupin over mounds of spaghetti. "Perhaps we should follow Barton for a while, get a handle on his speed, considering what we've heard of his preparation," cautioned Corbin.

"Look, Serge, *you* can follow, but you'll have to cut the canoe in half, 'cause *I'm* not following anybody tomorrow."

Tetrault has the machinery to back up his competitive nature. He resembles someone who swallowed a watermelon that lodged sideways in his chest before reaching his stomach. A roughneck who's seen a few sides of life as a sawmill operator, truck driver, and phys-ed teacher, Tetrault is enjoying life on the road as an integral, if less publicized, component of the world's fastest canoe team.

At 54 miles first place is settled; Corbin and Tetrault are now on a victory lap for the next 16 miles with the same three teams 7:35 behind, jockeying for position. Over the past 30 miles, second place in this race has become very acceptable. Appropriately, Toupin is well into his second Molson's; the brewer sponsors most of the races in Quebec. "Barton thought it was the boat last year when Serge beat him by six minutes during the first day of the Classique. Now he must think of something else because he's in one just like it this year."

Barton and Triebold and dozens of teams across North America paddle the "Corbin" model pro canoe made by Ev Crozier of Wisconsin. But the boat used by the namesake is a state-of-the-art $1,275 weapon. On the outside is two-ounce cloth. Then Kevlar is added and Hexcel honeycomb laced with carbon fiber. The hull's finish is as smooth as a baby's bottom. This 22-pound (Crozier's estimate) custom jobbie provides Corbin with a two- or three-pound advantage.

Crozier also makes the paddles for the team making a runaway of Cooperstown '83. Tetrault uses a 49-inch 14-degree bent-shaft made of graphite while Serge's is slightly longer at 51". Both paddles weight just 14 ounces.

An ounce with the paddles, a pound or two with the boat, five pounds at the start with no water and hauling 40 pounds less on their frames than Barton-Triebold . . . the addition explains some of that 7:35.

"One thing you can say about the Corbins," said Crozier, "they are not dumb. They've tried and tinkered with all the available equipment. They know their gear cold. They have all the angles figured out and working in their favor."

Summer has arrived in Bainbridge. The fairgrounds fill rapidly as the skies clear. The finish area is a quilt made of equal parts New England flea market, Breughel's *The Harvest* and Nat King Cole's "Down on the Boardwalk."

The aluminum leaders cross the finish to polite applause.

"Theprosinyet?"

There are no buoys in the water.

"When'sCorbincoming?"

The first amateur cruisers follow shortly.

"Corbinhere?"

Seven hours, 28 minutes and 6 seconds after starting in Cooperstown, Corbin and Tetrault cruise in at 68 strokes a minute. Down from 75 earlier, but still a tough way to make $80/hour apiece.

Ahh, yes, money. According to the International Canoe Federation (ICF), which governs amateur canoeing worldwide, Serge Corbin and Richard Tetrault are "amateurs." Don't laugh; so are Barton and Triebold. Here's how. At races where prize money is offered, Corbin's booty is presented to Toupin who passes it directly to a division of the governing body of canoeing in Quebec, Club Albatross. They assess a 10% handling fee and return the remainder to Corbin and Tetrault upon presentation of receipt for expenses incurred while training and racing.

One doesn't exactly get wealthy racing canoes. Corbin and Tetrault generated $7,000 to $8,000 in expenses last year. But $6,000 in winnings softens the blow.

Also, to conform to ICF regulations (so Corbin and Tetrault can race in the ICF World Marathon Championships in Europe), they are not allowed to display a sponsor's name on their boat. When and where through the years the Discosalon Val Mauricie logo has appeared on Corbin's boat is lost in translation; the French become difficult to understand at this point.

Butch and Brett Stockton arrive in 7:33:33. Mike Bohannon and Al Rudquist are next in 7:35:18 while Barton and Triebold limp in at 7:37:02. On the drive home Barton will vomit eight times, an indication that he was suffering from the flu during the race.

As Corbin and Tetrault walk slowly up the ramp from the water with Toupin and an elf in tow carrying the boat, the finish crowd parts deferentially. As in the morning on the banks of Otego, the crowd thickens but the level of whispering rises only slightly, interspersed with the whirr of cameras. There is a palpable distance between the onlookers and the visitors, a distance created perhaps by language, perhaps by awe, or perhaps by the fact that the American public does not yet feel at ease embracing a canoeing hero.

The Hyack results seem far away at this point, the word muted.

Corbin *could* be had.

But when and by whom?

*The test measures the amount of oxygen consumed per minute in relation to body weight. It indicates the overall efficiency of an athlete's cardiovascular system.

Bibliography

Part I—Acknowledgements

The author and publisher express their appreciation for permission to reprint the following works in whole or in part, listed in the order in which they appear in the text:

Olson, Sigurd F. "The Lonely Land," *The Lonely Land*. New York: Knopf, 1961. Copyright 1961 by Sigurd Olson. Reprinted by permission of Alfred A. Knopf, Inc.

Irving, Washington. *Astoria*. Clatsop ed. Portland, OR: Binfords & Mort, 1967.

Townsend, John Kirk. *Narrative of a Journey Across the Rocky Mountains to the Columbia River*. Introduction by Donald Jackson. Lincoln: University of Nebraska Press, 1978. By permission of University of Nebraska Press.

Russell, Osborne. *Journal of a Trapper (1834–1843)*. Edited from the Original Manuscript in the William Robertson Coe Collection of Western Americana in the Yale University Library. With a Biography of Osborne Russell and Maps of His Travels While a Trapper in the Rocky Mountains, by Aubrey L. Haines. Lincoln: University of Nebraska Press, 1965. By permission of University of Nebraska Press.

Schlissel, Lillian, ed. *Women's Diaries of the Westward Journey*. Preface by Carl N. Degler. New York: Schocken Books, 1982.

Carrey, John; Conley, Cort; and Barton, Ace. *Snake River of Hells Canyon*. Cambridge, Idaho: Backeddy Books, 1979.

Guthrie, A. B., Jr. *The Big Sky*. New York: W. Sloane Associates, 1947. Copyright renewed 1974 by A. B. Guthrie, Jr. By permission of Brandt & Brandt, Literary Agents, Inc.

Sumner, John Colton. "Lost Journal of John Colton Sumner." Utah Historical Quarterly, Vol. 37 No. 2 (Spring 1969).

Bonney, Orrin H., and Bonney, Lorraine. *Battle Drums and Geysers*. By permission of Lorraine Bonney.

Schwatka, Frederick. *Along Alaska's Great River*. Anchorage, Alaska: Alaska Northwest Pub. Co. (Box 4EEE, Anchorage, AK 99509), 1983. Originally published in 1885 by Cassell, New York.

Western Writers of America. "The Yukon River," by Archie Satterfield, *Water Trails West*. Garden City, NY: Doubleday & Company, 1978.

Murie, Olaus. *Journeys to the Far North*. Palo Alto, CA: American West Pub. Co., 1973.

Murie, Margaret E. *Two in the Far North*. New York: Knopf, 1967.

Patterson, Raymond M. *Dangerous River*. New York: W. Sloane Associates, 1954.

Faulkner, William. *Three Famous Short Novels*. New York: Random House, 1939. Renewed 1967 by Mrs. William Faulkner and Mrs. Paul Summers. By permission of Random House, Inc.

Steinbeck, John. *The Pearl*. New York: The Viking Press, 1947. Renewed 1973 by Elaine Steinbeck, Thom Steinbeck and John Steinbeck IV. By permission of Viking Penguin, Inc.

Hoagland, Edward. *Notes from the Century Before: A Journal from British Columbia*. San Francisco: North Point Press, 1982. Copyright 1969 by Edward Hoagland. By permission of Random House, Inc.

Pyle, Ernie. *Home Country*. Copyright 1940 by Scripps Howard Newspaper Alliance. Copyright 1947 by William Sloane Associates, Inc. By permission of William Morrow & Company.

Malo, John W. "Love Affair with a River." *Outdoor Illinois* 16 (May 1977).

Haig-Brown, Roderick. *A River Never Sleeps*. New York: W. Morrow, 1946. Copyright 1946, 1974 by Roderick L. Haig-Brown. By permission of New Century Publishers, Inc., Piscataway, NJ 08854 and Harold Ober Associates, Inc.

Eifert, Virginia. *River World: Wildlife of the Mississippi*. New York: Dodd, Mead, 1959. By permission of Larry Eifert.

Stegner, Wallace. "Glen Canyon Submersus," *The Sound of Mountain Waters*. Garden City, NY: Doubleday, 1969. By permission of Doubleday & Company, Inc.

Graves, John. *Goodbye to a River, a Narrative*. New York: Ballantine Books, 1971. Copyright 1959 by Curtis Publishing Co. Copyright 1960 by John Graves. By permission of Alfred A. Knopf, Inc.

Belknap, Bill. "Cataract Canyon's Rockbound Riddle." *Christian Science Monitor*, 21 August 1965, sec. 2, p. 1. Reprinted by permission from the *Christian Science Monitor*. Copyright 1964 The Christian Science Publishing Society. All rights reserved.

Frome, Michael. "Must This Be Lost to the Sight of Man?" *Field & Stream* 74 (July 1969). By permission of Michael Frome.

Brokaw, Tom. "That River Swallows People. Some It Gives Up. Some It Don't." *West (November 1, 1970): 11-18*. By permission of Tom Brokaw.

McPhee, John. *The Survvial of the Bark Canoe*. New York: Farrar, Straus, and Giroux, 1975. Copyright 1975 by John McPhee. This material first appeared in *The New Yorker*.

Vance, Joel. "The River." *Missouri Consevationist* (September 1975).

Norton, Boyd. *Rivers of the Rockies*. Chicago: Rand McNally 1975.

Maclean, Norman. *A River Runs Through It, and Other Stories*. Chicago: University of Chicago Press, 1976. By permission of University of Chicago Press.

Sumner, David. "Exploring a Desert Legend—The Dolores River." *Canoe* 4 (July-August 1976): 27-30.

Huser, Verne. "Wild and Scenic Rivers: Alive but Not Well," *American Forests* (November, 1982).

Collins, Robert O., and Nash, Roderick. *The Big Drops: Ten Legendary Rapids*. San Francisco: Sierra Club Books, 1978. By permission of the authors and Sierra Club Books.

Zwinger, Ann. *Run, River, Run: A Naturalist's Journey Down One of the Greatest Rivers of the West*. New York: Harper & Row, 1975. By permission of the author.

Lawrence, R.D. *Paddy: A Naturalist's Story of an Orphan Beaver*. New York: Knopf, 1977. By permision of Alfred A. Knopf, Inc.

Abbey, Edward. From *Down the River*. Copyright 1982 by Edward Abbey. Reprinted by permission of the publisher, E. P. Dutton.

Palmer, Tim. *Stanislaus, the Struggle for a River*. Berkeley: University of California Press 1982. By permission of The University of California Press.

Giddings, J. Calvin. "Kayak Adventuring in a Desert Gorge." *American Whitewater* 27–28 (November/December 1982–January/February 1983).

Evans, Eric. "Eighty-Five Strokes Per Minute." *Canoe* 11 (September/October 1983).

Part II—References

Abbey, Edward. *Desert Solitaire: A Season in the Wilderness*. New York: McGraw-Hill, 1968.

Amos, William H. *The Infinite River: A Biologist's Vision of the World of Water*. New York: Random House, 1970.

Austin, Mary. *The Land of Little Rain*. Introduction by T.M. Pearce. Albuquerque: University of New Mexico Press, 1974.

Bailey, Robert G. *Hell's Canyon: A Story of the Deepest Canyon on the North American Continent, Together with Historical Sketches of Idaho, Interesting Information of the State, Indian Wars and Mythology, Poetry and Stories*. Lewiston, Idaho: By the author, 1943.

_____. *River of No Return (The Great Salmon River of Idaho): A Century of Central Idaho and Eastern Washington History and Development Together with the Wars, Customs, Myths, and Legends of the Nez Perce Indians*. Rev. ed. Lewiston, Idaho: R.G. Bailey Print. Co., 1947 (i.e. 1948)

Bakeless, John. *Lewis & Clark, Partners in Discovery*. New York: W. Morrow, 1947.

Berry, Wendell. *The Long-Legged House*. New York: Harcourt, Brace & World, 1969.

Bonney, Orrin H., and Bonney, Lorraine. *Battle Drums and Geysers: The*

Life and Journals of Lt. Gustavus Cheyney Doane, Soldier and Explorer of the Yellowstone and Snake River Regions. Chicago: Sage Books, 1970.

Borland, Hal, ed. *Our Natural World: The Land and Wildlife of Ameria as Seen and Described by Writers Since the Country's Discovery.* Garden City, N.Y.: Doubleday, 1965.

Cantwell, Robert. *The Hidden Northwest.* Philadelphia: Lippincott, 1972.

Carrey, John. *The Middle Fork & The Sheepeater War.* Rev. ed. Cambridge, Idaho: Backeddy Books, 1980.

_____, and Conley, Cort. *River of No Return.* Cambridge, Idaho: Backeddy Books, 1978.

_____; Conley, Cort; and Barton, Ace. *Snake River of Hells Canyon.* Cambridge, Idaho: Backeddy Books, 1979.

Carver, Jonathan. *Travels through the Interior Parts of North-America in the Years 1766, 1767, and 1768.* 3d ed. London: C. Dilly, 1781.

Chittenden, Hiram Martin. *The American Fur Trade of the Far West: A History of the Pioneer Trading Posts and Early Fur Companies of the Missouri Valley and the Rocky Mountains and of the Overland Commerce with Santa Fe.* New York: F.P. Harper, 1902.

Collins, Robert O., and Nash, Roderick. *The Big Drops: Ten Legendary Rapids.* San Francisco: Sierra Club Books, 1978.

Conron, John. *The American Landscape: A Critical Anthology of Prose and Poetry.* New York: Oxford University Press, 1973.

Cox, Ross. *The Columbia River.* Norman: University of Oklahoma Press, 1957.

Dablemont, Larry. *The Authentic American Johnboat.* New York: David McKay, 1978.

Davidson, James West, and Rugge, John. *The Complete Wilderness Paddler.* New York: Knopf, 1976.

Dellenbaugh, Frederick S. *The Romance of the Colorado River: The Story of Its Discovery in 1540, with an Account of the Later Explorations, and with Special Reference to the Voyages of Powell through the Line of the Great Canyons.* 3d ed. New York: Putnam, 1909.

_____. *A Canyon Voyage: The Narrative of the Second Powell Expedition Down the Green-Colorado River from Wyoming, and the Explorations on Land in the Years 1871 and 1872.* Foreword by William H. Goetzmann. New Haven, Conn.: Yale University Press, 1962.

De Voto, Bernard. *Across the Wide Missouri.* With an Account of the Discovery of the Miller Collection by Mae Reed Porter. Boston: Houghton Mifflin, 1947.

Dickey, James. *Deliverance.* Boston: Houghton Mifflin, 1970.

Duncan, David James. *The River Why.* San Francisco: Sierra Club Books, 1983.

Eddy, Clyde. *Down the World's Most Dangerous River.* New York: F.A. Stokes, 1929.

Eifert, Virginia. *River World: Wildlife of the Mississippi.* New York: Dodd, Mead, 1959.

Eiseley, Loren. *The Immense Journey.* New York: Random House, 1957.

Evans, Eric, and Burton, John. *Whitewater Racing: A Comprehensive Guide to Whitewater Slalom and Wildwater Racing in Canoes and Kayaks.* New York: Van Nostrand Reinhold, 1980.

Faulkner, William. *Three Famous Short Novels.* Vintage Book, v. 149. New York: Random House, 1961.

Flint, Timothy. *A Condensed Geography and History of the Western States, or the Mississippi Valley.* Cincinnati, Ohio: E.H. Flint, 1828.

Freeman, Lewis R. *Down the Columbia.* New York: Dodd, Mead, 1921.

Frome, Michael. *Battle for the Wilderness.* New York: Praeger, 1974.

Graves, John. *Goodbye to a River, a Narrative.* New York: Ballantine Books, 1971.

Guthrie, A.B., Jr. *The Big Sky.* New York; W. Sloane Associates, 1947.

Haig-Brown, Roderick. *Return to the River: A Story of the Chinook Run.* New York: W. Morrow, 1941.

_____. *A River Never Sleeps.* New York: W. Morrow, 1946.

Hall, Leonard. *Stars Upstream: Life Along an Ozark River.* Rev. ed. Columbia: University of Missouri Press, 1969.

Hamilton, Joyce. *White Water: The Colorado River Jet Boat Expedition, 1960.* Christchurch, N.Z.: Caxton Press, 1963.

Hasbrouck, Louise Seymour. *LaSalle.* True Stories of Great Americans. New York: Macmillan, 1916.

Hemingway, Ernest. *In Our Time; Stories.* New York: Boni & Liverwright, 1925.

Hoagland, Edward. *Notes from the Century Before: A Journal from British Columbia.* San Francisco: North Point Press, 1982.

Holbrook, Stewart. *Holy Old Mackinaw: A Natural History of the American Lumberjack.* New York: Macmillan, 1938.

Huser, Verne. *Canyon Country Paddles: A Practical, Informative and Entertaining Guide to River Running Using the Kayak, Canoe, or Rubber Raft in Southeastern Utah.* Salt Lake City, Utah: Wasatch Publishers, 1978.

_____. *Grand Teton National Park Snake River Guide.* Boulder City, Nev.: Westwater Books, 1972.

_____. *River Camping: Touring by Canoe, Raft, Kayak, and Dory.* New York: Dial Press, 1981.

_____. *River Running.* Chicago: Regnery, 1975.

Irving, Washington. *The Adventures of Captain Bonneville, U.S.A., in the Rocky Mountains and the Far West, Digested from his Journal by*

Washington Irving. Edited and introduction by Edgeley W. Todd. Norman: University of Oklahoma Press, 1961.

_____. *Astoria.* Clatsop ed. Portland, Or.: Binfords & Mort, 1967.

Kolb, E.L. *Through the Grand Canyon from Wyoming to Mexico.* Foreword by Owen Wister. New York: Macmillan, 1914.

Lawrence, R.D. *Paddy: A Naturalist's Story of an Orphan Beaver.* New York: Knopf, 1977.

Lavender, David. *The Fist in the Wilderness.* Garden City, N.Y.: Doubleday, 1964.

_____. *The Rockies.* New York: Harper & Row, 1968.

Leopold, Aldo. *Round River, from the Journals of Aldo Leopold.* Edited by Luna B. Leopold. New York: Oxford University Press, 1953.

_____. *A Sand County Almanac, and Sketches Here and There.* New York: Oxford University Press, 1949.

Lewis, (Meriwether). *The Journals of Lewis and Clark.* Edited by Bernard De Voto. Boston: Houghton Mifflin, 1953.

Lopez, Barry Holstun. *River Notes: The Dance of Herons.* Kansas City, Kan.: Andrews and McMeel, 1979.

Mackenzie, Sir Alexander. *Exploring the Northwest Territory: Sir Alexander Mackenzie's Journal of a Voyage by Bark Canoe from Lake Athabasca to the Pacific Ocean in the Summer of 1789.* Norman: University of Oklahoma Press, 1966.

Madson, John. *John Madson, Out Home.* Edited by Michael McIntosh. New York: Winchester Press, 1979.

Malo, John W. *Malo's Complete Guide to Canoeing and Canoe-Camping.* New York: Quadrangle Books, 1969.

Manley, Atwood. *Rushton and His Times in American Canoeing.* With the assistance of Paul F. Jamieson. Syracuse, N.Y.: Syracuse University Press, 1968.

McGinnis, William *Whitewater Rafting.* New York: Quadrangle/New York Times Book Co., 1975.

McPhee, John. *Coming into the Country.* New York: Farrar, Straus, and Giroux, 1977.

_____. *Encounters with the Archdruid.* New York: Farrar, Straus, and Giroux, 1971.

_____. *The John McPhee Reader.* Edited by William L. Howarth. New York: Farrar, Straus and Giroux, 1976.

_____. *The Survival of the Bark Canoe.* New York: Farrar, Straus, and Giroux, 1975.

Melville, Herman. *The Confidence-Man: His Masquerade.* New York: Dix, Edwards & Co., 1857.

Morse, Eric W. *Fur Trade Canoe Routes of Canada, Then and Now.* 2d ed. Toronto: University of Toronto Press, 1979.

Muir, John. *The Mountains of California*. Garden City, N.Y.: Doubleday, 1961.

Murie, Margaret E. *Two in the Far North*. New York: Knopf, 1967.

_____, and Murie, Olaus. *Wapiti Wilderness*. New York: Knopf, 1966.

Murie, Olaus. *Journeys to the Far North*. Palo Alto, Calif.: American West Pub. Co., 1973.

Nash, Roderick. *Wilderness and the American Mind*. New Haven: Yale University Press, 1967.

Neihardt, John G. *The River and I*. New ed. New York: Macmillan, 1927.

_____. *The Splendid Wayfaring: The Story of the Exploits and Adventures of Jedediah Smith and His Comrades, the Ashley-Henry Men, Discoverers and Explorers of the Great Central Route from the Missouri River to the Pacific Ocean, 1822–1831*. Lincoln: University of Nebraska Press, 1970.

Nicollet, Joseph N. *The Journals of Joseph N. Nicollet: A Scientist on the Mississippi Headwaters, with Notes on Indian Life, 1836–37*. Publications of the Minnesota Historical Society. Trans. from the French by Andre Fertey; edited by Martha Coleman Bray. St. Paul: Minnesota Historical Society, 1970.

Norton, Boyd. *Rivers of the Rockies*. Chicago: Rand McNally, 1975.

_____. *Snake Wilderness*. San Francisco: Sierra Club, 1972.

Nute, Grace L. *The Voyageur*. Reprint ed. St. Paul: Minnesota Historical Society, 1955.

Olson, Sigurd F. *Listening Point*. New York: Knopf, 1958.

_____. *The Lonely Land*. New York: Knopf, 1961.

_____. *Runes of the North*. New York: Knopf, 1956.

Palmer, Tim. *Stanislaus, the Struggle for a River*. Berkeley: University of California Press, 1982.

Patterson, Raymond M. *The Buffalo Head*. New York: W. Sloane Associates, 1961.

_____. *Dangerous River*. New York: W. Sloane Associates, 1954.

_____. *Far Pastures*. Sidney, B.C.: Gray's Pub., 1963.

_____. *Finlay's River*. New York: W. Morrow, 1968.

_____. *Trail to the Interior*. New York: Morrow, 1966

Powell, John Wesley. *The Exploration of the Colorado River and Its Canyons*. New York: Dover, 1961.

Pyle, Ernie. *Home Country*. New York: W. Sloane Associates, 1947.

Raban, Jonathan. *Old Glory: An American Voyage*. New York: Penguin Books, 1982.

Russell, Osborne. *Journal of a Trapper (1834–1843)*. Edited from the Original Manuscript in the William Robertson Coe Collection of Western Americana in the Yale University Library. With a Biography of Osborne Russell and Maps of His Travels While a Trapper in the Rocky Mountains, by Aubrey L. Haines. Lincoln: University of Nebraska Press 1965.

Sandoz, Mari. *The Beaver Men: Spearheads of Empire.* New York: Hastings House, 1964.

_____. *Love Song to the Plains.* Lincoln: University of Nebraska Press, 1961.

Satterfield, Archie. *Exploring the Yukon River.* Seattle: Mountaineers, 1979.

_____. *The Lewis & Clark Trail.* Harrisburg, Pa.: Stackpole, 1978.

Schwatka, Frederick. *Along Alaska's Great River: A Popular Account of the Travels of the Alaska Exploring Expedition of 1883, Along the Great Yukon River, from Its Source to Its Mouth, in the British Northwest Territory, and in the Territory of Alaska.* New York: Cassell, 1885.

Seelye, John. *Prophetic Waters: The Rivers in Early American Life and Literature.* New York: Oxford University Press, 1977.

Sevareid, Eric. *Canoeing with the Cree.* Reprint ed. St. Paul: Minnesota Historical Society, 1968.

Simpson, Sir George. *Journal of Occurrences in the Athabasca Department by George Simpson, 1820 and 1821, and Report.* Edited by E.E. Rich; Foreword by Lord Tweedsmuir; Introduction by Chester Martin. Toronto: Champlain Society, 1938.

Stanton, Robert Brewster. *Colorado River Controversies.* Commentaries by Otis R. Marston and Martin J. Anderson. Boulder City, Nev.: Westwater Books, 1982.

Staveley, Gaylord. *Broken Waters Sing: Rediscovering Two Great Rivers of the West.* Boston: Little, Brown, 1971.

Stegner, Wallace. *Beyond the Hundredth Meridian: John Wesley Powell, and the Second Opening of the West.* Boston: Houghton Mifflin, 1962.

_____. *The Sound of Mountain Waters.* Garden City, N.Y.: Doubleday, 1969.

_____, ed. *This is Dinosaur: Echo Park Country and Its Magic Rivers.* New York: Knopf, 1955.

Strung, Norm; Curtis, Sam; and Perry, Earl. *Whitewater!* New York: Macmillan, 1976.

Tejada-Flores, Lito. *Wildwater: The Sierra Club Guide to Kayaking and Whitewater Boating.* San Francisco: Sierra Club Books, 1978.

Teller, Walter Magnes, ed. *On the River: A Variety of Canoe & Small Boat Voyages.* New Brunswick, N.J.: Rutgers University Press, 1976.

Thompson, David. *Narrative, 1784–1812.* New ed. Edited with an Introduction and Notes by Richard Glover. Toronto: Champlain Society, 1962.

Thoreau, Henry David. *The Maine Woods.* Notes by Dudley C. Lunt. New York: Bramhall House, 1950.

_____. *A Week on the Concord and Merrimack Rivers.* Foreword by Denham Sutcliffe. New York: New American Library, 1961.

Townsend, John Kirk. *Narrative of a Journey Across the Rocky Mountains to the Columbia River.* Introduction by Donald Jackson. Lincoln: University of Nebraska Press, 1978.

Twain, Mark. *The Adventures of Huckleberry Finn.* New York: Harper, 1884.

_____. *Life on the Mississippi.* Boston: J. R. Osgood, 1883.

Zwinger, Ann, and Teale, Edwin Way. *A Conscious Stillness: Two Naturalists on Thoreau's Rivers.* New York: Harper & Row, 1982.

Zwinger, Ann. *Run, River, Run: A Naturalist's Journey Down One of the Greatest Rivers of the West.* New York: Harper & Row, 1975.

East Woods Press Books

Backcountry Cooking
Berkshire Trails for Walking & Ski Touring
Best Bed & Breakfast in the World, The
California Bed & Breakfast
Campfire Chillers
Campfire Songs
Canoeing the Jersey Pine Barrens
Carolina Curiosities
Carolina Seashells
Carpentry: Some Tricks of the Trade from an Old-Style Carpenter
Catfish Cookbook, The
Charlotte: A Touch of Gold
Complete Guide to Backpacking in Canada
Creative Gift Wrapping
Day Trips From Cincinnati
Day Trips From Houston
Drafting: Tips and Tricks on Drawing and Designing House Plans
Exploring Nova Scotia
Fifty Years on the Fifty: The Orange Bowl Story
Fructose Cookbook, The
Grand Old Ladies
Grand Strand: An Uncommon Guide to Myrtle Beach, The
Healthy Trail Food Book, The
Hiking from Inn to Inn
Hiking Virginia's National Forests
Historic Country House Hotels
Hosteling USA, Third Edition
How to Afford Your Own Log Home
How to Play With Your Baby
Interior Finish: More Tricks of the Trade
Just Folks: Visitin' with Carolina People
Kays Gary, Columnist
Maine Coast: A Nature Lover's Guide, The
Making Food Beautiful
Mid-Atlantic Guest House Book, The
New England Guest House Book, The
New England: Off the Beaten Path
Ohio: Off the Beaten Path
Parent Power!
Race, Rock and Religion
River Reflections
Rocky Mountain National Park Hiking Trails
Saturday Notebook, The
Sea Islands of the South
Separation and Divorce in North Carolina
South Carolina Hiking Trails
Southern Guest House Book, The
Southern Rock: A Climber's Guide to the South
Sweets Without Guilt
Tar Heel Sights: Guide to North Carolina's Heritage
Tennessee Trails
Toys That Teach Your Child
Train Trips: Exploring America by Rail
Trout Fishing the Southern Appalachians
Vacationer's Guide to Orlando and Central Florida, A
Walks in the Catskills
Walks in the Great Smokies
Walks with Nature in Rocky Mountain National Park
Whitewater Rafting in Eastern America
Wildflower Folklore
Woman's Journey, A
You Can't Live on Radishes

Order from:

The East Woods Press
429 East Boulevard
Charlotte, NC 28203